AF251863

AMAZING GOD!
Light from Language
-Solving the Language Code-

Copyright © 2009 John Aaron Lee

For Worldwide Distribution

Amazing Ministries
ISBN – 978-0-9815676-3-1

www.leewordcodes.com

P. O. Box 3211
Brentwood, TN 37024

Sword & Spirit Publishing (SSP)
SAN: 855-9007

Cover design by Kyle Lopez

Printed in the United States of America

i

<u>*ACKNOWLEDGMENTS & DEDICATION*</u>

The devoted disciples of the Lord listed below all made important contributions to one or more areas relating to the development, writing, editing and quality of this book. I am very grateful for their friendship, support, skills and assistance. These individuals made important contributions in this book becoming a reality.

This book is dedicated to the individuals listed below.

Cecil Boswell

Tara Colwart

Dr. John Franklin

Kim Harrison

Christy Hummer

Kyle Lopez

Sandra Matthews

Joseph Weaver

_______________Table of Contents

Visit website for index and information about the author.

JOHN the **BAPTIST** was prophesied by Isaiah the Prophet over 700 years before his birth. The angel Gabriel announced to John's father Zechariah that his prayer had been heard and Elizabeth, his wife, would bear a son. His name would be called John, and he would be filled with the Holy Spirit from his mother's womb. Because Zechariah and his wife were both quite old, he asked Gabriel for a sign. The sign came in a most unusual way. Zechariah was struck dumb (unable to speak) which lasted until eight days after John's birth.

Five months after Elizabeth conceived, the angel went to Mary and told her that she would miraculously conceive, and she gave birth to the Son of God. There are different opinions, but there is substantial scholarly evidence that John the Baptist was born on Passover and that Jesus was born on the first day of the Feast of Trumpets. John's ministry was to turn many Israelites to the Lord their God. This was for the national preparation for the coming Messiah, Jesus, who has unquestionably had the greatest influence of any person that has ever lived.

The lesson here is that the Israelites were not ready for this event, so they needed to prepare. I submit that nothing has changed because at this time neither the Israelites nor the Gentiles are ready for the Lord's return. That need is there again for the Israelites to turn to the Lord, but not just Israel. The peoples of the world primarily are neither living by nor being governed by Biblical precepts and statutes. God is a stranger to billions of the current inhabitants of this planet. At the time of Christ's birth the announcement by the angel was, "I bring you good tidings of great joy, which shall be to <u>all</u> people." (Luke 2:10) This good news is for the whole world! Two purposes of this book are to provide fresh good news information and to sound a wake-up call to prepare for the Lord's second coming in this generation.

The New Testament account of John the Baptist reveals a man with a unique ministry and strange characteristics. There are two kinds of prophets, some were speaking and some were writing. John was a speaking prophet. John had the ministry to make people ready by preparing the way for the Messiah, Jesus Christ. He wore camel hair clothing and a wide leather belt. His diet was locusts and wild honey. His place of ministry was the wilderness area around the Jordan River, north of the Dead Sea. This was not a very pleasant climate or environment, being over 1000 feet below sea level. John's message was quite strong, since he referred to the Israelites as a "generation of vipers." But, not withstanding his dress, diet, and location, multitudes came from Jerusalem and all of Judea.

Jesus, himself, praised this man that many considered to be common, and even a little strange at the least. He was even blessed to baptize Jesus, the one called Yeshua. Yeshua said that of those born of woman there was not a greater prophet than John the Baptist. John the Baptist was the first prophet in 400 years and he called the people of Israel to repentance to prepare the way of the Lord. John's calling and ministry was unique; I also believe that this is a book birthed from a unique calling. And, that it was made possible by divine illumination for an approaching end time period called, "the day of the Lord."

When I was born it would have been difficult to find any end times signs as given in the Bible, but now these signs regularly are in the news. The single most important sign of the end times was Israel being reestablished as a nation in May 1948 after 1,878 years. There were twenty-five specific prophecies relating to this event that were fulfilled in exact detail. The dispersion of the Jews throughout the world and their return was prophesied 2,500 years before it was fulfilled in the twentieth Century.

Over twenty years ago, I spent some time in a rural area in a southern state. I met an older couple there that, at that time, had recently spent ten years traveling around the world on a beautiful yacht. The man was seventy years old, and was not a Christian. We had a discussion that disturbed him. I returned a couple of years later and this man saw me. He immediately proclaimed that he was at church all the time. And then he lowered his voice and advised me, "Around here you are known as John the Baptist." I knew I had some impact on a few people there, but I had no idea I had attained such an unworthy way of being identified. Just as my name, John, means "The Lord is gracious," I believe that these divine illuminations have been a gracious gift from the Lord.

I want to make the point that not everyone has the same spiritual experience, power, gifts or calling. Should not everyone be true to the light that they have received? Believers have the Holy Spirit, so we are able to receive from God. This includes illumination and/or revelation. I have received both, but I do not make any claim of spiritual infallibility as the prophets in the Bible. I do believe that God gifts some to proclaim or tell forth His truth and this book does contain Biblical truth and illumination. The Holy Spirit that Christian believers are sealed with is the "Spirit of truth."(John 15:26)

In 1st Thessalonians Chapter 5, Paul instructs the brethren not to despise prophesyings. That is because this is a special type of Christian communication that needs to be given attention. Prophetic revelation and illumination can be easily confused. The Holy Bible was by revelation and this book is almost exclusively by illumination, combined with experiences and understanding.

Well, besides a unique calling, "Does John the Baptist have anything else in common with this book written 2,000 years after his remarkable ministry?" I see a few other similarities. The preaching of John the Baptist was not just challenging to the religious elite of his day, but opened the eyes of thousands to repentance. John the Baptist was very blunt and challenging and similar dialog will especially be used in this book's last chapter.

I would like for this book to make truth easier for many to see. Repentance is just a turning or a change in what you think or believe. No one is born believing in God. Since most of humanity has missed knowing the one true God, it's my hope this book will be one more opportunity to assist individuals in finding the narrow way that leads to eternal life. There is only one truth, and my own acceptance of that truth was facilitated through a 192 page spiritual book I purchased in a store over twenty-five years ago.

In Revelation, the last book of the sixty-six books of the Bible, the spiritual condition of the church at Laodicea was described. The picture is not complimentary. The church is supposed to convert the world, but this church has primarily been converted by the world. Most members of this church are not born again and saved for an eternity in heaven. God loves those few that are, but even they need to repent and be zealous. When you get some understanding of all the false religions and misleading doctrines today, you see why being zealous is so important. Christian zeal is needed, but for the most part it is missing. "Enter ye in at the strait gate: for wide *is* the gate, and broad *is* the way, that leadeth to destruction, and many there be which go in thereat:" (Matthew 7:13).

Most Bible scholars believe that the seven churches of Revelation represent churches of all ages, but each age is characterized primarily by one of these churches. I and many other students of eschatology see evidence that we are fast approaching the "end times" and that the church at Laodicea (Rev. 3:14-19) primarily represents the condition of Christian churches in this period. Observation and statistics seem to verify that Laodicea is the church of our present time. Today, many Christians do not hold to many basic fundamental beliefs of the faith and I feel the need to distinguish between true believers and Christians. An example would be the deity of Jesus Christ. Respect for Jesus or believing that he is a prophet does not go far enough and is not sufficient for salvation. Jesus was fully man and fully God. He claimed to be equal with God. Have you examined that claim? What you believe about Jesus Christ is crucial to your standing with God. For me and countless others, He is Lord, Savior, King of Kings, the First born of the Resurrection and the unique Son of God. As He said, "He that has seen me has seen the Father." There is no neutral position – you either believe or you do not. Scripture states that non-believers are at enmity with the Almighty God.

Jesus sat His disciples down, "And beginning at Moses and all the prophets, he expounded unto them in all the scriptures the things concerning himself." Luke 24:27 The Bible is profound and deep and God hides many secrets within the sacred scriptures for man to search out. As an early example, Jesus might have used Genesis Chapter 5 listing the genealogies of Adam through Noah. The study of a Hebrew lexicon of the root meanings of the names of these ten men produces a surprise. Using the root meaning of each of their names and taken in order, you get a remarkable sentence that states the New Testament gospel. For information on the sentence from genealogies contact Koinonia House Ministry.

Amazing God does a similar thing using words throughout the Bible with this new holographic lexicon from Genesis to Revelation. This gives direct evidence from two witnesses – a Hebrew lexicon and this new discovery of the holographic lexicon. "In the mouth of two or three witnesses shall every word be established." 2 Corinthians 13:1

When I was eleven, I was required to regularly attend a neighborhood church. I remember I had to wear itchy wool Sunday clothes. One day the pastor called me to his office. He suggested I consider the ministry. I laughed. He was offended because he was serious. He replied that whenever I spoke before the church everyone in the church sat up and listened, and they did not even do that for him. I said that I did not have anything important to say. He said that did not matter. Well, it is now decades later, and I am persuaded that I do have spiritual truths to share. I hope many people will listen and hear with their hearts as well as their heads.

Isn't it remarkable that approximately fifty percent of the current world's population claim either to be physically or spiritually related to Abraham? That is several billion people who include Catholics, Protestants, Muslims, Arabs, Jews and others. Thousands of years ago the God of Abraham, asked him a question, and Abraham did not know the answer. You do not know the answer either. In this book, you will get both the question, and because of divine revelation, you will get the answer. If you can not wait, the question is in Genesis 15:5 and it is about the stars.

I would hope that the billions of people that claim a kinship with Abraham might want to listen to the person who could answer a question that this great man of faith could not. This is a question that no one could correctly answer without the benefit of supernatural revelation. It is a question about the Cosmos that even NASA with super computers would not be able to solve.

Christianity is not an esoteric religion; rather it is about having a personal relationship with the real God. By God's grace, I have had many answered prayers and personal experiences with the living God for over a quarter of a century. I believe that because of God's amazing grace, this writer is one of many disciples that have been allowed to have some special privileges with the Creator. These privileges of faith, answered prayer and illumination are to produce fruit that will be a blessing to others.

The words of Jesus, "Feed my sheep" moved me through the indwelling Holy Spirit to write this book. Therefore, these privileges do not give pride, but rather a sense of responsibility. I have long realized any spiritual work I attempt should be started and finished through faith. I have had multiple opportunities to see work done with faith produce results that exceeded any of my natural skills or abilities.

Faith is clarity, vision, belief, trust, dependence, and confidence. Not being a writer by profession (except thesis, grant writing & articles), I undertook this writing on faith. I have experienced that God has given the grace, including Christian editors, to complete this work. "But God hath chosen the foolish things of the world to confound the wise; and God hath chosen the weak things of the world to confound the things which are mighty." 1 Corinthians 1:27

In the Bible, God proclaims to Israel that He is a jealous God. He had that right because he was in a covenant relationship with Israel. This is just like jealousy that might occur in a marriage because the union is a covenant that pledges fidelity. I find that just as God is jealous, so am I jealous for the God of Abraham, Isaac and Jacob. I know that this is the true God and this God is really worth knowing.

ix

I feel burdened for those that have not found God and entered into His experiences, peace and rest. I say with confidence that the advantages of being in God's family are superior to anything else that you could have in this world. God desires for you to seek Him. I pray you will seek truth and with God's grace find Jesus Christ, the second person of the Godhead.

The Bible reveals that there is only one God, but three distinct persons of the Godhead that exist simultaneously, which is referred to as the Trinity. The three persons of the Godhead are Father, Son, and Holy Ghost or Holy Spirit. It is one essence, one God, but the three persons existing simultaneously. The Bible revels that "God's ways are not our ways." God is beyond our complete comprehension and the Trinity is only known by revelation from the Bible. "Go ye therefore, and teach all nations, baptizing them in the name of the Father, and of the Son, and the Holy Ghost." (Matthew 28:19)

Jesus is referred to this way - "In the beginning was the Word, and the Word was God and the Word was with God." (John1:1) Since Jesus is called the Word, apparently words are very important to God. *Amazing God* will demonstrate that God put an enormous amount of design, detail and logic into words.

In the lexicon, section two, you will see evidence supporting the statement about the design of words. As the word design has the letters for sign – this book is a new sign revealing the complex design of language by the Creator God.

Christians should have a reverence for a Holy God and also have the utmost appreciation for the Holy Bible. I believe that it is the inspired, magnificent and miraculous word of God. The Bible should be the final authority on all matters in the Christian faith.

I have several reasons for believing and trusting God. First, is the profound creation that includes such variety and complexity of life. Next, is the written word of God which answers all of the major issues of life; such as where we came from, the meaning of life, morality, man's eternal destiny, and prophecy about future events. The third reason involves the observation of God's will and purposes demonstrated throughout history. This includes the profound rebirth of the nation of Israel. And last, but not least, is my own personal relationship and experiences with the Creator God, the Maker of heaven and earth.

This book is intended to complement the sacred Scriptures and generate a fresh interest in the Scriptures and a clearer understanding for many. I believe the Holy Bible is the inspired, magnificent and miraculous word of God.

My prayer is that reading this book will be a stimulating, strengthening, satisfying and significant spiritual blessing to you. This book is a start in solving the language code. I hope you enjoy your reading journey through this discovery that decodes words to reveal their spiritual meaning.

<u>SECTION ONE</u>

Chapter One explains the discovery of the spiritual meaning of words from the letters in words.

CHAPTER ONE – THE PRESENCE OF GOD

GMAIL was a term used to describe "God mail" that is faster than e-mail. The term was first used in 2002. Gmail developed from a discovery, by divine illumination, that English language words contain letters that when properly combined reveal deeper meanings. This is a type of cryptic message or code within words that seems to have mostly been overlooked, missed or lost. There are more to words than meets the eye. Gmail words reveal the spiritual meaning of the word and they are by illumination, therefore they are not just regular anagrams.

In *Amazing God* you will see how over 170 words contain the letters for other words which display the nature and wisdom of God. *Amazing God* offers a new view of language that uncovers its divine construction and the spiritual DNA of language. This DNA of language supports the truth of Scripture. DNA, the substance that makes each and every person unique is in the word individual. This was no accident!

Gmail started in 2002 as instant understanding of words within words. This is like instant messaging from God. People exposed to some of this Gmail recognized the significance of words from words, but many thought that they just came from tinkering around with the letters. Once you see examples of words from words you can "tinker with letters in words" and make interesting discoveries. But, these are anagrams and not true Gmail anagrams. The most profound word examples in this book, including the title, did not come from tinkering with letters, but rather they came from an instantaneous understanding.

For a Gmail example, I will use the word pirate. In the word there are the letters for words RAPE and TRAP. Rape means to seize by force, or plunder or have sex by force. Does that describe pirates? Pirates are also known for setting traps for their victims, which is even still true today with increasing internet piracy. This example shows that the word has letters within the word that support the meaning and use of the word. Some of the Biblical words in the lexicon are far more profound than this secular word example.

The following is a small sample list of Gmail words: **Universe** – (<u>uni verse</u>) One verse and it is the first verse in the Bible. "In the beginning God created the heaven and the earth." There is a universe because God brought it into existence. **Earth** – (<u>heart</u>) This planet is called earth because it is of prime importance to God's heart. **World** – (word and Lord) It is appropriate to be here because of God's word and the Lord Jesus Christ. **Life** – (file) God has a file on every person that will ever live. The Bible refers to the Book of <u>Life</u>. **Person** – (<u>per</u> <u>Son</u>) You are who you are <u>per</u> the <u>son</u>. "No man cometh unto the Father, but by the Son." **Deity** - (<u>Die</u>) Why would die be in <u>deity</u>? Could God possibly die? No, God is eternal and will always live. However, when God became fully man while still fully God (theological term is hypostatic union) he was separated from the Father (separation from God is death) and he willingly died physically on a cross in Jerusalem. **Character** – (<u>heart</u> <u>chart</u>) Character is evaluated by God, with a chart on everyone's heart (the essence of who you are and the seat of emotion and reason) **Bibliography** – (<u>Bible</u> <u>holy graph</u>) The Bible is the authentic sacred book, and I believe everyone's biography should be influenced by this divine inspired Holy book. Actually, it is 66 books combined together that were written on three continents, in three languages by forty different men over 1,500 years. A <u>bibliography</u> is a compilation of works by a specific author. The Holy Bible was written by the Holy Spirit through the writings of forty men who gave us history, knowledge, wisdom, and guidance directly from God. **Scripture** – (<u>your</u> <u>script</u>). God's will is important for you to know, and there is a script for you from the Bible. It has some room for improvisation (individualism), but you are responsible for that script. If you stay ignorant that is no excuse. **Stone** – The word note is in stone. Every time you cast a stone at someone else God makes a note of it and it will come back to you. Jesus knew this and he said, "Let he that is without sin among you cast the first stone at her." (John 8:7)

Shortly after Gmail began, my wife, who first had the experience of meanings revealed within words stated, "I think that God and Noah Webster had fun together." Noah Webster said, "Language as well as the faculty of speech, was the immediate gift of God."

This author definitely agrees with Noah Webster. *Amazing God* will provide extensive evidence that language reveals a pattern of design, so sophisticated, it would surpass the ability of modern super computers to duplicate. This pattern in language shows further proof of God's design in yet another aspect of creation. Billions believe, including this author, that God created the universe. And the evidence of this divine design or fingerprints of God, are manifested in numerous ways.

God provides numerous clues to His reality. Many of these clues are not as clear as the physical laws of gravity and the sun always rising. There are aspects of human existence such as poverty, suffering, pain, and death that confuse many. Actually, suffering and death confirm that man is under a judgment curse because of sin. People lacking faith, unfortunately miss the clues and miss truly knowing God. These evidences of a power much higher than mankind have included, but are not limited to; the marvelous design of the cosmos, balance in nature, complex life on earth, and the Old and New Testaments with hundreds and hundreds of accurately fulfilled prophecies.

There is astonishing evidence of God in both a macro (large) and a micro (small) examination of existence. As science advances, the macro view is expanded across trillions of miles of space and countless galaxies (estimate a trillion). In one of the most distant galaxies named Whirlpool Galaxy (or M51) a NASA photo shows a dark cross in a circle of white light. If, as Christians maintain the cross at Calvary does represent the single most important event in the history of planet earth, you might expect it to be showcased even in a far distant galaxy.

Man's knowledge continues to increase in the micro universe as well. Science has discovered laminins, glycoproteins, which are the structural scaffolding in almost every human and animal tissue. Laminins are secreted and incorporated into cell-associated extra-cellular matrices. These micro components are shaped like a cross. "And he (Jesus) is before all things and by him all things consist." (Colossians 1:17) Consist means He holds everything together! Without laminins we would be a pile of jelly. The Gmail words for laminins - I am in man. Sin is in man.

Cross contains the word ross, meaning refuse and that means denied or rejected. "He came unto his own, and his own received him not." John 1:11 I have a cross story I would like to share. My wife had a white gold cross with diamonds. In a store she saw a more expensive diamond cross that caught her eye. She said to me that if I would buy her that cross I could give my daughter the cross she was wearing. I decided to go back and buy the new cross. I boxed and wrapped her first diamond and 14k gold cross and sent it to my daughter for Christmas. Later, after Christmas, I spoke with my daughter and I got the "Paul Harvey rest of the story." She said my granddaughter, young at that time, asked her what she wanted for Christmas. She told her that the only thing she really wanted for Christmas was a cross. My granddaughter processed the request and told her mother that she did not have any money for a cross. My daughter told her that if she would just draw a picture of a cross that would be fine. When my granddaughter saw the shiny gold and diamond cross her mother opened, she enthusiastically said to her mother, "God does answer prayer."

Kabbalah, originated from ancient Jewish mysticism, and was the source for a line in the movie *Bee Season* starring Richard Gere. It states that the letters in words contain the secrets of the universe. This book agrees with, and provides verification, for that statement. I am not an authority on Kabbalah, but I understand sometimes it presents a non-Biblical view of God. *Amazing God* supports an uncompromising belief in the God of the Bible. Primary purposes for *Amazing God* are to support scripture and show that words reveal a design structure that is beyond human ability. This design evidence would add human language for consideration as one more component to the list of "God's clues or fingerprints."

The second person of the Godhead is called the Word, and "Heaven and earth shall pass away, but my words shall not pass away." There is clearly a divine essence within language; and Scripture provides the primary window with which God is revealed to mankind. Thus, it stands to reason that language was with God before creation and is part of His being.

The Bible could be the only book you would ever have and it would be all you would need. It is so important that is why we have bibliography (Bible - Holy Graph)

> "For now we see through a glass, darkly; but then face to face: now I know in part; but then shall I know even as also I am known." - 1 Corinthians 13:12

Holy Scripture is a window to God. The result of *Amazing God* is to bring a sharp focus view on one word at a time. *Amazing God* provides a laser like light and magnifying glass for each word examined. Scripture reveals the truth and glory of God and this book shows the importance and significance of many words in that window view. Word has the phonetic letters for door. Each word in *Amazing God* opens a door to a treasure room of understanding. *Amazing God* gives the reader a thought provoking view of the divine DNA of language and the uncanny ways in which God has left His fingerprints on words. If a regular English word dictionary is important and useful, how valuable and useful is a spiritual lexicon (special dictionary)?

The word hologram has meaning both from the definition of holocryptic and holograph. The first of these two words means to effectively conceal, and the second word means whole or entire.

The equipment for making a hologram includes a laser, mirror and diffusers. The hologram is a frequency record, and when viewed with a laser of the same frequency, it reveals a three-dimensional image of the original object. A profound quality of a hologram is that the image is distributed throughout the entire media. If the hologram is cut into pieces, each piece contains the complete image.

In his excellent book, *Cosmic Codes*, Dr. Chuck Misler discussed the similarities between a hologram and the Bible. I do agree with Dr. Misler that the Bible is like a hologram, and that God's plan for redemption of mankind is distributed from Genesis in the Old Testament to Revelation in the New Testament. Even the idea of God in the form of a man started in Genesis. This man, God as a man, made three appearances to Abraham and Abraham worshiped him. If Abraham accepted and ran to meet God in the form of a man why should not you do the same?

This hologram concept then makes words the smallest segment of the Bible that still conveys an accurate message or picture. Just like each piece of a hologram contains the complete image. When letters from words are reformed to make other words, it provides compelling evidence to the accuracy of the Bible and for the hologram theory.

For several years, there was only one person that received regular Gmail. For this person, it started during a Henry Blackaby small group Bible study of *Experiencing God*. About the time that a group of three of us agreed to do some collaboration on this book lexicon, we all started getting regular and significant numbers of Gmail. This continued for about three months, and then we realized that all three of us had, at about the same time, stopped getting Gmail. Later, the Gmail started again, but they came at a slower rate. Later, two editors of this book received some Gmail. This further substantiates that this is not something that we are able to do or control merely just with our intellect. The five of us are convinced that there is a definite component of illumination with receiving Gmail. Some of you that read this book will experience the ability to discern the spiritual meaning contained in words.

A few years ago I had an interesting experience in a medical doctor's office. The doctor is an endocrinologist, and I was there waiting for an appointment. His first name is George, and I started writing all the words that I could make with the letters in his name. I had written several, and then I saw the word ego. I placed it at the top of the list even though I had written several other words before I saw this one. When the doctor entered the room he immediately saw the list and asked if I had made it. I said yes. He quickly went to the telephone and made a call. When he returned, he said, "Last night my wife and I had a long conversation about my ego." This example, though not exactly Gmail, illustrates God using a word from a word to get a doctor's attention. I believe it was not a coincidence or accident that ego was placed at the top of the list.

It is hoped readers will find these words within words insightful, inspiring, and thought provoking. Christian and Messianic pastors and apologists should find these many word examples to be a valuable tool to compliment their ministries. Other Christian believers should enjoy the many insights from word revelations that support the God of the Bible, and the Christian worldview. Anyone who values the Bible should love the Gmail lexicon as a Biblical aide.

This book was written for God's sheep, both those that know they are sheep and those that will hear God and become sheep. Jesus said, "I am the good shepherd, and know my sheep and am known of mine." John 10:14 It is hoped that those who are genuinely seeking to find meaning and purpose to life may discover some helpful answers from reading *Amazing God.*

Also, it is suspected that God wants to leave enough important word codes unsolved so that some others might enjoy this same experience. Revelations from words are an exhilarating experience that you really want to share with others. When you receive a true Gmail you know it. It is both insightful and thrilling to hear from God in this special way. It is always great to experience the presence of God!

What do we know about the origin of language? Scientists cannot answer with 100% certainty questions of origin because they were not there. This is a question similar to the origin of the universe because we do not have any eye witnesses. In a book, *The Word,* written by Isaac Mozeson, evidence is presented that demonstrates that Hebrew is the patriarch of language. Mozeson's book demonstrates that all languages come from a single original source. Mozeson supports language having a divine origin. A book by Kang and Nelson with a 1979 Copyright demonstrates that events, like Noah's Ark, recorded in the Book of Genesis are hidden in the Chinese language. And, as quoted earlier, Noah Webster believes that language and speech were both instant gifts from God.

This writer takes as accurate and inspired revelation, the Biblical accounts of both the origin of the universe and the origin of language. As the reader progresses through this book, he/she will encounter a lot of evidence to support both of these Biblical claims through many Gmail examples, along with additional information. The following is what the Word of God says about the source of language. "And the whole earth was of one language, and of one speech. And it came to pass, as they journeyed from the east, that they found a plain in the land of Shinar; and they dwelt there. And they said one to another, Go to, let us make brick, and burn them thoroughly. And they had brick for stone, and slime had they for mortar. And they said, Go to, let us build us a city and a tower, whose top may reach unto heaven; and let us make us a name, lest we be scattered abroad upon the face of the whole earth. And the LORD came down to see the city and the tower, which the children of men built. And the LORD said, Behold, the people is one, and they have all one language; and this they begin to do: and now nothing will be restrained from them, which they have imagined to do. Go to, let us go down, and there confound their language, that they may not understand one another's speech. So the LORD scattered them abroad from thence upon the face of all the earth: and they left off to build the city. Therefore is the name of it called Babel; because the LORD did there confound the language of all the earth: and from thence did the LORD scatter them abroad upon the face of all the earth. (Genesis 11:1-9) These are the families of the sons of Noah, after their generations, in their nations: and by these were the nations divided in the earth after the flood." (Genesis 10:32)

Separate nations are God's plan for this planet, and this necessitated many different languages. According to this account written by Moses and recorded in the first chapter of the Old Testament, the languages (thousands) in the world came directly from God early in human history. Of course, over time there are additions and changes to language, but each original language had a divine origin. Gmail will provide evidence to help substantiate that claim.

It is understood there are many individuals that do not have personal experiences with God. That is unfortunate because the Bible gives assurance that true believers have direct access to God. "Let us therefore come boldly unto the throne of grace, that we may obtain mercy, and find grace to help in time of need." (Hebrews 4:16)

Some believers do not think that God provides any new revelations since the Bible is complete. The writer's position is that the Bible is the inspired word of God and the ultimate authority. Anything contradicting the inspired Word of God should be rejected. However, through a personal relationship with the God of Abraham, Isaac and Jacob, I am convinced, both by experiences and Biblical text there is divine help with understanding and new spiritual illuminations. The original word for "word" in the New Testament substantiates just this. The Greek word 'logos' refers to the written Word of God. And the word 'rhema' refers to 'words' or revelations from God that are always based on Scripture. Throughout history, God has revealed Himself not only through the written word, but through divine revelation and illumination.

In 1905, when Albert Einstein was only 26 years old, he published a paper on relativity. At the time of the publication on the theory of relativity, it was met with skepticism and ridicule. As other papers were published, they were viewed the same way. Since these papers were so advanced, only a few physicists even understood them. Only slowly over time did people start to realize that Einstein was actually a true genius. He developed the theory of relativity. The greatest result of relativistic physics was Einstein's famous relation, $E=mc^2$. The equation demonstrates that for a small amount of mass you get an enormous amount of energy. That is precisely what occurs with an atomic bomb. Did you know that Einstein claimed to have gotten his understanding for $E=mc^2$ from the Bible? He said that you will not see it, but it is there in the first book, the Book of Genesis. Using letters in the name of the Jewish Albert Einstein you are able to spell <u>liberate Israel</u>, so will God liberate Israel from her enemies by $E=mc^2$?

Besides being a great physicist, Albert Einstein is also famous for his many quotes. One quote is, "One cannot help but be in awe as he [one] contemplates the mysteries of eternity, of life, of the marvelous structures of reality." For many years, prior to $E=mc^2$ and the atomic bomb, skeptics made fun of the Bible because of a verse that said the "elements shall melt with a fervent heat." (2 Peter 3:10) This contradicted the science of the day. Today, if you ask a physicist to describe an atomic reaction, they will talk about tremendous heat that occurs in a split second, because of the energy released when atoms split. The heat parallels that of our sun. So once again, the Bible proved to be right – elements, indeed, shall melt. The more science discovers, the smarter the Bible becomes. Since this period of the explosion of knowledge began, the Bible has proven to be hundreds or even thousands of years ahead of its time on many issues.

Isaac Newton died 280 years ago and is the scientist known for laying much of the foundation for modern physics, astronomy, math (calculus) and optics. This man considered by many to be the world's greatest scientist, had an intense interest in the Bible. Newton studied the Book of Daniel and concluded that the world would not end (Battle of Armageddon) earlier than 2060. (The world will never actually end, but it will go through major changes) Newton was convinced that the Bible contained cryptic messages and I think he would enjoy this book that reveals cryptic messages in language! As you read, I hope that this decoding of words will be an enjoyable and informative adventure for you. You may even find yourself decoding some words yourself.

<u>SECTION TWO</u>

Section Two of this book provides an alphabetical listing of
GMAIL words with commentary and Bible verses.
This section is referred to as the

GMAIL LEXICON

Section Two is the heart of *Amazing God*.

A

Abraham

Am - Bar (son) - Arab

Hebrew - This author believes that this is the only pure language and that it was the language used in the Garden of Eden. The Lexicon shows Hebrew for two lexicon words to honor this amazing language.

אברהם – Avraham – Father of Many
בר – Bar – Son
רב – Rav – Many
אמה – Umah – People, Nation
רם – Ram – High, Exalted
הר – Mountain

Abraham's name originally was Abram, and God changed it to Abraham. This was very significant because it represented a change had occurred within the man. His former name looked back to his father and pagan roots, and his new name looked to a very different future. This future through his descendants would eventually include the Messiah and bring blessing to the entire world.

You might find it interesting that <u>Abraham</u> was from the area of modern day Iraq, and that he has Arab in his name. His parents would have been Arab. Bar means son and <u>Abraham's</u> name means father of many. When God gave Abraham his name he had not even fathered one child. Now, Abrahams' descendents would be in the millions. His two best known sons are Ishmael and Isaac. Many Arabs are descended from Ishmael, and Jews are descended from Isaac. He is a father of multitudes of Arabs, as well as, the father of the Jews. Jews are simply Arabs that God separated and made a distinct people group to serve His purposes. Israel is God's servant. The Jewish people group and the Arabs are close relatives.

Abraham is a special man – God identified him as both "a friend of God" and "the father of faith." Today, over half of the world's population claims either a physical or spiritual connection to father Abraham. Abraham pleased God, and I wonder how many of the Arab, Jewish, Catholic, Christian/Protestant and other groups that identify with this man would receive similar compliments from God. I see evidence indicating God would like to see major spiritual changes in every one of these groups that claim Abraham as their Father. Being a physical descendent does not mean that spiritually your father is Abraham.

God made a covenant with Abraham that is important to all of mankind. He promised to multiply Abrahams' descendents, and to bless all nations through his lineage. A faithful God has accomplished both of these promises in His covenant with Abraham. Twice Satan has tried unsuccessfully to eliminate the Jewish people in devilish ways. The first time Satan used Hiram, and the second time he used Hitler. Satan is not finished with attempts to accomplish this objective. Make sure you are not another pawn being used by Satan in his unholy spiritual war against these descendents of Abraham. God will always preserve a remnant of the Jewish people.

Satan is the main enemy of God, and he is also an enemy of mankind. Do you think Satan would spare the Ishmael side of Abraham's family tree? Could the Devil be pleased with any descendants from God's friend and this man of great faith? God desires to bless all of the descendants of Abraham. I have to believe that Abraham would be disappointed to see the fruit of his loins in so much division and opposition. I pray for the peace of Jerusalem and for the faith and blessing of Abraham for all his millions of descendents.

God spoke to Moses from the burning bush over 3,500 years ago and told him that His name was "I am." Fourteen centuries after Moses heard the words "I am" the significance is revealed in God's only begotten Son. Jesus explained: "I am the Good Shepherd (laid down His life for the sheep), I am the Bread of Life, I am the Way, the Truth and the Life," etc. The blessing from God through Abraham's descendants was His own Son that became the perfect Lamb that died for the sins of the world. This lineage of God's Son, the Messiah, included <u>Abraham</u>, Isaac, Jacob, Joseph, Boaz, Jesse, David, Solomon, the Virgin Mary and her husband, Joseph of Nazareth, the legal father.

"And I will make thy seed to multiply as the stars of heaven, and will give unto thy seed all these countries; and in thy seed shall all the nations of the earth be blessed;" - Genesis 26:4

"And as for Ishmael, I have heard thee: Behold, I have blessed him, and will make him fruitful, and will multiply him exceedingly; twelve princes shall he beget, and I will make him a great nation." - Genesis 17:20

"Ye are of *your* father the devil, and the lusts of your father ye will do. He was a murderer from the beginning, and abode not in the truth, because there is no truth in him. When he speaketh a lie, he speaketh of his own: for he is a liar, and the father of it." - John 8:44

"That if thou shalt confess with thy mouth the Lord Jesus, and shalt believe in thine heart that God hath raised him from the dead, thou shalt be saved." - Romans 10:9

"And they came to the place which God had told him of; and Abraham built an altar there, and laid the wood in order, and bound Isaac his son, and laid him on the altar upon the wood. And Abraham stretched forth his hand, and took the knife to slay his son. And the angel of the LORD called unto him out of heaven, and said, Abraham, Abraham: and he said, Here *am* I. And he said, Lay not thine hand upon the lad, neither do thou any thing unto him: for now I know that thou fearest God, seeing thou hast not withheld thy son, thine only *son* from me. And Abraham lifted up his eyes, and looked, and behold behind *him* a ram caught in a thicket by his horns: and Abraham went and took the ram, and offered him up for a burnt offering in the stead of his son. And Abraham called the name of that place Jehovahjireh: as it is said *to* this day, In the mount of the LORD it shall be seen. *"* – Gn.22:9-14

Accountability

Action – You – Ability - Account

You are accountable to God for your own actions, based on your God given ability. This principle has an effect both in time (now) and eternity (later). The credit in your account is determined on what you accomplished for the Master based on your ability.

Heaven is not earned by works, and is a privilege given by God's grace because it is a price that none of us could pay. I know that because Jesus asked his Father three times if there was any other way to let that cup pass from Him. The Father in Heaven did not know another way for mankind to be saved.

It does not matter how rich or poor you are because one day, everyone's bank account on earth goes to zero. Then for those that have accepted God's free gift of salvation through Jesus, there will be a judgment that will evaluate their works and the good works will result in rewards. Those works determined of value by God's standards, not by man's standards. Heaven is not general admission and the rewards there are based on what you have sent ahead by faith with good works.

"Oh let the wickedness of the wicked come to an end; but establish the just: for the righteous God trieth the hearts and reins."- Ps. 7:9
"For it is written, *As* I live, saith the Lord, every knee shall bow to me, and every tongue shall confess to God. So then every one of us shall give <u>account</u> of himself to God." - Romans 14:11-12

Adoration

Adorn - Radiant - Art

Adoration for God's beauty is a form of worship. His creation is a radiant work of art not only created for us to enjoy, but for us to recognize God's hand in it: so that we know that He is God. This brings Him glory. Every plant that sprouts vibrant, fragrant flowers, every colorful bird that sings long, captivating songs, and every clear blue tide that washes up on snow white sands could make us say or think, "God, You are awesome! This beauty was not created by accident!" Even the complexity of living things should make us stop and praise God. We see this by realizing that only an all knowing God could create insects that look exactly like a thorn, or a leaf, or a stick; and creatures under the sea that create their own light; or are able to change the color of their skin to blend in flawlessly with rocks and coral. The Milky Way galaxy and millions of other galaxies that adorn an otherwise cold and dark universe should be a reminder of how vast God's is creation. It is easy to worship the Creator when you know the Savior.

"For the invisible things of Him from the creation of the world are clearly seen, being understood by the things that are made, even His eternal power and Godhead; so that they are without excuse;" - Romans 1:20

"The heavens declare the glory of God; and the firmament sheweth his handywork." - Psalm 19:1

Albert Einstein

See – El (God) – Is - Able – Liberate – Israel – Sin – Test

The Bible states that the elements will melt with great heat and science said that was ridiculous because it contradicted the "Law of the conservation of matter and energy." Albert Einstein developed his formula of $E=MC^2$, which stood for energy equaled mass times the speed of light per cubic centimeter. This meant that you would get an enormous amount of energy from a small amount of mass. That was exactly what happened with an atomic bomb detonation. In a split second the heat approximated that of the sun.

The God who stated in His word that the elements will melt is able preserve and to liberate Israel. Israel, re-established sixty-one years ago, is a test for the nations of the world because each nation will be judged by what they do regarding the "apple of God's eye." His word regarding Israel is as sure as His word about the elements melting.

"After many days thou shalt be visited: in the latter years thou shalt come into the land *that is* brought back from the sword, *and is* gathered out of many people, against the mountains of Israel, which have been always waste: but it is brought forth out of the nations, and they shall dwell safely all of them." Ezekiel 38:8

"But the day of the Lord will come as a thief in the night; in the which the heavens shall pass away with a great noise, and the elements shall melt with fervent heat, the earth also and the works that are therein shall be burned up." 2 Peter 3:10

Almighty

I – Am – Light

When you flip on a light switch what happens? The dark disappears immediately if the switch is connected to a power source. Darkness has no power against light and God is light. God is <u>Almighty</u> and by His power, He created everything we see and things that we can't see. When Moses asked God what his name was, He replied, "I Am that I Am." We are to praise, worship, and exalt Him because without Him, we have nothing. In the New Testament, it says that Jesus is the light of the world. We should be drawn to him like moths to a flame; otherwise, we are just walking in the dark without the <u>Almighty</u> "I am the way" guiding.

"And God said unto Moses, 'I Am that I Am' and He said, 'Thus shalt thou say unto the children of Israel, I Am hath sent me unto you" - Exodus 3:14

"This then is the message which we have heard of Him, and declare unto you, that God is light, and in Him is no darkness at all. If we say that we have fellowship with Him, and walk in darkness, we lie, and do not the truth: But if we walk in the light, as He is in the light, we have fellowship one with another, and the blood of Jesus Christ His Son cleanseth us from all sin."- 1 John 1:5-7

"Then spake Jesus again unto them, saying, I am the light of the world: he that followeth me shall not walk in darkness, but shall have the light of life." - John 8:12

Amazing

I am – A-Z – Gain – Again – In – Zing

Again, I am in A-Z. On a Sunday I had a discussion with one of the persons that helped add to the Gmail lexicon about the book title. I said that I had not gotten anything yet. The following Tuesday I received the word, AMAZING, and I knew that I now had the main word for the book title. This was his response to my email with the word for new title: "*Amazing*". That is great! I love it! Cheers to the Holy Spirit for that one. Very good! I received this Gmail complete at four a.m. on May 3, 2007. When you add up all the numbers in the date and time you get *twenty-one*. That is seven times three. One seven for each person in the trinity, and each person of the Godhead is in the book. Seven is a special and important number in Bible numerology. That was not planned by the human author. God is truly <u>amazing</u>. Jesus is the light of the world, and without that light this world would indeed be very dark.

The word for a high pitched sound, like something moving at very high speed, is zing. I believe this zing was present when God spoke the creation into existence.

In Hebrew the first letter is alef and the last is tav. Since Jesus was a Jew he may have actually said, "I am the alef and the tav." The original Hebew alphabet had word pictures. The picture for alef was an ox head and the picture for tav was a cross or plus sign. Was the Hebrew language representing God's plan of redemption from animal sacrifice to the cross? It looks like Jesus has tried to make believing easy because He is the Alef and Tav, the "Alpha and Omega," and the Am and Zing.

"I am Alpha and Omega, the beginning and the ending, saith the Lord, which is, and which was, and which is to come, the Almighty." - Revelation 1:8

"If you would gain the whole world, but do not know the Lord Jesus and lose your soul, you would not have profited from the opportunity of life. For what shall it profit a man, if he shall gain the whole world, and lose his own soul?" - Mark 8:36

"Jesus said unto her, I am the resurrection, and the life: he that believeth in me, though he were dead, yet shall he live:" - John 11:25

"If any man serve me, let him follow me; and where I am, there shall also my servant be: if any man serve me, him will *my* Father honour." - John 12:26

"I am come a light into the world, that whosoever believeth on me should not abide in darkness." – John 12:46

"Ye call me Master and Lord: and ye say well; for *so* I am." – John 13:13

"Now I tell you before it come, that, when it is come to pass, ye may believe that I am *he*." – John 13:19
"Jesus saith unto him, I am the way, the truth, and the life: no man cometh unto the Father, but by me." – John 14:6

"Believest thou not that I am in the Father, and the Father in me? the words that I speak unto you I speak not of myself: but the Father that dwelleth in me, he doeth the works. Believe me that I *am* in the Father, and the Father in me: or else believe me for the very works' sake." – John 14:10-11

"At that day ye shall know that I *am* in my Father, and ye in me, and I in you." – John 14:20

"I am the true vine, and my Father is the husbandman." – John 15:1

"I am the vine, ye *are* the branches:" He that abideth in me, and I in him, the same bringeth forth much fruit: for without me ye can do nothing." – John 15:5

Pilate therefore said unto him, Art thou a king then? Jesus answered, Thou sayest that I am a king. To this end was I born, and for this cause came I into the world, that I should bear witness unto the truth. Every one that is of the truth heareth my voice." John 18:37

American - United States of America (USA)

I Am – Can - Care – Merci (mercy) - USA

The nation of <u>America</u> was established on principles of faith and freedom, by men of strong conviction. <u>America</u> began as a God fearing, God loving, God worshipping nation. God has given <u>America</u> an abundance of blessings, and this nation has served God and has shone to the world like a city on a hill.

Historically, this nation has shown mercy and care to all areas and different people groups of the world.

America claims to be an ally, friend and supporter of Israel, which is very important because God blesses and curses nations on this one issue. The city of Jerusalem, the Capitol of Israel, has USA in the middle of the word, and I believe that this is not a coincidence, but rather the plan of God. I Am is involved in the affairs and destiny of mankind. America owes her freedom and achievement to the providence of God.

Americans have believed in the "American dream" that you can be anything you want to be. You could be born poor and become the President. Unfortunately, as a nation, America has been sliding away from God for a long time. This is having, and will continue to have an adverse effect on continued blessings from God. The problem might be too much emphasis on the "I can" instead of the "I Am." God has and would love to continue to bless America. Nations that turn away from God eventually receive judgment, not blessings. America may be there now!

"Ye are the light of the world. A city that is set on an hill cannot be hid." - Matthew 5:14

"And he shall judge among the nations, and shall rebuke
many people: and they shall beat their swords into plowshares, and their spears into pruninghooks: nation shall not lift up sword
against nation, neither shall they learn war any more." - Isaiah 2:4

Anxiety

Next – Yet – Exit

Anxiety is the fear of not knowing what will happen next, or what is yet to come. It is a form of worry, which is a sin because it shows a lack of trust in God. Therefore, the best way to get anxiety to exit your mind is to stop and realize that God has everything worked out for His divine purposes. He will take care of those things that are yet to come because He knows all and sees all. Worry and <u>anxiety</u> may come about from many different circumstances, such as finances, job status, relationships, etc. All of these things, which we worry about, are things that can and will be provided by God. He will provide if we place our trust in Him and He will take care of our needs. This allows us to have peace and joy in times that are normally stressful.

"Therefore I say unto you, Take no thought for your life, what ye shall eat, or what ye shall drink; nor yet for your body, what ye shall put on. Is not the life more than meat, and the body than raiment? Behold the fowls of the air: for they sow not, neither do they reap, nor gather into barns; yet your heavenly Father feedeth them. Are ye not much better than they? Which of you by taking thought can add one cubit unto his stature? And why take ye thought for raiment? Consider the lilies of the field, how they grow; they toil not, neither do they spin: And Yet I say unto you, That even Solomon in all his glory was not arrayed like one of these. Wherefore, if God so clothe the grass of the field, which to day is, and to morrow is cast into the oven, shall he not much more clothe you, O ye of little faith? Therefore take no thought, saying, What shall we eat? or, What shall we drink? or, Wherewithal shall we be clothed? (For after all these things do the Gentiles seek:) for your heavenly Father knoweth that ye have need of all these things. But seek ye first the kingdom of God, and his righteousness; and all these things shall be added unto you. Take therefore no thought for the morrow: for the morrow shall take thought for the things of itself. Sufficient unto the day is the evil thereof."- Matt. 6:25-34

Argument

True men are great – Grate – Rage - Anger

      Grate means to offend or irritate; as, harsh words grate the heart. An <u>argument</u> can escalate to the point of creating rage in one or both parties. Rage is anger on steroids, because it is furious and usually uncontrolled. This is why an <u>argument</u> might cause a response leading to injury or even death. The condition of rage is a sin or transgression against God. Any <u>argument</u> that reaches this level is another example of the sin nature that is in all mankind.

If a thing is true, it is not false, and it agrees with reality. In the Bible, men are telling Joseph, their brother who they did not recognize, that they are true men. Years earlier these brothers had sold him into slavery for twenty pieces of silver, and lied to their father that his son Joseph had been killed. They were not such true men back then.

Joseph tested his brothers to see if they had changed. They told Joseph they were not spies and were all sons of one man. Reality is the best <u>argument</u> for the truth. They were honest in what they told their brother Joseph, who had become a ruler in Egypt. They passed his testing and the family was reunited. This Old Testament account of Jacob, Joseph, and his brothers showed that true men are great. One reason they are great is they are all citizens of heaven.

"Then Job answered and said, Even to day *is* my complaint bitter: my stroke is heavier than my groaning. Oh that I knew where I might find him! *that* I might come *even* to his seat! I would order *my* cause before him, and fill my mouth with <u>argument</u>s. I would know the words *which* he would answer me, and understand what he would say unto me. Will he plead against me with *his* great power? No; but he would put *strength* in me. There the righteous might dispute with him; so should I be delivered for ever from my judge. Behold, I go forward, but he *is* not *there*; and backward, but I cannot perceive him: On the left hand, where he doth work, but I cannot behold *him*: he hideth himself on the right hand, that I cannot see *him*: But he knoweth the way that I take: *when* he hath tried me, I shall come forth as gold." - Job 23:1-10

"We *are* all one man's sons; we *are* true *men*, thy servants are no spies. If ye *be* true *men*, let one of your brethren be bound in the house of your prison: go ye, carry corn for the famine of your houses: And we said unto him, We *are* true *men*; we are no spies: And the man, the lord of the country, said unto us, Hereby shall I know that ye *are* true *men*; leave one of your brethren *here* with me, and take *food for* the famine of your households, and be gone: And bring your youngest brother unto me: then shall I know that ye *are* no spies, but *that* ye *are* true *men: so* will I deliver you your brother, and ye shall traffick in the land."- Genesis 42:11-19, 31-34

"It is an honour for a man to cease from strife: but every fool will be meddling." - Proverbs 20:3

"Where no wood is, *there* the fire goeth out: so where *there is* no talebearer, the strife ceaseth." - Proverbs 26:20

"An angry man stirreth up strife, and a furious man aboundeth in transgression." - Proverbs 29:22

"Be ye angry, and sin not: let not the sun go down upon your wrath:" - Ephesians 4:26

Atonement

One – Man - Amen – Meant

The Old Testament requirement of animal sacrifice for <u>atonement</u> was only a type, but was needed because "without the shedding of blood there is no remission of sin." Jesus was without sin and the only acceptable sacrifice acceptable to God the Father. The type was meant to point to Jesus, the Lamb of God.
"Wherefore, as by one man sin entered into the world, and death by sin; and so death passed upon all men, for that all have sinned:" - Romans 5:12

"Nevertheless death reigned from Adam to Moses, even over them that had not sinned after the similitude of Adam's transgression, who is the figure of him that was to come. But not as the offense, so also is the free gift. For if through the offense of one many be dead, much more the grace of God, and the gift by grace, which is by one man, Jesus Christ, hath abounded unto many."– Romans 5:14, 15

"For as in Adam all die, even so in Christ shall all be made alive." - 1 Corinthians 15:22

"And walk in love, as Christ also hath loved us, and hath given himself for us an offering and a sacrifice to God for a sweet smelling savour." - Ephesians 5:2

"The next day John seeth Jesus coming unto him, and saith, Behold the Lamb of God, which taketh away the sin of the world." - John 1:29

"I am Alpha and Omega, the beginning and the ending, saith the Lord, which is, and which was, and which is to come, the Almighty." - Revelation 1:8 Amen!

Authority

Author – Thy - Truth

God's Word, the Holy Bible, is the ultimate <u>authority</u> because He is the author of truth. God is not only the author of the Bible (Through the divine inspiration of 40 men covering a period over 1,500 years), but He is the author of all life. Unbelievers cannot accept the Bible as <u>authority</u> because the natural man is not receptive to the things of God. They think it is just religion and foolish, but through the Spirit, we can see and understand clearly. Some people think that faith is blind, but nothing is clearer because you have to hear from God to have faith.

"So then faith *cometh* by hearing, and hearing by the word of God." - Romans 10:17

"Looking unto Jesus the author and finisher of *our* faith; who for the joy that was set before him endured the cross, despising the shame, and is set down at the right hand of the throne of God." - Hebrews 12:2

"Now we have received, not the spirit of the world, but the spirit which is of God; that we might know the things that are freely given to us of God. Which things also we speak, not in the words which man's wisdom teacheth, but which the Holy Ghost teacheth; comparing spiritual things with spiritual. But the natural man receiveth not the things of the Spirit of God: for they are foolishness unto him: neither can he know them, because they are spiritually discerned. But he that is spiritual judgeth all things, yet he himself is judged of no man. For who hath known the mind of the Lord, that he may instruct him? But we have the mind of Christ."- 1 Corinthians 2: 12-16

"Sanctify them through thy truth: thy word is truth"- John 17:17

Awesome

Awe – Some

Only some have awe for God, but all should.

"Let all the earth fear the LORD: let all the inhabitants of the world stand in awe of him."- Psalm.33:8

B

Baptism

Past

Baptism is a church sacrament, and to be <u>baptized</u> is an important part of becoming a follower of Jesus. The late B. R. Lakin said, "A baptismal certificate will not get you into heaven." I agree that <u>baptism</u> does not save one's soul, but it does serve an important purpose.

Many people struggle with the guilt of past sins, and though those sins are forgiven as soon as one has saving faith in the Lord Jesus Christ, most times it takes something physical for a new believer's mind to grasp the spiritual. <u>Baptism</u> provides a physical means in which one can feel the washing away of that guilt. It represents a spiritual death of our past nature, and resurrection in the Holy Spirit, buried with Christ to be raised with Him as a new creation. It is a symbolic action that Jesus has "wiped the slate clean" so to speak, and the guilt of past sins washes away.

This is not to say that a born again, baptized Christian will not sin. Because of our human nature, we will all inevitably sin until we are perfected in Heaven. However, we are no longer slaves to sin because its power has been broken. Even death's power is a thing of the past.

"What shall we say then? Shall we continue in sin, that grace may abound? God forbid. How shall we, that are dead to sin, live any longer therein? Know ye not, that so many of us as were baptized into Jesus Christ were baptized into his death? Therefore we are buried with him by baptism into death: that like as Christ was raised up from the dead by the glory of the Father, even so we also should walk in newness of life. For if we have been planted together in the likeness of his death, we shall be also in the likeness of his resurrection: Knowing this, that our old man is crucified with him, that the body of sin might be destroyed, that henceforth we should not serve sin.

"For he that is dead is freed from sin." - Romans 6:1-7

"For Christ sent me not to <u>baptize</u>, but to preach the gospel: not with wisdom of words, lest the cross of Christ should be made of none effect." 1 Corinthians 1:17

"The like figure whereunto even baptism doth also now save us (not the putting away of the filth of the flesh, but the answer of **a** good conscience toward God,) by the resurrection of Jesus Christ."- 1 Peter 3:21

Believed

Bled – Die – Live

The Lord Jesus suffered and bled on a Roman cross to die, so that we may live. He was resurrected to show that He could overcome death; and to show those who <u>believed</u> in Him that they could do the same. As Christians, we have Jesus' resurrection power through his precious blood. When we believe through faith that He gave His life for our forgiveness and salvation, and we die we will immediately be present with Christ.

"Jesus said unto her (Martha, regarding Lazarus), 'I am the resurrection, and the life: he that believeth in me, though he were dead, yet shall he Live: And whosoever Lives and believes in me shall never die."- John 11:25-26

Began

Bang

For many years, scientists have used the Big Bang theory to try to prove that the universe was created by an explosion of matter from a single point. It states that there was nothing in the beginning. It goes further to say that a process known as Vacuum

Fluctuation created a dime-sized singularity, or a dense mass of matter, which exploded to form the ever-expanding universe we see today. On the surface, the Big Bang theory as stated by scientists looks like an absolute mockery of God's divine blueprint of the universe. And that generally is their whole aim: To try to disprove God's hand in creation. However, they may be closer to the scriptural truth of creation than they realize! In accepting the Big Bang theory, scientists also accept the event of a beginning, which is what is stated in Genesis 1:1. We know that in the beginning there was "nothing", as the scientists say (That compressed mass of matter had to come from somewhere!), but rather there was God who spoke the universe into existence. The key word here is "Spoke". This would obviously indicate a sound of some sort, be it actual words, or a simple bang. There was a bumper sticker that said, "I believe the Big Bang Theory: *God said, 'Bang' and there it was!*"

"By the Word of the Lord were the heavens made; and all the host of them by the breath of His mouth. He gathereth the waters of the sea together as an heap: He layeth up the depth in storehouses. Let all the earth fear the Lord: let all the inhabitants of the world stand in awe of Him. For He spake, and it was done; He commanded, and it stood fast."- Psalm 33:6-9

"In the beginning was the Word, and the Word was with God, and the Word was God. The same was in the beginning with God. All things were made by Him; and without Him was not any thing made that was made. In Him was life; and the life was the light of men. And the light shineth in darkness; and the darkness comprehended it not. There was a man sent from God, whose name was John. The same came for a witness, to bear witness of the Light, that all men through Him might believe. He was not that Light, but was sent to bear witness of that Light. That was the true Light, which lighteth every man that cometh into the world. He was in the world, and the world was made by Him, and the world knew Him not. He came unto His own, and His own received Him not. But as many as received Him, to them gave He power to become the sons of God, even to them that believe on His name: Which were born, not of blood, nor of the will of the flesh, nor of the will of man, but of God. And the Word was made flesh, and dwelt among us, (and we beheld his glory, the glory as of the only begotten of the Father,) full of grace and truth." - John 1:1-14

Believer

Rebel - Re-live (live what you believe) – Ever - El (God)

Mankind from the beginning was a rebel against God and God has ever since been at work to restore that broken relationship. God wants even the wicked to find life.

A person who is a <u>believer</u> in Jesus Christ has received eternal life and been sealed by the Holy Spirit. This may mean their spirit is protected and is now incorruptible. From the Scriptures I find man has received the "breath of life" and in addition to a spirit has a, soul, and body. The soul has the letters for us, so that is who we are.

A sealed person then embarks on a spiritual journey and this process is called sanctification. This means that a believer should be set apart (spiritually) for God and lives a life that demonstrates what they believe. A <u>believer</u> is not saved by works, but a <u>believer</u> should have works of faith that show they really believe in the God of the Bible. The just are saved by faith and they are supposed to continue to live and re-live faith experiences. Prayer, Bible reading and church attendance are three faith experiences that you re-live.

"Have I any pleasure at all that the wicked should die? saith the Lord GOD: *and* not that he should return from his ways, and live?" Ezekiel 18:23

"Therefore we are buried with him by baptism into death: that like as Christ was raised up from the dead by the glory of the Father, even so we also should walk in newness of life." Romans 6:4

"These things have I written unto you that believe on the name of the Son of God; that ye may know that ye have eternal life, and that ye may believe on the name of the Son of God." 1 John 5:13

Benevolence

Be - Noble - Love

It is easy to see that <u>benevolence,</u> or kindness, is tied tightly with all other fruit of the Spirit. One can't have kindness without love, and kindness and love birth goodness. All three of these together help each of us to be noble to our neighbors and to God. The definition of the word noble is *"possessing, characterized by, or arising from superiority of mind or character or of ideals or morals."* Our noble character as Christians should reflect the love that God showed to us.

"For God so loved the world, that he gave his only begotten Son, that whosoever believeth in him should not perish, but have everlasting life." - John 3:16

"For we ourselves also were sometimes foolish, disobedient, deceived, serving divers lusts and pleasures, living in malice and envy, hateful, and hating one another. But after that the kindness and love of God our Saviour toward man appeared, Not by works of righteousness which we have done, but according to his mercy he saved us, by the washing of regeneration, and renewing of the Holy Ghost;" - Titus 3:3-5

Bibliography

Bible – Biography - Holy

A <u>bibliography</u> is a compilation of works by a specific author. The Holy Bible is compiled of the writings of forty men who were inspired by the Holy Spirit to give us history, knowledge, wisdom, and guidance directly from God.

A biography is a written account of someone's life composed by someone other than the subject of the biography. A biography written about another person may have flaws and misinformation, but the Bible is an infallible biography because it was inspired by the Holy Spirit. It's a paradox, in that it is fully the Word of God, but fully penned by the hands of men. God is the author, yet man is the author. The mystery in this paradox is revealed in the person of Jesus Christ, the living word: fully God, and fully man.

"And the Word was made flesh, and dwelt among us, and we beheld his glory, the glory as of the only begotten of the Father, full of grace and truth" - John 1:14

"All scripture is given by inspiration of God, and is profitable for doctrine, for reproof, for correction, for instruction in righteousness."- 2 Timothy 3:16

Blameless

Lamb – Less – Me – El (God)

In the Old Testament at the Passover Feast, the high priest brought an unblemished lamb to the altar to be sacrificed as an offering to God, in order for sins to be forgiven. The blood of the unblemished Lamb (or other animals) was a symbol of a pure, clean life. And the spilling of the blood symbolized death, because the wages of sin is death. The act of offering this sacrifice was done once a year. When Jesus came to this world, He lived a sinless life. He was <u>blameless</u>, yet He was condemned to die for sins He did not commit, but rather for the sins which mankind committed. He became the sacrificial Lamb. His blood which was spilled took away all our sin for all time.

We can rejoice as Christians because we know that what Jesus did for mankind justifies us as righteous before God. Yes, all sins, past, present and future are forgiven and not remembered (called to account for action) by God. To have a successful life he/she realizes that God is the vine and they are the branches. The vine supplies strength to the branch, so Christians should rely less on themselves (me) and more on God

"And almost all things are by the law purged with blood; and without shedding of blood is no remission." - Hebrews 9:22

"And he shewed me a pure river of water of life, clear as crystal, proceeding out of the throne of God and of the Lamb. In the midst of the street of it, and on either side of the river, *was there* the tree of life, which bare twelve *manner of* fruits, *and* yielded her fruit every month: and the leaves of the tree *were* for the healing of the nations. And there shall be no more curse: but the throne of God and of the Lamb shall be in it; and his servants shall serve him:" - Revelation 22:1-3

Blessed

Bleed – Seed

Jesus Christ had to be crucified on the cross, pierced and bleed to death to take away the sins of the world. Jesus was of the seed of David and fulfilled the covenant that God made with Abraham that through him all nations would be <u>blessed</u>.

"And I will make thy seed to multiply as the stars of heaven, and will give unto thy seed all these countries; and in thy seed shall all the nations of the earth be blessed;" - Genesis 26:4

"I am the door: by me if any man enter in, he shall be saved, and shall go in and out, and find pasture" - John 10:9

"Of this man's seed hath God according to *his* promise raised unto Israel a Saviour, Jesus:" - Acts 13:23

But with the precious blood of Christ, as of a lamb without blemish and without spot:"- 1 Peter 1:19

Blood

Bold

Under the old covenant, no one was allowed to enter the Holy of Holies. This was the innermost area of the temple, where God's presence dwelt behind a thick curtain. Only the high priest could enter, and only then if he brought <u>blood</u> to sprinkle on the Holy Seat. Otherwise, he would be struck dead because of his sinful nature. When Jesus died on the cross, his <u>blood</u> replaced that of the animals that were sacrificed under the Old Covenant laws. It took away our sins and made us clean, allowing anyone who has accepted Jesus' sacrifice to enter into God's presence whenever and wherever, without fear of being struck down. We can boldly come before God because of the <u>blood</u> of Jesus.

"Having therefore, brethren, boldness to enter into the holiest by the blood of Jesus" - Hebrews 10:19

Boundaries

Sound – Around – Abide – Sad – Sin – End

Skeptics and unbelievers have a misunderstanding about the commandments, precepts and laws of God. They see God as a kill-joy that takes away their fun. God acknowledges that there is "pleasure in sin for a season." However, God knows the ultimate consequence of disobedience and sin. Respect for <u>boundaries</u> and honoring <u>boundaries</u> actually increases freedom. Traffic lights establish legal <u>boundaries,</u> but they improve traffic flow and safety. It is the same with God's boundaries because they bring about a better society and richer, fuller, longer lives.

Boundaries should be sound, not established by man but by God. A nation built around sound boundaries will prosper, but if the people of that nation depart from those boundaries it will bring a sad end. Today, it appears that most of the nations of the world have not continued to abide in God's boundaries. This falling away is exactly what the Bible describes as the end approaches.

"But we are bound to give thanks alway to God for you, brethren beloved of the Lord, because God hath from the beginning chosen you to salvation through sanctification of the Spirit and belief of the truth:" - 2 Thessalonians 2:13

"See that none render evil for evil unto any *man*; but ever follow that which is good, both among yourselves, and to all *men*." –
1 Thessalonians 5:15

Breath

Heart

God is love and has a heart for human life which is sacred and distinguished from animals. Because we are made in the image and likeness of God and we have a living soul. Man became a living soul when he received the breath of life from God. Once the man Adam committed sin in the Garden of Eden mankind and all of the creation came under a curse. That is why there is no paradise anywhere in the universe because it was lost.

"But God, who is rich in mercy, for his great love wherewith he loved us," Ephesians 2:4

"The Spirit of God hath made me, and the breath of the Almighty hath given me life." - Job 33:4

C

Called

El (God) – Lead - Deal

Any person becoming a prophet, pastor, evangelist, teacher or Christian writer is supposed to be <u>called</u> by God. When God calls you He is making a deal with you. Jesus said, "Follow me." That is the deal. A person that is called into Christian service should be led by God. Unfortunately, this is not always the case and those that are self called often do harm to the faith. I would not want to be in a church were the leader had not been called by God.

Moses saw a burning bush that was not consumed and he turned aside to see this great sight. At this burning bush God spoke to Moses and <u>called</u> him to deliver the Hebrews out of the hand of the Egyptians. This was a profound and important call, but like Moses everyone in ministry should have heard a call from God and responded with an acceptance. Moses could not lead the people out of Egypt if he had not been led by God throughout his assigned task. Have you been called or chosen and not responded?

"For many are <u>called</u>, but few *are* chosen." - Matthew 22:14

"Many will say to me <u>in</u> that day, Lord, Lord, have we not prophesied in thy name? and in thy name have cast out devils? and in thy name done many wonderful works? And then will I profess unto them, I never knew you: depart from me, ye that work iniquity." – Matthew 7:22-23

"And the angel of the LORD appeared unto him (Moses) in a flame of <u>fire</u> out of the midst of a <u>bush</u>: and he looked, and, behold, the bush burned with fire, and the bush *was* not consumed."- Exodus 3:2

Character

Heart – Chart – React – Rate - Tear

Because of original sin by Adam in the Garden of Eden, mankind inherited a fallen sin nature. The Bible states, "Jesus wept." Our <u>character</u> has been corrupted by sin and that causes weeping and tears. In a conversation with Cain, God said, "If thou doest well, shalt thou not be accepted? And if thou doest not well, sin lieth at the door. And unto thee *shall be* his desire, and thou shalt rule over him." - Genesis 4:7

God will never lower His standard and excuse sin, so Cain was told that he must conquer sin. No one that has ever lived has done that except Jesus Christ, the anointed Messiah. That is why our own righteousness or works is never adequate to meet God's standard. That is why we all need a Savior that does meet the righteous standard of God. In salvation that righteousness is applied to us and never removed.

The sin nature has an effect on our <u>character</u> and on how we react to circumstances, events and choices in life. God knows your heart better than you do and has a "heart chart" on you and everyone else. You have heard the expression he/she has a good heart. Yes, even people will rate the heart of others, but it is God's view that really counts. What does God think of your heart? Is it hardened toward God? Does it have hatred, envy, or covetousness? Does your heart demonstrate the fruit of the Holy Spirit?

The Finisher – Devie Anderson (American)
o o o For "The Finisher" is the author of faith

The completer of all

The essence

The "Way"

For better for worse

For winning the stand

"The Finisher" looks

At the heart of the man.

"But the fruit of the Spirit is love, joy, peace, long-suffering, gentleness, goodness, faith," - Galatians 5:22

"The heart *is* deceitful above all *things*, and desperately wicked: who can know it?" - Jeremiah 17:9

"For out of the heart proceed evil thoughts, murders, adulteries, fornications, thefts, false witness, blasphemies:" - Matthew 15:19

Children

Heir – hide

Just as <u>children</u> naturally enjoy playing hide-and-seek, there is a need to seek God who is hidden from the five senses. The loving creator God wants to draw us into a relationship with Him. He hides, but wants to be found. When you do find God through faith you become an heir of righteousness. All true believers are included in God's family, and in the New Testament are referred to as <u>children</u> because we are God's <u>children</u>. In heaven there will be people from every kindred, tongue, and nation on this planet. This means that they will be heirs and receive an astounding eternal reward.

"My little <u>children</u>, these things write I unto you, that ye sin not. And if any man sin, we have an advocate with the Father, Jesus Christ the righteous:" - 1 John 2:1

"And if <u>children</u>, then heirs; heirs of God, and joint-heirs with Christ; if so be that we suffer with *him*, that we may be also glorified together." - Romans 8:17

"By faith Noah, being warned of God of things not seen as yet, moved with fear, prepared an ark to the saving of his house; by the which he condemned the world, and became heir of the righteousness which is by faith." - Hebrews 11:7

Christian

Christ – In – His

When we have faith to believe in the divinity of Jesus and the truth of His death and resurrection, we become <u>Christians</u>. We are in Christ, and we as the church function as His body. The Bible says that we are "the light of the world."

"So we, *being* many, are one body in Christ, and every one members one of another." - Romans 12:5

"For we must all appear before the judgment seat of Christ; that every one may receive the things *done* in *his* body, according to that he hath done, whether *it be* good or bad." - 2 Corinthians 5:10 (Rewards only and applies to all who are saved)

Committed

Come – Tied – To – Time

I come tied to time (we are only able to commit for a time). In this world, time is very short, just a breath, compared to eternity. Unfortunately, many trade time for eternity. Like the television show, "Deal or No Deal" would you trade your short time or life span here for an eternity that you do not understand very well? Eternity is like the case that is holding ten billion dollars, and your case here has only ten cents. That is a reasonable analogy, and yet many trade their eternal birthright (salvation is eternal life) for the short time they might have in this fallen and corrupt world. Men reject light because their deeds are evil. They make a bad deal.

"I would seek unto God, and unto God would I commit my cause:" - Job 5:8

"But, beloved, be not ignorant of this one thing, that one day *is* with the Lord as a thousand years, and a thousand years as one day." - 2 Peter 3:8

"And saying, The time is fulfilled, and the kingdom of God is at hand: repent ye, and believe the gospel." - Mark 1:15

Compassion

Compass – Son

Christians should have <u>compassion</u> for those who are in need, be it physical or spiritual; we should show them care in the way that Jesus showed us care while He was here on Earth. Through our <u>compassion,</u> we allow them to see Christ in us, pointing their eyes in the direction of Jesus. God will use a <u>compassion</u>ate Christian as a compass to point the lost to His Son.

"And Jesus, moved with <u>compassion,</u> put forth *his* hand, and touched him, and saith unto him, I will; be thou clean." - Mark 1:41

"Then we which are alive *and* remain shall be caught up together with them in the clouds, to meet the Lord in the air: and so shall we ever be with the Lord." - 1 Thessalonians 4:17

Complete

Temple – Come

Most evangelical Christians have an expectation for the return of Jesus, and this is referred to as the "second coming." According to Bible prophecy, the Jewish Temple in Israel will be desecrated by the Anti-Christ exactly three and one half years before the Battle of Armageddon. The last Temple was destroyed by the Roman army in 70 A.D. So if there is no temple how could it be desecrated? The answer is that the Temple must be rebuilt for the prophesy of its desecration to be fulfilled.

There is probably a connection between a <u>complete</u> rebuilt Temple and Christ's return for believers, which is commonly called the Rapture. If you would like to make a donation for the construction of the new Temple send it to: Rabbi Chaim Richman The Temple Institute PO Box 31876 Jerusalem, Israel 91317

"But when ye shall see the abomination of desolation, spoken of by Daniel the prophet, standing where it ought not, (let him that readeth understand,) then let them that be in Judea flee to the mountains:" - Mark 13:14

"Then we which are alive *and* remain shall be caught up together with them in the clouds, to meet the Lord in the air: and so shall we ever be with the Lord." - 1 Thessalonians 4:17

Consecrated

Sacred - Center - Secret

The word sacred is not in the Bible, but <u>consecrated</u> is a synonym for sacred. To have fear (awe, respect, and reverence) of the Lord opens a gate of understanding to the secret of His covenant. New Age practitioners like to refer to being "centered." What you really need is for the center of your being (heart) to understand a secret that makes you sacred (belong to God) by a covenant relationship with the Lord.

"For Moses had said, Consecrate yourselves to day to the LORD, even every man upon his son, and upon his brother; that he may bestow upon you a blessing this day." - Exodus 32:29

"The secret of the LORD *is* with them that fear him; and he will shew them his covenant." - Psalm 25:14

Conscience

Con – Science – See - Seen

Knowledge (science) alone only yields an unbeliever, but faith in God and science (knowledge) yields a believer. The human <u>conscience</u> exists universally, and is another witness to the existence of God. Values of morality are understood instinctively through the <u>conscience</u> producing general agreements of right and wrong. If man was the product of random organization through processes of nature, why would any moral values exist? Those relying only on science have been conned and are blind to spiritual truth. See and seen is in the word science because that is required for it to be true science. If it is not observable it is not science.

"But have renounced the hidden things of dishonesty, not walking in craftiness, nor handling the word of God deceitfully; but by manifestation of the truth commending ourselves to *every man's* <u>conscience</u> in the sight of God." - 2 Corinthians 4:2

Conservative

Con (with) Verse – Vote – Reactive

Most <u>conservatives</u> use verse whether they are Republicans, Democrats, Catholics, Evangelical Christians, Orthodox Jews, Mormons, Jehovah Witness, Amish, or Wahabi Muslims, etc. They also vote and are reactive to conserve their views. Some <u>conservatives</u> serve the true God, but some do not. Some persons that use verse do so for their own agenda and/or personal gain and others try to follow truth and principles.

Most of America's founding Fathers were greatly influenced by the Christian Bible (1611 King James Version). This influence resulted in the recognition of the Creator God and the establishment of freedom and liberty in the Declaration of Independence and the Constitution of the United States. A foundation in moral principals and religious freedom was an important part of their concept of self-government. Jonathan Krohn born March 1, 1995 wrote a book titled *Define Conservatism*. The young Mr. Krohn has gained a lot of notoriety from his book and a February 2009 speech at CPAC. He contends that not everyone who calls themselves a conservative really understands the meaning of conservatism. His book outlines four fundamental principles of conservative thought: support for the United States Constitution, respect for life, less government, and more personal responsibility. Jonathan says, "Conservatism is based on principle and it is an ideology of protecting people and people's rights."

"Ye are the salt of the earth: but if the salt have lost his savour, wherewith shall it be salted? it is thenceforth good for nothing, but to be cast out, and to be trodden under foot of men." Matthew 5:13

Consume

Come - Use - Me

When we let the Holy Spirit <u>consume</u> us, we are saying to God, "Come use me." The Holy Spirit is the part of the Godhead that lets Him be within us so that He can work on us to build character, faith, obedience, and wisdom. He can then use us as part of the body of Christ to build His Kingdom.

"So we, *being* many, are one body in Christ, and every one members one of another." - Romans 12:5

Converse (con-with)

Con – Verse

Let your conversation be influenced with Bible verses.

"But as he which hath called you is holy, so be ye holy in all manner of conversation;" - 1 Peter 1:15

"All scripture *is* given by inspiration of God, and *is* profitable for doctrine, for reproof, for correction, for instruction in righteousness:" - 2 Timothy 3:16

"For the word of God *is* quick, and powerful, and sharper than any two edged sword, piercing even to the dividing asunder of soul and spirit, and of the joints and marrow, and *is* a discerner of the thoughts and intents of the heart." - Hebrews 4:12

"And *that* every tongue should confess that Jesus Christ *is* Lord, to the glory of God the Father." – Philippians 2:11

Covenant

One – Tent – Conven *(Convene)* – Ten

A <u>covenant</u> is a formal sealed agreement between two parties. Our God is a <u>Covenant</u> God, as we can see throughout the entire Bible. He made <u>covenant</u>s with mankind including Noah, Abraham, Moses, David, and believers in Jesus, the anointed Messiah. All of the promises God made in these <u>covenants</u> have been kept by Him because God is not a <u>covenant</u> breaker. The Old Testament contains the <u>covenant</u> revealed to Moses in the form of the Ten Commandments. The new <u>covenant</u> by Jesus' blood is different, however. It is not only for one group of people (the Jews), but for all who accept it and enter into the <u>covenant</u> and promises through Jesus Christ. The new <u>covenant</u> allows us to come together as one people, not Jew and Gentile, but as one new man, and convene as one body.

Moses was commanded by God to create a place for his

people to worship, called the Tabernacle. The very first Tabernacle was a tent, called "The tent of Meeting", where all of his people came together. The Christian church is much like this tent of Meeting in the Old Testament. Since we are one body through Christ, we are all under His tent. He is the High Priest of the Tabernacle which resides in every Christian's heart. This tent covers every church that is rooted in His truth and acknowledges God's only son as High Priest, Prophet and King.

"And the bow shall be in the cloud; and I will look upon it, that I may remember the everlasting <u>covenant</u> between God and every living creature of all flesh that *is* upon the earth." - Genesis 9:16

"And the LORD said unto Moses, Write thou these words: for after the tenor of these words I have made a <u>covenant</u> with thee and with Israel. And he was there with the LORD forty days and forty nights; he did neither eat bread, nor drink water. And he wrote upon the tables the words of the <u>covenant</u>, the ten commandments." - Exodus 34: 27, 28

"For he is our peace, who hath made both one, and hath broken down the middle wall of partition *between us*;" - Ephesians 2:14

Creation

Art – Ate – Reaction – Action

The word <u>creation</u> has eight letters and eight is the spiritual number for a new beginning. A week is seven days and the eighth day starts a new week. In music, seven notes complete an octave and the eighth note starts a new octave. Noah and his family that survived the Genesis flood were a total of eight souls. <u>Creation</u> was something entirely new because it required a cause; and was not there until that cause or beginning took place.

The <u>creation</u> is certainly a masterpiece containing phenomenal design, function and beauty. God's creation is in a fallen condition because of the curse that came from Adam's fall. God did not create sin, but did create the potential for sin because man was equipped with a self will.

Because of this freedom we also have the potential to generate real love for others and for the Creator. What is your reaction to this <u>creation</u> that you have the privilege of experiencing? I believe God is worth knowing, loving and worshiping beyond words. If you have not already, you should take action and pursue the Creator.

"In the selfsame day entered Noah, and Shem, and Ham, and Japheth, the sons of Noah, and Noah's wife, and the three wives of his sons with them, into the ark;" - Genesis 7:13

"And thou shalt love the LORD thy God with all thine heart, and with all thy soul, and with all thy might." - Deuteronomy 6:5

D

Daniel

I – And - El (God) - Land

<u>Daniel</u> had a life that fulfilled God's purposes for him, because <u>Daniel</u> was in a relationship with the true and living God of Israel. He had confidence in God's power, even when facing hungry lions. <u>Daniel</u> was a Prophet that God revealed precise information to about all the future kingdoms of the world. Of course, kingdoms involve land. Also, he spoke with King Cyrus who had conquered the Babylonian Empire and showed him that he had been prophesied by name in the Bible. King Cyrus allowed the Jews to return to Jerusalem and their land.

"Now God had brought Daniel into favour and tender love with the prince of the eunuchs." - Daniel 1:9

"In the third year of Cyrus king of Persia a thing was revealed unto Daniel, whose name was called Belteshazzar; and the thing *was* true, but the time appointed *was* long: and he understood the thing, and had understanding of the vision." - Daniel 10:1

"Thus saith Cyrus king of Persia, All the kingdoms of the earth hath the LORD God of heaven given me; and he hath charged me to build him an house in Jerusalem, which *is* in Judah. Who *is there* among you of all his people? The LORD his God *be* with him, and let him go up." - 2 Chronicles 36:23

Deceitful

Lie –Feud (strife) **– Life – Die**

The first <u>deceitful</u> act took place in the Garden of Eden when Satan deceived Eve. Today, the worst deceits are still the deceptions that lead away from the true God and into serious errors like following secularism, materialism, humanism or any false gods or false religion.

"Take heed to yourselves, that your heart be not <u>deceived,</u> and ye turn aside, and serve other gods, and worship them;" - Deuteronomy 11:16

"Who is a liar but he that denieth that Jesus is the Christ? He is antichrist, that denieth the Father and the Son." - 1 John 2:22
"It *is* an honour for a man to cease from <u>strife</u>: but every fool will be meddling." - Proverbs 20:3

"But of the tree of the knowledge of good and evil, thou shalt not eat of it: for in the day that thou eatest thereof thou shalt surely die." - Genesis 2:17 "And the serpent said unto the woman, Ye shall not surely die:" - Genesis 3:4

"By mercy and truth iniquity is purged: and by the fear of the LORD *men* depart from evil." - Proverbs 16:6

"With him *is* strength and wisdom: the <u>deceived</u> and the deceiver *are* his." - Job 12:16

"Be not <u>deceived</u>; God is not mocked: for whatsoever a man soweth, that shall he also reap." - Galatians 6:7

"And he said, Take heed that ye be not <u>deceived</u>: for many shall come in my name, saying, I am *Christ*; and the time draweth near: go ye not therefore after them." - Luke 21:8

Deception

Deep – Pit

Satan's first big <u>deception</u> on earth was in the Garden of Eden when he talked with Eve through the serpent. Satan is a deceiver that is out to deceive the whole world. He was a murderer and a liar from the beginning. The intent of His <u>deception</u> is to lead souls away from the truth of the Living God, so their end will be a deep pit that is bottomless.

"Now the serpent (Satan) was more subtle than any beast of the field which the LORD God had made. And he said unto the woman, Yea, hath God said, Ye shall not eat of every tree of the garden?" – Genesis 3:1

"Take heed to yourselves, that your heart be not <u>deceived</u>, and ye turn aside, and serve other gods, and worship them;" – Deuteronomy 11:16

"I made the nations to shake at the sound of his fall, when I
cast him down to hell with them that descend into the pit:
and all the trees of Eden, the choice and best of Lebanon, all
that drink water, shall be comforted in the nether parts of the
earth." - Ezekiel 31:16

"Put on the whole armour of God, that ye may be able to stand
against the wiles of the devil." - Ephesians 6:11

"And the fifth angel sounded, and I saw a star fall from heaven
unto the earth: and to him was given the key of the bottomless pit.
And he opened the bottomless pit; and there arose a smoke out of
the pit, as the smoke of a great furnace; and the sun and the air
were darkened by reason of the smoke of the pit."- Rev.9:1-2

Default

Fault – Ate

In the beginning man was created as a blameless soul with
a sinless nature. He was without fault. But when Satan tempted
Adam and he ate the forbidden fruit and all mankind had inequity
or sin from that point on. Mankind's natural <u>default</u> is now that of
sin. We are born of the flesh and are sinners when we enter the
world. Our natural inclination is that of sin, and we are separated
from God. When we are born again through belief in the deity and
sacrifice of Jesus Christ, the righteousness of Christ is applied to
us, and we are free from bondage to sin.

"But of the tree of the knowledge of good and evil, thou shalt not
eat of it: for in the day that thou eatest thereof thou shalt surely
die." - Genesis 2:17

"For if by one man's offence death reigned by one; much more
they which receive abundance of grace and of the gift of
righteousness shall reign in life by one, Jesus Christ.)" – Rom. 5:17

Denial

Lied - End – Die

In the Garden of Eden Satan made a <u>denial</u> of the truth of the word of God and lied to Eve. Faith comes by hearing the word of God – everyone either accepts God's word, or like Satan, denies God's word. All die because the wages of sin is death, and in the end you will either have eternal life or experience the second death because of a <u>denial</u> of the Son of God.

"Ye are of *your* father the devil, and the lusts of your father ye will do. He was a murderer from the beginning, and abode not in the truth, because there is no truth in him. When he speaketh a lie, he speaketh of his own: for he is a liar, and the father of it." - John 8:44

"And the serpent said unto the woman, Ye shall not surely die:" Genesis 3:4

"If we suffer, we shall also reign with *him*: if we deny *him*, he also will deny us:" - 2 Timothy 2:12

Dependence

Deepen – Need – Depend

We need God and should depend on Him for everything. Greater <u>dependence</u> upon Him will allow us to be delivered, sustained and will deepen our relationship with Him.

"Were not the Ethiopians and the Lubims a huge host, with very many chariots and horsemen? yet, because thou didst rely on the LORD, he delivered them into thine hand." - 2 Chronicles 16:8

"Cast thy burden upon the LORD, and he shall sustain thee: he shall never suffer the righteous to be moved." - Psalm 55:22

"For all these things do the nations of the world seek after: and your Father knoweth that ye have need of these things." - Luke 12:30

Depravity

Yet – I –Pray – Party - Pity

The word <u>depravity</u> is **not** cited in the Bible. It means innate corruption. Total <u>depravity</u> theology presents that every person born into the world is enslaved to the service of sin and, apart from the efficacious or grace of God, is utterly unable to choose to follow God or choose to accept salvation as it is freely offered. In Reformed Theology, God **must** predestine individuals into salvation since man is incapable of choosing God.

I believe in Biblical predestination and election. God had a determined plan of redemption for both Jews and Gentiles. I accept that God is sovereign and He rightfully exercises His will and purpose. Those thoughts are grand; however I do find some problems with the above doctrine commonly known today as Calvinism (Selective salvation), which was named for John Calvin (1509-1564), a French reformation theologian.

As I stated the Bible does present election and pre-destination and there are elements of Biblical truth in Calvinistic doctrine. However, I do not believe that God elected anyone to go to hell. Calvin's five-point doctrine (Total depravity, Unconditional election, Limited atonement, Irresistible grace, Preservation of the saints) presents salvation and eternal life by predestination or election. There is a lot of debate and difference of opinion on this topic. There are many respected scholars and studied Christians who have opposing views.

Calvinism has five points and I am a "zero point" Calvinist. Calvin's first point is TOTAL <u>DEPRAVITY</u>. I have chosen to use this first point to make my point. All men/women have <u>depravity</u> (innate corruption) and the word itself is serious because it implies 100%. Therefore, I believe that adding total in front of it is not correct. The word total means absolute and is a red flag to me in theology. Any <u>depravity</u>, even one sin, separates an unsaved person from God. I see Biblical problems with a doctrine claiming the gift of salvation is not freely available to everyone.

I do strongly agree with this that Calvin wrote, "For anyone to arrive at God the Creator he needs Scripture as his Guide and Teacher." The Bible makes many appeals to everyone to receive God's grace. Abraham's faith, not election, was counted for righteousness. Since there are over one hundred verses stating salvation is offered to everyone it must be an important doctrine.

Mankind is made in God's image, has a conscience, moral virtues and the influence of <u>depravity</u> (innate corruption) can either increase or decrease in a society. All major religions teach the importance of prayer. Muslims are supposed to pray five times a day and New Age practitioners have prayer. Some prayers could be more spiritually correct than others, but prayer is usually not depraved. However, there is a warning of damnation for long prayer that is done just for show. (Luke 20:47)

It is because of partial <u>depravity</u> that many people think that they are basically good. The heathen do like to party. Because mankind has <u>depravity</u> God has taken pity on us. That is one reason He made a universal offer of salvation to everyone.

I suggest Christians should be cautious about selective salvation. This doctrine faded away after Augustine and in this writer's view is it should fade away once again.

"And GOD saw that the wickedness of man *was* great in the earth, and *that* every imagination of the thoughts of his heart *was* only evil continually." - Genesis 6:5

"And he is the propitiation for our sins: and not ours only, but also for the sins of the whole world." 1 John 2:2

"The Lord is not slack concerning his promise, as some men count slackness; but is long-suffering to us-ward, not willing that any should perish, but that all should come to repentance." 2 Peter 3:9

But without faith it is impossible to please him: for he that cometh to God must believe that he is, and that he is a rewarder of them that diligently seek him." Hebrews 11:6

Desire

Reside

Desire can be a longing, an appetite, including sexual desire which is lust; or a wish to obtain something. Desire can be selfish or unselfish. You might wish for something good for someone else. Desires reside in the heart, and they can produce cravings and emotions to attain that which is desired. The desire of something sinful and morally wrong can be difficult to overcome because of this tendency for desire to reside in us. Even born again believers that have been set free from sin could slip into fleshly desires that war against the spirit. A Christian is either walking in the spirit or walking in the flesh. The Bible says to crucify the flesh. The Lord's model prayer states, "Lead us not into temptation, but deliver us from evil." (Matthew 6:13)

"If thou doest well, shalt thou not be accepted? and if thou doest not well, sin lieth at the door. And unto thee *shall be* his desire, and thou shalt rule over him." - Genesis 4:7

"He will fulfil the desire of them that fear him: he also will hear their cry, and will save them." - Psalm 145:19
"Better *is* the sight of the eyes than the wandering of the desire: this *is* also vanity and vexation of spirit." - Ecclesiastes 6:9

"For thus saith the LORD of hosts; Yet once, it *is* a little while, and I will shake the heavens, and the earth, and the sea, and the dry *land*; And I will shake all nations, and the <u>desire</u> of all nations shall come: and I will fill this house with glory, saith the LORD of hosts." - Haggai 2:6-7

"Brethren, my heart's <u>desire</u> and prayer to God for Israel is, that they might be saved." - Romans 10:1

"But now, after that ye have known God, or rather are known of God, how turn ye again to the weak and beggarly elements, whereunto ye <u>desire</u> again to be in bondage?" - Galatians 4:9

"For if after they have escaped the pollutions of the world through the knowledge of the Lord and Saviour Jesus Christ, they are again entangled therein, and overcome, the latter end is worse with them than the beginning." - 2 Peter 2:20

"Therefore I say unto you, What things soever ye <u>desire</u>, when ye <u>pray</u>, believe that ye receive *them*, and ye shall have *them*." - Mark 11:24

Devil

Lived – Vile – Evil - Die

When Jesus was in the wilderness for forty days he was tempted by the <u>devil</u> (Satan), and you too have been tempted by the <u>devil</u>. The work and deeds of the <u>devil</u> are evil and vile before God. The Devil was a murderer from the beginning, so how many millions will die or have died because of his activity? Many people today do not even believe in a literal devil, but these are deceived.

"And he was there in the wilderness forty days, tempted of Satan; and was with the wild beasts; and the angels ministered unto him." - Mark 1:13

Deity
Deity

Yet – I – Die – Ye (You)

Why would die be in <u>deity</u>? Could God possibly die? No, God is eternal and will always live. However, when God became fully man while still fully God (theological term is hypostatic union) he was separated from the Father (separation from God is death) and he willingly died physically on a cross in Jerusalem.

Jesus was fully God and this was attested to by Old Testament scripture, John the Baptist, the Apostles, by Jesus, by the Angels and by God the Father. Jesus himself declared that he was equal to God. Since about 2000 years ago when he died, was buried and rose again after three days, millions of believers have accepted that as fact and believed it with all their heart. It is part of the Good News that Jesus, the Lamb of God, died in our place and took the sins of mankind upon him. He left the glory of heaven to suffer and physically die for you and me.

"Jesus saith unto him, Have I been so long time with you, and yet hast thou not known me, Philip? He that hath seen me hath seen the Father; and how sayest thou *then*, Shew us the Father?" - John 14:9

"In whom we have redemption through his blood, *even* the forgiveness of sins: Who is the image of the invisible God, the firstborn of every creature." - Colossians 1:14-15

Dimension

Dime – Mind – Men – Son

Scientists have a theory that was developed from advanced geometry that there are ten <u>dimensions</u>. Because dime means a tenth, I agree that reality has 10 <u>dimensions</u>.

The concept of the Trinity, one God, but three distinct persons in the Godhead is hard for many people to comprehend. This pattern of one thing with three components is demonstrated over and over in nature. Matter exists in one of three states, solid, liquid, or gas. The water molecule has three atoms, but water is one substance. Time has the three tenses of past, present and future. All matter has the three <u>dimensions</u> of length, width and height. A line drawn on a sheet of paper that might look two dimensional actually has three <u>dimensions</u>. The Trinity; Father, Son, and Holy Spirit, is a complex concept, but for me it is easier to grasp than 10 <u>dimensions</u>.

"For God hath not given us the spirit of fear; but of power, and of love, and of a sound mind." - 2 Timothy 1:7

"Go ye therefore, and teach all nations, baptizing them in the name of the Father, and of the Son, and of the Holy Ghost:"– Matt.28:19

Disciple

Is – Led

Faith is not developed or nurtured by force or compulsion. Following unfeigned faith is a calling for those that had the real faith to become believers. Believing and being a <u>disciple</u> are two separate things. The salvation from believing is by grace alone, but discipleship involves following a call to be fishers of men. You could actually be a <u>disciple</u> and not be a believer – be saved. An example is Judas Iscariot. He was a <u>disciple</u>, but will spend eternity in Hell because he never believed in Jesus.

You see the true God does not use force to win followers. Cattle can be driven, as seen in many old Hollywood westerns, but sheep cannot. Sheep need a shepherd, and they are required to be led. The Spirit of God draws, convicts, reveals, and leads, but does not force. Whenever the method is force, you can be sure that this is the beast, or Satan, and not God. God does not force His will upon you and violate the self-will that you were given.

The Apostle Paul, who had been thoroughly taught on the law, did not say in his instructions on giving to keep on tithing. The New Testament is silent on tithing for Christian believers. Christianity does not give any exact percentage of money that should be given away. For some, the Old Testament rule of a tenth is good for guidance, but is not a requirement nor is it necessary for God to bless you. For Christians their giving should be done cheerfully, and to the glory of God.

My understanding is that the Muslin religion does require the giving (Zakat) of 1/40 (2.5%) of their capitol plus voluntary charity (Sadaqa). Both of these religions support giving, but a difference is that Islam teaches that it helps achieve salvation, and Christianity teaches that it should result from salvation.

Generosity was a characteristic of believers in the early church, and God likes the first fruits (not the leftovers). Christians should support a local church along with other giving. Giving should be a cheerful and pleasant experience. God is love and following Him is best when we want to, and not out of fear or force.

Being led by God is by far the best choice, but everyone has the freedom to reject God and sadly many do just that. First, a Christian <u>disciple</u> is a person who believes in the Jesus of the Bible. This Jesus is the Messiah, the Savior, the Lord and the King of Kings. He became a man, but was always God, the second person of the Godhead. Disciples are told (imperative tense) to share the gospel (good news) throughout the world. <u>Disciples</u> are supposed to do four things: Follow the Apostles doctrine, have fellowship, break bread (eat together), and have prayer.

Essentially, a <u>disciple</u> is indwelt by the Holy Spirit and is led by Jesus Christ. <u>Disciples</u> should have a love for God and demonstrate love to others, especially other believers. Christians are supposed to become more Christ like through fellowship (with man and God) and discipleship by the Good Shepherd. Discipleship is a lifelong process, because our character will never be perfected until we reach Heaven. Perfect discipleship is faithfulness to God's heart and will. Regardless of the condition or maturity of true believers Jesus said that we are the light of the world. That is important – all other religion is darkness because Christians are the light on this planet called Earth.

"I am the good shepherd: the good shepherd giveth his life for the sheep." - John 10:11

"The disciple is not above *his* master, nor the servant above his lord." - Matthew 10:24

"Ye are the light of the world." - Matthew 5:14

"Go ye therefore, and teach all nations, baptizing them in the name of the Father, and of the Son, and of the Holy Ghost:" - Matthew 28:19

"Every man according as he purposeth in his heart, *so let him give*; not grudgingly, or of necessity: for God loveth a cheerful giver." - 2 Corinthians 9:7

"And that no man might buy or sell, save he that had the mark, or the name of the beast, or the number of his name." - Revelation 13:17

Dominion

Domino

Man has a God given authority to rule over the earth. That right was compromised, or usurped, by Satan when Adam sinned in the Garden of Eden. Now all of creation is under a curse and in a fallen state, so really there is no paradise anywhere. Today, you can just look at the nightly news to see the domino effect of sin.

"And God blessed them, and God said unto them, Be fruitful, and multiply, and replenish the earth, and subdue it: and have <u>dominion</u> over the fish of the sea, and over the fowl of the air, and over every living thing that moveth upon the earth." - Genesis 1:28

"For unto the angels hath he not put in subjection the world to come, whereof we speak. But one in a certain place testified, saying, What is man, that thou art mindful of him? or the son of man, that thou visitest him? Thou madest him a little lower than the angels; thou crownedst him with glory and honour, and didst set him over the works of thy hands: Thou hast put all things in subjection under his feet. For in that he put all in subjection under him, he left nothing *that is* not put under him. But now we see not yet all things put under him." Hebrews 2:5-8

"For sin shall not have <u>dominion</u> over you: for ye are not under the law, but under grace." - Romans 6:14

E

Earth

Heart – Art

This universe is so enormous that our minds really cannot grasp the distances involved throughout space and galaxies. The light from our closest star travels at 186,000 miles per second for four years before it reaches the earth – traveling 24 trillion miles. Scientists estimate that there are 200 billion stars in the Milky Way galaxy, and now with modern telescopes approximate the number of galaxies at one trillion. With this enormity, the amazing thing is that the <u>earth</u> is where God has His heart.

Of course, the art the <u>earth</u> displays is astonishing. Just the variety of colors and patterns in the atmosphere are remarkable. Not to mention that the <u>earth</u> primarily is watered by the atmosphere, and by the various happenings of our weather. Who does not think that a beautiful sunset is anything but art?

"Of old hast thou laid the foundation of the earth: and the heavens *are* the work of thy hands." - Psalm 102:25

"For God so loved the world, that he gave his only begotten Son, that whosoever believeth in him should not perish, but have everlasting life." - John 3:16

English

His – Hinges – Sign –El (God) – Single

The English language is the most widely used and known language in the world. Often the ability to do business hinges on knowing English because this single language is the language of business around the world. In His wisdom, God provided another sign to know him through the letters of English language words.

"And Solomon's wisdom excelled the wisdom of all the children of the east country, and all the wisdom of Egypt." 1 Kings 4:30

"And ye shall be unto me a kingdom of priests, and an holy nation. These *are* the words which thou shalt speak unto the children of Israel." Exodus 19:6

Entirety

Enter – Ten – Eternity

We will not know God in His <u>entirety</u> unless we have an eternity with God once we enter Heaven. The <u>entirety</u> of the law of God is contained in the Ten Commandments.

"And he (Moses) was there with the LORD forty days and forty nights; he did neither eat bread, nor drink water. And he wrote upon the tables the words of the covenant, the ten commandments." - Exodus 34:28

"And after these things I heard a great voice of much people in heaven, saying, Alleluia; Salvation, and glory, and honour, and power, unto the Lord our God:" - Revelation 19:1

Established

Stable – Slab –Base – Able - Blessed

In Ephesians, Paul talks about being rooted and <u>established</u> in love. To describe God is to describe Love. He is fully love. If we are <u>established</u> in love, we are <u>established</u> in God. Most homes today are built on what is called a slab foundation. This is the base on which the home is built and supported. If the slab is not poured on stable ground, the foundation will sink. The home will have problems ranging from cracked walls and ceilings, unleveled flooring, separated brick joints, and a host of other issues. It is the same in our spiritual walk. If we become established in God's love, then the slab foundation is poured on stable ground, and we will be able to support the wood and bricks that make our hearts a home to Jesus and the Holy Spirit. Being firmly <u>established</u> with Love as our base, we will also become able to be used by God. We will be blessed and others in our life will be also.

"For this cause I bow my knees unto the Father of our Lord Jesus Christ, Of whom the whole family in heaven and earth is named, That he would grant you, according to the riches of his glory, to be strengthened with might by his Spirit in the inner man that Christ may dwell in your hearts by faith; that ye, being rooted and grounded in love, may be able to comprehend with all saints what is the breadth, and length, and depth, and height, and to know the love of Christ, which passeth knowledge, that ye might be filled with all the fullness of God." - Ephesians 3:14-19

Eternal

God (El) – Tern (sounds like turn) – Al (sounds like All)

God is <u>eternal</u> and did not have a cause or beginning as we did. Eternity has no end, and those born again receive <u>eternal</u> life at the time of their salvation. The Bible reveals that all will have their turn with God. Another way to say that is, whether you know it or not, you have an appointment with God. There will be a resurrection of life and a resurrection of damnation. Unfortunately, the lost have an appointment for judgment at the Great White Throne. After that they will have an <u>eternal</u> separation from God that is called the second death. Believers will have <u>eternal</u> access and relationship to the Everlasting God of Glory.

"I am Alpha and Omega, the beginning and the end, the first and the last." - Revelation 22:13

Evangelist

Save - Give - Live – Gentiles – Angel - Angle

The primary responsibility of an <u>evangelist</u> is to preach the gospel as presented in the New Testament. Usually an evangelist travels and brings the gospel to the Gentiles to save their souls. The Bible says that the Jews are enemies for the gospel's sake. And God imposed their spiritual blindness for the "times of the Gentiles." As a nation they were restored to their Promised Land in unbelief, but in God's timing their blindness will be lifted. The remnant of Jewish believers is increasing. So it appears that we might be in a transitional time as it was 2,000 years ago, when the transition was going from the Jews to the Gentiles. The nations will benefit enormously from a spiritual Israel.

The word for angel signifying, both in the Hebrew and Greek, a "messenger," and hence employed to denote any agent God sends forth to execute His purposes. I have heard many

<u>evangelists</u> and find that the great majority are excellent messengers for God. Their primary message, the gospel (good news), will give the believer eternal life. Many years ago a senior pastor told me he thought I should be an evangelist.

"But watch thou in all things, endure afflictions, do the work of an <u>evangelist</u>, make full proof of thy ministry." - 2 Timothy 4:5

"As concerning the gospel, *they are* enemies for your sakes: but as touching the election, *they are* beloved for the fathers' sakes." - Romans 11:28

Examine

I am man – I test (exam) me

Christians have a responsibility to do a self-exam where they confess and agree with God regarding sin in their lives. This process is not just important for spiritual health, but for physical health as well. The Bible warns that sin that is not confessed could even be a cause for premature death. Probably, the process would include some chastening by God to change a behavior. If that did not solve the problem then more serious consequences might need to follow.

Unfortunately, I do not care how good modern medicine is it will not be effective in this situation. So, the physical or medical problem would actually have a spiritual cause. Therefore, it would need a spiritual solution before it became too late!

"Wherefore whosoever shall eat this bread, and drink *this* cup of the Lord, unworthily, shall be guilty of the body and blood of the Lord. But let a man <u>examine</u> himself, and so let him eat of *that* bread, and drink of *that* cup. For he that eateth and drinketh unworthily, eateth and drinketh damnation to himself, not discerning the Lord's body. For this cause many *are* weak and sickly among you, and many sleep. For if we would judge ourselves, we should not be judged." 1 Corinthians 11:27-31

Expectant

Tent – Tax – Text – Next – Exact

A pregnant woman is called an <u>expectant</u> mother. She would be waiting for and looking forward to the arrival of her child. She would hope that the timing of her delivery would be ideal for a healthy baby. People are <u>expectant</u> for many different reasons and it involves waiting for something to occur.

When Adam sinned in the Garden of Eden why did God not send his son immediately, but wait about 4,000 years? In Galatians 4:4 an answer is provided. God sent his son forth when the fullness of time was come.

God sent his son at the exact perfect time that is called "the fullness of time." The birth of Jesus probably occurred during the Feast of Tabernacles (tents) and he was born in Bethlehem where his parents had to go to pay their tax. His arrival fulfilled many Messianic prophecies contained in the scriptures. He completely fulfilled the letter and spirit of the Torah (law). The text of scripture provided for the <u>expectant</u> hope of His arrival. Today, many Christians are <u>expectant</u> of His return, and this next visit is referred to as the second coming. Many followers of Judaism also have an <u>expectant</u> Messianic hope.

The following reasons taken as written from <u>www.gotquestions.org /fullness-of-time.html</u> provide answers of why the timing of His coming was perfect.

"There were many things occurring at the time of the first century that, at least by human reasoning, seemed to make it ideal for Christ to come then. Those included the following:
1) There was a great anticipation that the Messiah would come among the Jews of that time. The Roman rule over Israel made the Jews hungry for the Messiah's coming. 2) Rome had unified much of the world under its government, giving a sense of unity to the

various lands. Also, because the empire was relatively peaceful, travel was possible by the early Christians to spread the gospel that would not have been possible during other times. 3) While Rome had conquered militarily, Greece had conquered culturally. A "common" form of the Greek language (different from classical Greek) was the trade language and was spoken throughout the empire, making it possible to communicate the gospel to many different people groups through that one common language. 4) The fact that many people's idols had failed to give them victory over the Roman conquerors caused many to abandon their worship. At the same time in the more "cultured" cities, the Greek philosophy and science of the time left others spiritually empty in the same way that the atheism of Communist governments leaves a spiritual void today. 5) The mystery religions of the time emphasized a savior-god and required worshipers to offer bloody sacrifices, thus making the gospel of Christ, involving one ultimate sacrifice, not unbelievable to them. The Greeks also believed in the immortality of the soul (but not of the body. 6) The Roman army recruited soldiers from among the provinces, introducing these men to Roman culture and to ideas (such as the gospel) that had not reached those outlying provinces yet. The earliest introduction of the gospel to Britain was the result of the efforts of Christian soldiers stationed there."

Again, the above statements are based on men looking at that time and their speculation why that particular point in history was a good time for Christ to come. But we understand that God's ways are above our ways and these may or may not have been some reasons for why He chose that particular time to send His Son. From the context of Galatians 3 and 4, it is evident that God sought to lay a foundation through the Jewish Law that would prepare for the coming of the Messiah. The Law was meant to help people understand the depth of their sinfulness (in that they were incapable of keeping the Law) so that they might more readily accept the cure for that sin in Jesus the Messiah (Galatians 3:22-23; Romans 3:19-20). The Law also served as a "tutor" (Galatians 3:24) to bring people to Jesus as the Messiah. It did this through its many prophecies concerning the Messiah which Jesus fulfilled. Add to this the sacrificial system that pointed to the need for a sacrifice for sin as well as its own temporary nature (with each sacrifice always requiring later additional ones). Old Testament history also painted pictures of the person and work of Christ through several events and religious feasts (such as the willingness of Abraham to offer up Isaac or the details of the Passover during the exodus from Egypt, etc.).

Lastly, Christ came when He did in fulfillment of specific prophecy. Daniel 9:24-27 speaks of the "seventy 'weeks'" or the seventy "sevens." From the context, these "weeks" or "sevens" refer to groups of seven years, not seven days. We can examine history and line up the details of the first sixty-nine weeks (the seventieth week will take place at a future point). The countdown of the seventy weeks begins with "the going forth of the command to restore and build Jerusalem" (verse 25). This command was given by Artaxerxes Longimanus in 445 B.C. (see Nehemiah 2:5). After 7 "sevens" plus 62 "sevens," or 69 x 7 years, it states that "Messiah shall be cut off, but not for Himself and that the city and the sanctuary would be destroyed" and that the "end of it shall be with a flood" (meaning major destruction) (verse 26). Here we have an unmistakable reference to the Savior's death on the cross.

A century ago in his book The Coming Prince, Sir Robert Anderson gave detailed calculations of the sixty-nine weeks, using 'prophetic years,' allowing for leap years, errors in the calendar, the change from B.C. to A.D., etc., and figured that the sixty-nine weeks ended on the very day of Jesus' triumphal entry into Jerusalem, days before His death. Whether one uses this timetable or not, the point is that the timing of Christ's incarnation ties in with this detailed prophecy recorded by Daniel over five hundred years beforehand."

F

Faithfulness

Fasten - Lean – Safe

Fasten your eyes on the Lord and lean on Him to be safe. The Bible demonstrates that being faithful means to know and do God's will.

"Thy <u>faithfulness</u> *is* unto all generations: thou hast established the earth, and it abideth." - Psalm 119:90

"And I will raise me up a faithful priest, that shall do according to that which is in mine heart and mind." 1 Samuel 2:35

Father

Fear - Hear – Heart – Her - Fate - Hate

The similarities between our earthly <u>father</u>s and God, our Heavenly <u>Father</u>, are amazing. Naturally, parents hold a special place in a child's heart, and love for their father is different than love for their mother. Yet, at the same time, they are equal. Just as a child loves their earthly father, we are commanded to love God with all of our heart, with a love even greater than that for our parents. A <u>father</u>'s role in the family is vital. He offers protection, discipline and direction, just like God the <u>Father</u>. Just as an earthly <u>father</u> tells his child what is best for him/her, so God speaks to His children in the same fashion. It is our responsibility as children of God to hear and apply what He is telling us. Our natural response is not to listen, thinking we know what is best for ourselves, which often results in mistakes and/or discipline. I know from my own experience that daughters really need their fathers when the issue involves her fate.

A child should fear his <u>father</u>. This doesn't mean he or she should be scared of him or afraid for their safety, but each child should have a fear out of respect knowing their father has authority over them. <u>Fathers</u> should be, as God is, slow to anger. An angry <u>father</u> raises an angry, frightened, discouraged child. We fear God out of reverence knowing that He is the ruler of all creation and we are under His authority. Your eternal fate is determined by whether you have a faith-based fear (awe, reverence, appreciation, believe) of God.

"Hear, ye children, the instruction of a <u>father</u>, and attend to know understanding."- Proverbs 4:1

"Thou shalt not bow down thyself to them, nor serve them: for I the LORD thy God *am* a jealous God, visiting the iniquity of the fathers upon the children unto the third and fourth *generation* of them that hate me; And shewing mercy unto thousands of them that love me, and keep my commandments. Thou shalt not take the name of the LORD thy God in vain; for the LORD will not hold him guiltless that taketh his name in vain." Exodus 20:5-7

"For ye have not received the spirit of bondage again to fear; but ye have received the Spirit of adoption, whereby we cry, Abba, <u>Father</u>. The Spirit itself beareth witness with our spirit, that we are the children of God: And if children, then heirs; heirs of God, and joint-heirs with Christ; if so be that we suffer with him, that we may be also glorified together." - Romans 8:15-17

"<u>Fathers</u>, provoke not your children to anger, lest they be discouraged" (Some translations; Lose Heart) - Colossians 3:21

Fear

Far – Ear

Do you <u>fear</u> God? Do you hear Him? God does not want your heart to be far from Him. And when it is perfect (pure) toward God, He will make astonishing demonstrations for the sake of His name and His word. I learned from Pastor Cecil Boswell

Psalm 138:2 reveals that God has actually magnified His word above His name. And that 2 Peter 1:19-21 verifies the certainty of His word.

"The _fear_ of the LORD _is_ the beginning of wisdom: and the knowledge of the holy _is_ understanding." - Proverbs 9:10

"Wherefore the Lord said, Forasmuch as this people draw near _me_ with their mouth, and with their lips do honour me, but have removed their heart far from me, and their _fear_ toward me is taught by the precept of men:" - Isaiah 29:13

Feelings

Life – Lies –Flee - Sing

You could have strong _feelings_ about a person, politics, religion, an issue, or about God. What are your _feelings_ or convictions about life? What are your _feelings_ about God? What is your perception of God, and do you have any emotion about Christianity, church, or God?

Sometimes _feelings_ are emotional, or based on false perceptions or biases. Therefore, _feelings_ are not always rational or reliable. The Christian faith is not based on changing emotions, or an exciting experience. Faith is based on revealed knowledge of God and a relationship with God through Jesus Christ.

It would be impossible for me not to believe in God and the Jesus Christ of the Bible. Flee anything and everything that would keep you from knowing God for yourself. Believe in the Son of God and receive eternal life. You will be glad you did, because one day you will be in heaven and will sing a new song.

"Who being past _feeling_ have given themselves over unto lasciviousness, to work all uncleanness with greediness." - Ephesians 4:19

"For we have not an high priest which cannot be touched with the feeling of our infirmities; but was in all points tempted like as *we are, yet* without sin." - Hebrews 4:15

Fellowship

Fish – Flow - Whole - Self – Help - Ship – Fellows

Fellowship is a very important part of the Christian life. Fellowship applies both to a Christian's relationship with God and relationship with other believers. That real and personal relationship with God provides extraordinary fellowship. Yet, while every Christian should set aside a quiet time to study Scripture and talk with God on their own, it's not a wise idea to think that because you have Jesus you need no other fellowship. There should be no such thing as a 'Lone Ranger Christian'. The Bible encourages us to put others above self and to love your brothers and sisters in the faith. We are commanded in the Bible to fellowship with other believers.

We, as Christians, are like a school of fish. If we stay close to the other believers God has put around us, we have a better sense of where we are going. But if we try to swim alone and not go with the flow of the "school", we lose the guidance, encouragement and help that they offer.

The church cannot be whole without fellowship. Likewise, a solitary Christian cannot be whole without it either. Through fellowship, we get encouragement from other believers. We also get help in tough times, we have an outlet to which we can share our praises and our needs, and we learn to grow in grace and knowledge of His truth. These are all made possible by our unique spiritual gifts. Jesus made a promise that if two or more people should come together in His name, He would be there with them. So when we fellowship with others, we are fellowshipping with Jesus as well. We are all fellows in a ship, and that ship is headed for golden shores. We may be able to make it to the shore in our own little dingy, but that would be one very rough ride!

"That which we have seen and heard we declare unto you, that ye also may have <u>fellowship</u> with us: and truly our <u>fellowship</u> is with the Father, and with his Son Jesus Christ." - 1 John 1:3

"For where two or three are gathered together in my name, there am I in the midst of them."- Matthew 18:20

"Two are better than one; because they have a good reward for their labor. For if they fall, the one will lift up his fellow: but woe to him that is alone when he falleth; for he *hath* not another to help him up. - Ecclesiastes 4:9-10

Finances

I – Can - Sin – Insane/Sane – Inane

Insanity is unsoundness and folly. In America the real estate market demonstrated insanity in finances. Homes became ridiculously overpriced, the mortgage lenders were making unsound loans, Wall Street was selling unsound securities and individuals were making unsound decisions by buying property or properties that were beyond their means. Some of us remained sane, but millions did not and their sin has had dire economic consequences. Inane means senseless or foolish. Folly and foolishness combined with the sins of covetousness and greed greatly contributed to crippling the current economy in America. It is apparent that government and everyone else commit sin in some way relating to acquiring and spending of money. The ways mankind (you and I) can sin with <u>finances</u> are numerous.

"A good name is rather to be chosen than great riches, and loving favor rather silver and gold." Proverbs 22:1

'The rich ruleth over the poor, and the borrower is servant to the lender." Proverbs 22:7

Flesh

Self - Shelf

Natural man is primarily interested in self and his attention is focused on the <u>flesh</u>. If you were to look at the essence of sin it would be the desire to be your own captain – to put yourself in the position of independently setting your own course. The natural man is on the shelf – put aside, out of use to God. There is no neutral ground, and until a person is born again he/she is an enemy of God. For this reason I do not believe that a person earns any eternal rewards until after they have been born again. They may do lots of good works such as; give away large sums of money, etc. But he/she will receive no eternal credit or reward until after they are a part of the Kingdom of God.

"But seek ye first the kingdom of God, and his righteousness; and all these things shall be added unto you." - Matthew 6:33

"But the natural man receiveth not the things of the Spirit of God: for they are foolishness unto him: neither can he know *them*, because they are spiritually discerned." – 1 Corinthians 2:14

"My <u>flesh</u> and my heart faileth: *but* God *is* the strength of my heart, and my portion for ever." - Psalm 73:26

"No man can serve two masters: for either he will hate the one, and love the other; or else he will hold to the one, and despise the other. Ye cannot serve God and mammon." - Matthew 6:24

"We love him, because he first loved us." - 1 John 4:19

Friend

End – Die – Find

You are born with your relatives, but you have to find and make a friend. It might be just like the lyrics in the Tom Petty song "It's hard to find a friend." God found a friend in Moses and vice versa. If you want to define success I would say that the designation of "friend of God" would have to be at the top. A friendship with God is the only one guaranteed to never end and never die.

"And the LORD spake unto Moses face to face, as a man speaketh unto his <u>friend</u>." Exodus 33:11

"Ye adulterers and adulteresses, know ye not that the friendship of the world is enmity with God? whosoever therefore will be a <u>friend</u> of the world is the enemy of God." James 4:4

I am the door: by me if any man enter in, he shall be saved, and shall go in and out, and find pasture." John 10:9

Fruits

First - Ruts *(Phonetic pronounciation: Roots)*

The Bible uses the word <u>fruit</u> to represent the visible action of the Holy Spirit in our lives, and also prosperity from God's blessings. They come from God and only God, which means we should give them back to Him. The first Fruit of the Spirit is love, and from it comes the rest of the <u>fruits</u>: Joy, Peace, Patience, Benevolence (Kindness), Faithfulness, Meekness, and Temperance (Self Control). The Holy Spirit allows this fruit to grow in us so that the seeds may be planted in others around us. But those seeds will not grow into fruit-producing vines without the Spirit; and for the Spirit, you need Jesus. This is the essence of loving your neighbor. By bearing <u>fruit</u>, we let people see there is something different about the way we live. Then they may seek what we have in Jesus Christ and truly live. Christians want to share their joy with all. Yet, sadly, many Christians are hated because of their joy.

God is love, but the Adversary is a murderer. How will there be peace when the "Prince of Peace" is rejected and hated?

Jesus says that we are like a branch on a vine, and that He is the vine and we are the branches. Each branch has the ability to produce fruit. But those that are dead will not produce fruit, so God cuts them off. A dead branch on a vine will draw nutrients away from the branches that are producing fruit. So if they are removed, the fruit producing ones will be able to bear more fruit and grow new branches. The implications of Jesus as the vine are very important because, He was sent by God as our source. The vine is nourished by roots and fed by God. This allows us, through Jesus Christ, to be rooted in love.

"But the <u>fruit</u> of the Spirit is love, joy, peace, longsuffering, gentleness, goodness, faith." - Galatians 5:22

"And other fell on good ground, and did yield <u>fruit</u> that sprang up and increased; and brought forth, some thirty, and some sixty, and some an hundred." - Mark - 4:8

G

Giants

Ant – Saint – Ain't

Goliath, a giant warrior, was killed by David when he was a very young man. This giant man was actually just an ant compared to God. Do you think that Goliath had any idea that he was actually facing a giant in David? When David took the field and faced the giant warrior no one had recognized David as a giant, including his own family. After David had defeated the giant he was recognized as a giant.

David's faith in God was very strong, and because of that

this saint got the victory. The true giants with God are the saints. If you ain't a saint you are not a true giant. All giants have weakness including nations and empires. That is why all need to rely on God and not on our own devices.

"And there went out a champion out of the camp of the Philistines, named Goliath, of Gath, whose height was six cubits and a span (over 9 feet)." – 1 Samuel 17:4

Gifts

Fits – Fit

According to Scripture, every believer receives at least one spiritual <u>gift</u> at the time of his/her salvation. Believers have nothing to do with which <u>gift(s)</u> they receive. These gifts are supernatural and remain with each believer throughout his earthly life, regardless of behavior. The purpose of receiving a gift(s) is to use it to benefit the church. Scripture explains that the church functions as the body of Christ on earth, and Christ is the head of the church. The church is a supernatural organization that is fit together by the Holy Spirit. The spiritual <u>gifts</u> that the members bring to the church provide the church with multiple supernatural strengths. The gifts vary, but each is important just as it is with the different parts of our physical bodies. Understanding of your particular spiritual <u>gift(s)</u> helps a Christian in knowing where he or she fits in the church body for service. The <u>gifts</u> are numerous; a few are prophecy, pastors, evangelism, teaching, knowledge, wisdom, service, giving, exhortation, mercy, administration, etc.

"Now concerning spiritual <u>gifts</u>, brethren, I would not have you ignorant. Ye know that ye were Gentiles, carried away unto these dumb idols, even as ye were led. Wherefore I give you to understand, that no man speaking by the Spirit of God calleth Jesus accursed: and that no man can say that Jesus is the Lord, but by the Holy Ghost. Now there are diversities of <u>gifts</u>, but the same Spirit.

And there are differences of administrations, but the same Lord. And there are diversities of operations, but it is the same God which worketh all in all. But the manifestation of the Spirit is given to every man to profit withal. For to one is given by the Spirit the word of wisdom; to another the word of knowledge by the same Spirit; To another faith by the same Spirit; to another the gifts of healing by the same Spirit; To another the working of miracles; to another prophecy; to another discerning of spirits; to another divers kinds of tongues; to another the interpretation of tongues: But all these worketh that one and the selfsame Spirit, dividing to every man severally as he will. For as the body is one, and hath many members, and all the members of that one body, being many, are one body: so also is Christ."-1Corinthians 12:1-12

Glorified

God - Lord - Life

It is appropriate for God to be in the word <u>glorified</u> because the greatest honor and praise belongs to God, and God only is worthy of worship. There is none other like God. A magnificent 15th century castle in England has glory. There are glorious earthly mansions, and there are many large and beautiful churches that show physical glory. I visited Thomas Roads Baptist Church in Lynchburg, Virginia. The beautiful lobby in this modern facility is over 23,000 square feet and this church had a main auditorium that would seat thousands. This is an example of a facility built at great expense to honor the God that is worshipped there.

I think of the glory throughout nature. Have you ever stood in awe at the glory in the sunset, or in a starry night sky? There is glory on earth, but all earthly glory is inferior to heavenly glory and especially to God's glory. God is covered with majesty and surrounded with glory.

Lord is in the word <u>glorified</u>, because Jesus honored and <u>glorified</u> the name of the Father; and the Father has exalted Him above all others. The greatest glory comes from God, and without God there would be no glory. In heaven, authentic (real), Christians will be <u>glorified</u> by God. The sum of eternal truths of life and God are revealed in the Lord. Every religion must answer four questions: Origin, meaning, morality, and destiny. The coherent answers that Christianity provides cannot be matched by any other religion, philosophy, or science. Other religions make claims, but Jesus claimed to be equal with God and He backed it up by glorious works and miracles. He was crucified and rose from the dead after three days. Not only was His claim the greatest, but the amount of evidence for the truth of His claim is unequaled in all of history. Maybe this is why some of the countless millions in the past and present have encountered the Lord and believed in Him as their Savior.

"Then Moses said unto Aaron, This *is it* that the LORD spake, saying, I will be sanctified in them that come nigh me, and before all the people I will be <u>glorified</u>. And Aaron held his peace." - Leviticus 10:3

"And said unto me, Thou *art* my servant, O Israel, in whom I will be <u>glorified</u>." - Isaiah 49:3

"Insomuch that the multitude wondered, when they saw the dumb to speak, the maimed to be whole, the lame to walk, and the blind to see: and they <u>glorified</u> the God of Israel." - Matthew 15:31

"And if children, then heirs; heirs of God, and joint-heirs with Christ; if so be that we suffer with *him*, that we may be also <u>glorified</u> together." - Romans 8:17

"Wherefore God also hath highly exalted him, and given him a name which is above every name:" - Philippians 2:9

"Now unto him that is able to keep you from falling, and to present *you* faultless before the presence of his glory with exceeding joy" - Jude 1:24

Gnosticism (2nd century heresy)

Misticism (ph. Mysticism) - No – Sin – Son

Gnosticism claimed spiritual knowledge developed from mystical religious and philosophical doctrines. In the second century, these beliefs were combined with Christianity and the Gnostic sects were denounced as heretical by church fathers. The Gnostic teachings about evil and about Christ were not Biblical. They taught that matter was evil, but the spirit was good, so no sin. One sect of the Gnostics denied the humanity of Christ and the other denied the identity of Jesus as Christ, so no Son.

Mysticism and New Age teachings continue to claim a higher level of knowledge, but they lead away from truth. They are wise in their own minds, but they really are just plain dumb. (See Gmail on wisdom and philosophy)

"Beware lest any man spoil you through philosophy and vain deceit, after the tradition of men, after the rudiments of the world, and not after Christ. For in him dwelleth all the fulness of the Godhead bodily." Colossians 2:8-9

Grace

Care – Race

God's unfailing <u>grace</u> shows that He cares for us, enough to redeem us by sending Jesus to die on the cross for our sins. In Greek, the word for grace is *charis*. Sounds a lot like care, doesn't it? His grace is poured out over every nationality and people group because He cares for all whom He created. Some grace is common, like rain that falls on all. Other grace is reserved for those that are in the family of God.

Believers are in a race to produce works of eternal value and God provides much grace for us to finish the race. I like very much grace as the following acronym (not original by this author): **G**od's **R**iches **A**t **C**hrist's **E**xpense.

"Concerning His Son Jesus Christ our Lord, which was made of the seed of David according to the flesh; And declared to be the Son of God with power, according to the spirit of holiness, by the resurrection from the dead: By whom we have received grace and apostleship, for obedience to the faith among all nations, for His name." - Romans 1:3-5

"Wherefore seeing we also are compassed about with so great a cloud of witnesses, let us lay aside every weight, and the sin which doth so easily beset us, and let us run with patience the race that is set before us." – Hebrews 12:1

Gratitude

Great – Atitude (Phonetically - Attitude)

Gratitude is the joyful feeling one has when a favor is done for him undeservingly. Gratitude, as a Christian, is grace reflected back to the Father in the joy that we have in Jesus, and His grace towards us. It should give us a great attitude, even in difficult circumstances. Paul had such gratitude even when he was beaten or in prison.

In Greek, Grace is *Charis* and gratitude is *eucharistian*. Notice that the Greek word for care is in the word for gratitude. This is because gratitude is a response to grace. So be grateful, *You Christian! (euchiaristian)* Unfortunately, much of the human race blasphemes God instead of expressing gratitude. That will ultimately bring God's wrath upon the earth and the unbelievers.

"For all things are for your sakes, that the abundant grace might through the thanksgiving of many redound to the glory of God."- 2 Corinthians 4:15

"And said to the mountains and rocks, Fall on us, and hide us from the face of him that sitteth on the throne, and from the wrath of the Lamb:" - Revelation 6:16

Good

God

God is in <u>good</u> because only God is truly <u>good</u>. The word <u>good</u> as we use it today is from the Old English word for God. When we say "Goodbye" to someone, we are actually using the Old English contraction for "God Be With You". But the word <u>good</u> is often used today as a way to describe things that are simply acceptable by man's standards. For example: A <u>good</u> movie, a <u>good</u> game of golf, good luck, <u>good</u> food, or a <u>good</u> argument. These things may not have anything at all to do with God, but we still use the word <u>good</u> for everything and anything that isn't necessarily bad. So knowing the true origin of the word <u>good</u>, we can clearly see that Scripture uses the word to describe things that are of God. When the word <u>good</u> is found in the Bible, you can put "of", "by" or "from" in front of it and see the implications of the word as it is meant to be read. A <u>good</u> person in the Bible is essentially being described as Godly.

"And Jesus said unto him, Why callest thou me <u>good</u>? *There is* none <u>good</u> but one, *that is*, God." – Mark 10:18

Guidance

Aid – Nudge

A nudge is a gentle touch, which is the method of the true God. There is a tremendous contrast because the self-serving Satan, and the God that loves us. Satan says to hell with you, but Jesus left heaven and went to the cross for us. What a contrast! Jesus came to our aid by paying a price, with a blood sacrifice, that no one could pay by themselves. God nudges us to seek and to find Him because that is to our greatest benefit. Do not take your council from the ungodly. But seek to follow God and He will guide you.

"Blessed *is* the man that walketh not in the counsel of the ungodly, nor standeth in the way of sinners, nor sitteth in the seat of the scornful." - Psalm 1:1

H

Hardened

Hear - Ended

Once your heart has sufficiently hardened your ability to hear God has ended. The more times you say no to God the harder your heart will become. In believing in Jesus through faith God is able to replace our stony hearts with a new spirit and a new heart.

"And when Pharaoh saw that the rain and the hail and the thunders were ceased, he sinned yet more, and <u>hardened</u> his heart, he and his servants. And the heart of Pharaoh was <u>hardened</u>, neither would he let the children of Israel go; as the LORD had spoken by Moses. Exodus 9:34-35
"A new heart also will I give you, and a new spirit will I put within you: and I will take away the stony heart out of your flesh, and I will give you an heart of flesh." Ezekiel 36:26

"O LORD, why hast thou made us to err from thy ways, *and* hardened our heart from thy fear? Return for thy servants' sake, the tribes of thine inheritance." Isaiah 63:17

"But even unto this day, when Moses is read, the veil is upon their heart." 2 Corinthians 3:15

Harvest

Earth – Star – Save – Have – Heart - Tares

The earth is going to continue to have a harvest of food as long as it exists. Besides a harvest time for food, there will be a time of spiritual harvest, and the wheat (saved) will be separated from the tares (lost). God has a heart for a large harvest because He takes no delight in the death of the wicked. And in fact, there will be a great harvest of people of faith from the four corners of the world and from every spoken language. Do you know the "Star out of Jacob" and the "seed of David?" Jesus is called the "Bright and Morning Star" and He is the "Lord of the Harvest."

"While the earth remaineth, seedtime and harvest, and cold and heat, and summer and winter, and day and night shall not cease." - Genesis 8:22

"He that gathereth in summer *is* a wise son: *but* he that sleepeth in harvest *is* a son that causeth shame." - Proverbs 10:5

"When thou cuttest down thine harvest in thy field, and hast forgot a sheaf in the field, thou shalt not go again to fetch it: it shall be for the stranger, for the fatherless, and for the widow: that the LORD thy God may bless thee in all the work of thine hands." - Deuteronomy 24:19

"Pray ye therefore the Lord of the harvest, that he will send forth labourers into his harvest." - Matthew 9:38

"And another angel came out of the temple, crying with a loud voice to him that sat on the cloud, Thrust in thy sickle, and reap: for the time is come for thee to reap; for the <u>harvest</u> of the earth is ripe." - Revelation 14:15

"I shall see him, but not now: I shall behold him, but not nigh: there shall come a Star out of Jacob, and a Sceptre shall rise out of Israel, and shall smite the corners of Moab, and destroy all the children of Sheth." - Numbers 24:17

"Neither is there salvation in any other: for there is none other name under heaven given among men, whereby we must be saved." - Acts 4:12

"Remember that Jesus Christ of the seed of David was raised from the dead according to my gospel:" - 2 Timothy 2:8

"As therefore the tares are gathered and burned in the fire; so shall it be in the end of this world." - Matthew 13:40

Hatred

Heart – Death

<u>Hatred</u> is an intense ill will toward a person, persons, or even God. Hatred causes harm. Any <u>hatred</u> always shows a heart problem, and hating harms you. Everyone is made in the image of God, receives life from God, has a soul, and has sacred value.

Even though He has made us, loves us, and has made a way for salvation, many still hate Him. Do you know that many people actually hate God? Jesus said that you are either for Him or against Him. There is no neutrality toward God, so you are on one side or the other.

"Thou shalt not bow down thyself to them, nor serve them: for I the LORD thy God *am* a jealous God, visiting the iniquity of the fathers upon the children unto the third and fourth *generation* of them that <u>hate</u> me;" - Exodus 20:5

"Blessed are ye, when men shall <u>hate</u> you, and when they shall separate you *from their company*, and shall reproach *you*, and cast out your name as evil, for the Son of man's sake." - Luke 6:22

"But I say unto you which hear, Love your enemies, do good to them which <u>hate</u> you," - Luke 6:27

"He that saith he is in the light, and <u>hateth</u> his brother, is in darkness even until now." - 1 John 2:9

"He that is not with me is against me: and he that gathereth not with me scattereth." - Luke 11:23

"But he that sinneth against me wrongeth his own soul: all they that <u>hate</u> me love death." - Proverbs 8:36

Heart

Hear - Hate – Rate - Heat

The human <u>heart</u> is regarded as the seat of emotions, personality, will, disposition, conscience, feelings, and thoughts. This is the center or core of your soul, of who you are as a person. The Lord God knows your heart better than you do. God wants you to hear Him in your <u>heart</u>. God wants you to have His Word in your <u>heart</u>. God wants you to fear Him in your <u>heart</u> because "the fear of God is the beginning of wisdom." God commands that we love him with all our <u>heart</u>. That is passion and heat or fire for God. You have a heart rate which determines your pulse. God also takes your rate or pulse, which reveals your opinions and feelings.

If you have any hate in your heart for anyone, including God, you have a heart problem.

"The <u>heart</u> *is* deceitful above all *things*, and desperately wicked: who can know it?" - Jeremiah 17:9

"Idolatry, witchcraft, hatred, variance, emulations, wrath, strife, seditions, heresies," - Galatians 5:20

History

This - Is - His - Story

When we are reading the Bible, we can clearly see that "This Is His Story." The Bible is a book that reveals Jesus Christ, and it is a book about Jehovah. Everything from before creation, the six-day creation itself, all the way through the last days of earth, and the end of time is recorded in the Bible. Even in the Old Testament there are carefully woven evidences of Jesus throughout. The Bible is truly the story of His glory. It tells His Story. There is no such thing as "Prehistory" since we have the Holy Bible. Job was on earth at the same time as the dinosaurs. A dinosaur called behemoth is described in the thirty-ninth chapter of the Book of Job.

About one-third of the Bible is actually future <u>history</u>, which is called prophecy. God is omniscient, all knowing, and that includes complete knowledge of the future. The atomic bomb, satellites, Israel's return to the land, the explosion of knowledge, and transportation are all foretold in the Bible. All these just mentioned occurred after I was born. The Bible contains at least one hundred fifty accurately fulfilled prophecies about the first coming of Jesus. There are an even greater number of prophecies regarding His return, or second coming. The Bible explains both our <u>history</u> and our future from God's perspective. The Bible is a great treasure, and the greatest <u>history</u> and only accurate prophecy book ever written. It is a huge benefit to have an understanding of all of the most important events that lie in the future.

"For the prophecy came not in old time by the will of man: but holy men of God spake *as they were* moved by the Holy Ghost." - 2 Peter 1:21

"Behold, I come quickly: blessed *is* he that keepeth the sayings of the prophecy of this book." - Revelation 22:7

Holograms

Logos – Goal – Solo

Words must be important to God because the second person of the Godhead is called the Word. The Greek word that Word was translated from is the word logos. "In the beginning was the Logos, and the Logos was with God and the Logos was God." (John 1:1) This Logos accomplished the goal of submitting to the Father's will to be the solo acceptable and perfect Lamb of God to take away the sins of the world.

The word <u>hologram</u> has meaning both from the definition of holocryptic and holograph. The first of these two words means to effectively conceal, and the second word means whole or entire. The equipment for making a <u>hologram</u> includes a laser, mirror and diffusers. The <u>hologram</u> is a frequency record, and when viewed with a laser of the same frequency it reveals a three-dimensional image of the original object.

A profound quality of a <u>hologram</u> is that the image is distributed throughout the entire media. If the <u>hologram</u> is cut into pieces, each piece contains the complete image. A <u>hologram</u> also can reflect the full color spectrum of the rainbow. The rainbow is a symbol of a covenant God made with Noah. Sometimes <u>holograms</u> are used to prove that something of value is authentic. You might see a <u>hologram</u> on a driver's license or on credit cards.

I agree with the concept that the Bible is like a <u>hologram,</u> and God's plan for the redemption of mankind is distributed from Genesis in the Old Testament to Revelation in the New Testament. This then makes words the smallest segment of the Bible that still conveys an accurate message or picture. When letters from words are reformed to make other words, it provides compelling evidence to the accuracy of the Bible and the <u>hologram</u> theory. Like a <u>hologram</u> for words to be converted to Gmail they need to be seen with the correct frequency, and this writer believes that frequency to be none other than the Spirit of God.

"And the Word (Logos) was made flesh, and dwelt among us, (and we beheld his glory, the glory as of the only begotten of the Father,) full of grace and truth." - John 1:14

"And this is the Father's will which hath sent me, that of all which he hath given me I should lose nothing, but should raise it up again at the last day." - John 6:39

"Enter ye in at the strait gate: for wide *is* the gate, and broad *is* the way, that leadeth to destruction, and many there be which go in thereat:" - Matthew 7:13

"And I saw another mighty angel come down from heaven, clothed with a cloud: and a rainbow *was* upon his head, and his face *was* as it were the sun, and his feet as pillars of fire:" - Revelation 10:1

I

Idolatry

Lord - Dolar (Dollar) - Dirty - Try – A - Idol

Idolatry is certainly a serious matter to God because two of the Ten Commandments dealt with this issue. In its strictest form idolatry denotes worship of deity in a visible form. This is a satanic counterfeit because the essence of God is spiritual and unseen. Satan tried to get the Lord to commit idolatry because he asked Jesus to bow down and worship him. Since Satan desires to be worshipped as God you can be sure that he is involved in idolatry. Satan's message is "try a idol," and everyone has. In the broadest sense, idolatry would be anything that persons or nations elevate above God. Much of modern idolatry is less obvious than ancient forms. But whatever is sought and valued above God is idolatry. For example, some people make pleasure, wealth, materialism, science, sports, education, politics, national defense, religion, etc. more important than having a relationship with God. If enjoying those things is more important than having a relationship with God they are idolatry. Wealth itself is fine, but if the pursuit of money or wealth is put above God it would be sinful.

I consider atheism to be idolatry because the person is stubbornly putting their unbelief above God. Denial of God is a category of ignorance. Agnostics are stubbornly skeptic, which is another one of the three forms of ignorance described in the Bible. Stubbornness is identified in the Bible as idolatry. If a nation relies more on its own defenses for protection than on God, it is an idolatrous nation.

God takes idols very seriously because idolatry is misleading and is always in competition with truth and the real Creator of the universe. In the Bible, the first example of idols among the Israelites is Genesis 31:19, where Rachael stole her father's gods. Idolatry has, and does appear, all over the world in nations and in all religions, even including some that profess to be Christian. The Israelites, despite severe warnings, had a past with multiple influences of idol worship. The nations that become more reliant on resources and dollars (U$A) than on the Sovereign God are idolatrous nations.

The worship of heavenly bodies, such as the sun and moon, were the most prevalent in systems of idolatry. Idols are carved from stone and made with hands. Idols started in the plains of Chaldea (Babylon) and spread through Egypt, Greece, Roman Empire, Asia and the whole world. Idols seduce others to false worship. Idols are attractive because they are tangible, visible and provide an outward sign that attracts the senses of man. The Christmas season that is widely practiced in our culture is a mix of pagan custom and Christianity. This holiday is extremely popular and many individuals get quite caught up either in the pagan aspects,the spiritual aspects, or both. Easter is likewise a mix of pagan custom (eggs - fertility) and Christianity. Wealth, luxury, pageantry, parades, artistry, and the licentious revelries that accompanied much of false worship appealed to a natural attraction to sensual passion and gave <u>idolatry</u> broad appeal. The amount of internet pornography and the explosion of and sale of pornography and pornographic materials in America is an example of how addictive these desires can be. They are not called dirty books and movies for nothing. This is a gross industry and if you are involved with this industry in any way, consider repenting and getting out fast.   This includes large hotel chains that sell pornography to guests in their rooms. Do not think there is not a judgment for <u>idolatry</u>. After the Israelites made and worshipped a golden calf, God required men with swords to go throughout the camp and about 3,000 were killed that day.

"Thou shalt have no other gods before me. Thou shalt not make unto thee any graven image, or any likeness *of any thing* that *is* in heaven above, or that *is* in the earth beneath, or that *is* in the water under the earth:" - Exodus 20:3-4

"Now while Paul waited for them at Athens, his spirit was stirred in him, when he saw the city wholly given to <u>idolatry</u>."- Acts 17:16

"For all the gods of the nations *are* <u>idols</u>: but the LORD made the heavens." - Psalm 96:5

"Cursed *be* the man that maketh *any* graven or molten image, an abomination unto the LORD, the work of the hands of the craftsman, and putteth *it* in *a* secret *place.* And all the people shall answer and say, Amen." - Deuteronomy 27:15

"And the devil said unto him, All this power will I give thee, and the glory of them: for that is delivered unto me; and to whomsoever I will I give it. If thou therefore wilt worship me, all shall be thine. And Jesus answered and said unto him, Get thee behind me, Satan: for it is written, Thou shalt worship the Lord thy God, and him only shalt thou serve." - Luke 4:6-8

Immanuel (Hebrew) and **Emmanuel** (variation of Immanuel)

Me – Man – El (Eloheim - God) – Name –I -Am

Jesus Christ is God incarnate. He is both fully man and fully God (Me man, Me God). The literal Hebrew meaning is God (el) with (im) us (anu). The Hebrew Gmail is I am man, I am God. Jesus is the visible image of the invisible God, who is I Am. He was the Lamb slain before the foundation of the world. The Messiah, a sinless sacrifice, was God's divine plan for salvation by grace. He took on flesh and became the "Son of Man."

His virgin birth is essential to the Christian faith. Some Islamic sects correctly teach the virgin birth of Christ, but belief in His birth does not save you. It is faith in His deity, death, resurrection and shed blood for your sin that saves you. Jesus was rejected, condemned, and nailed to a cross and crucified. He rose from the grave and He is the Resurrection and the Life. He has been given all power in heaven and on earth, and His name is above every name. The Christian hope is that we live because He lives. He and God are one (one God, but three persons of the Godhead).

"Therefore the Lord himself shall give you a sign; Behold, a virgin

shall conceive, and bear a Son, and shall call his Name <u>Immanuel</u>."
- Isaiah 7:14

"Who being the brightness of *his* glory, and the express image of his person, and upholding all things by the word of his power, when he had by himself purged our sins, sat down on the right hand of the Majesty on high;" - Hebrews 1:3

"And every creature which is in heaven, and on the earth, and under the earth, and such as are in the sea, and all that are in them, heard I saying, Blessing, and honour, and glory, and power, *be* unto him that sitteth upon the throne, and unto the Lamb for ever and ever." - Revelation 5:13

Individual

DNA – Dual – In – I Divide You All (Phonetically)

A discovery in 1953 found that each person has contained in his/her microscopic cells a language called Deoxyribon Nucleic Acid (DNA). Each cell in the human body, except red blood cells, has about six feet of DNA. Since there are trillions of cells the human body contains billions of miles of DNA. That is some science for you to contemplate.

This DNA code in each cell is a type of language and is equal to a gigabyte of information. This language is the genetics design in all physical life. DNA is an extremely complex message and any message requires a messenger. This message was from the Giver of Life, the one true Living Almighty Creator God.

DNA is an <u>individual</u> code that produces a unique person for a relationship with God and for a special job. The Creator holds the patent/copyright, and each human life is sacred because we are made in the image of God. We owe eternal allegiance and gratitude to God for this precious gift of life.

Every person is born in sin and has a sin nature. Man in this state is called the natural man. Only those <u>individuals</u> that have a second birth, a spiritual birth, have a dual nature. They still have the natural side. But they have the precious advantage of having a spiritual nature, and they are reconciled to God. Scripture says that we are partakers in the Divine Nature, so maybe DNA = "Divine Nature Applied." This is so important that is why it is the front cover of *Amazing God*.

"So God created man in his *own* image, in the image of God created he him; male and female created he them." - Genesis 1:27

"And they went in unto Noah into the ark, two and two of all flesh, wherein *is* the breath of life." - Genesis 7:15

"But the natural man receiveth not the things of the Spirit of God: for they are foolishness unto him: neither can he know *them*, because they are spiritually discerned." - 1 Corinthians 2:14

"For the invisible things of him from the creation of the world are clearly seen, being understood by the things that are made, *even* his eternal power and Godhead; so that they are without excuse:" - Romans 1:20

"For this cause shall a man leave his father and mother, and shall be joined unto his wife, and they two shall be one flesh." - Ephesians 5:31

"Whereby are given unto us exceeding great and precious promises: that by these ye might be partakers of the divine nature, having escaped the corruption that is in the world through lust." - 2 Peter 1:4

Insight

His - In - Sight - Sign

Without God there would be no sight, period. Forty men wrote the sixty-six books of the Holy Bible over a period of approximately 1,500 years on three continents and in three languages. The first five books (Genesis 1,400 BC) were written by Moses and the last book by the Apostle John around 95 AD. God's ways are not simple, and God's true Word was not produced in a simple way. These writers had an unparalleled <u>insight</u> into the mysteries of God's ways, because they were being led and inspired by the Holy Spirit. The profoundness and prophecy contained in the Bible are astonishing. The Holy Spirit allowed the writers to see reality in His sight, through His eyes. As opposed to seeing it through their own flawed, human eyes that could not grasp the full truth and wonder of God's mind and heart. This special <u>insight</u> allowed some of the Biblical writers, notably prophets, to receive a vision or sign through a dream that uncovered a mystery, or foretold a future event. Hundreds of prophecies have been fulfilled that provided many exact details.

Israel's dispersion and return to the land had twenty-five ancient prophecies that were fulfilled in detail. Nations need to pay attention because you may think that you are measuring Israel, but the Sovereign God is measuring you by Israel. Nations, religions, churches, and individuals are being weighed in the balances and many will be found wanting.

"For the LORD *is* good; his mercy *is* everlasting; and his truth *endureth* to all generations." - Psalm 100:5

"All scripture *is* given by inspiration of God, and *is* profitable for doctrine, for reproof, for correction, for instruction in righteousness:" - 2 Timothy 3:16

"For the word of God *is* quick, and powerful, and sharper than any two-edged sword, piercing even to the dividing asunder of soul and spirit, and of the joints and marrow, and *is* a discerner of the thoughts and intents of the heart." - Hebrews 4:12

"Receiving the end of your faith, even the salvation of your souls. Of which salvation the prophets have enquired and searched diligently, who prophesied of the grace that should come unto you: Searching what, or what manner of time the Spirit of Christ which was in them did signify, when it testified beforehand the sufferings of Christ, and the glory that should follow. Unto whom it was revealed, that not unto themselves, but unto us they did minister the things, which are now reported unto you by them that have preached the gospel unto you with the Holy Ghost sent down from heaven; which things the angels desire to look into."-1 Peter 1:9-12

"And I will bless them that bless thee, and curse him that curseth thee: and in thee shall all families of the earth be blessed." - Genesis 12:3

Inspiration

Anoint – In - Spirit – Pastor

The writers of the Bible were inspired by the Holy Spirit to write the thoughts and exact words of God Almighty. The writing, though inerrant, was flavored by their personality and era in which they were living. Also, that divine <u>inspiration</u> didn't stop with the Apostles Peter, Paul or John. God still to this day, uses the Spirit to inspire His people. Believers are sealed by the Holy Spirit at their time of salvation, through faith in Jesus Christ. The Spirit is able to anoint our hearts and minds to be instruments of encouragement, teaching, and further <u>inspiration</u> to others. The Holy Spirit will work through all believers that allow Him to do so, and divine <u>inspiration</u> can come to anyone who is in the Spirit. When led by the Spirit you are not under the law. For where the Spirit of the Lord is there is freedom. God can take the weak and confound the wise. Spiritual gifts are supernatural. So a regular musician, writer, speaker, artist, teacher, doctor, athlete, or any other individual, may become a spiritual giant that will be used for God's purposes. One can be even greater than he could ever imagine, all for the glory of God. A spiritual gift(s) remains with an individual during his entire life. Yet they are not needed on the other side of eternity, since we will be with the Lord in our glorified state.

But to whom much is given, much is required. There is a certain responsibility that comes with this transformation from ordinary to extraordinary. When it comes to writers, teachers, evangelists, and pastors, this <u>inspiration</u> should be used very wisely. Scripture, the original Divine inspiration of God, should back up spiritual teachings and writings. This is that the truth revealed to those original writers will be fortified and supported. It is important to keep in mind that God's Spirit is what inspires, so we know it is from God and not our own minds. This is so that He gets the glory only He is worthy to receive.

"For it is not ye that speak, but the Spirit of your Father which speaketh in you."-Matthew 10:20

"Are they not all ministering Spirits, sent forth to minister for them who shall be heirs of salvation?"-Hebrews 1:14

"And grieve not the holy Spirit of God, whereby ye are sealed unto the day of redemption." - Ephesians 4:30

Instruction

To -Trust – In – Son

The best instruction that mankind can receive is <u>to</u> <u>trust</u> <u>in</u> the <u>Son</u>. That teaching or <u>instruction</u> should go out to nations all over the world.

"Then he openeth the ears of men, and sealeth their <u>instruction</u>," Job 33:16

"Take fast hold of <u>instruction</u>; let *her* not go: keep her; for she *is* thy life." - Proverbs 4:13

"Apply thine heart unto <u>instruction,</u> and thine ears to the words of knowledge." - Proverbs 23:12 ¶

Intimate

In - Time - Mate – Team

To be <u>intimate</u> is to be in close association or be very familiar. Usually, in an intimate relationship things are exclusively shared. You and your mate are a team and should be in an intimate relationship. In time you and your mate should learn more and more about each other, and grow stronger as a team. This team should make each of you stronger than you would be alone.

These same principles work in a relationship with God. A close personal, intimate relationship with God is something that is attainable. In time, God wants you to find Him, learn about Him, and grow into a personal relationship with Him. Proper worship includes a relationship with God that has emotion. To be on God's team has amazing advantages. You have a soul and God has a soul. Your soul mate is supposed to be the Living Almighty God.

"For I determined not to know any thing among you, save Jesus Christ, and him crucified." - 1 Corinthians 2:2

"And the scripture was fulfilled which saith, Abraham believed God, and it was imputed unto him for righteousness: and he was called the Friend of God." - James 2:23

"For ye have not received the spirit of bondage again to fear; but ye have received the Spirit of adoption, whereby we cry, Abba, Father." - Romans 8:15

"Let us therefore come boldly unto the throne of grace, that we may obtain mercy, and find grace to help in time of need." - Hebrews 4:16

"And thou shalt love the LORD thy God with all thine heart, and with all thy soul, and with all thy might." - Deuteronomy 6:5
"I will greatly rejoice in the LORD, my soul shall be joyful in my God; for he hath clothed me with the garments of salvation, he hath covered me with the robe of righteousness, as a bridegroom decketh *himself* with ornaments, and as a bride adorneth *herself* with her jewels." - Isaiah 61:10

Image

I Am – Me – Game - Age

The <u>image</u> you have of yourself may be different from the <u>image</u> that God has of you. Many people get the spiritual <u>image</u> of themselves by comparing themselves with others. Many think that this is the standard that God uses for entrance into heaven. Where did they get that standard? Is it God's standard? It is not God's standard according to the Bible. Standing before God is different from standing before men. Based on your merit the standard is 100% sinless perfection. Do you measure up to that standard? No, you do not measure up to God's standard. If you could, Jesus would not have crucified for sin. He is God's only acceptable standard, therefore, His righteousness must be applied to you. The formula for righteousness is not works, but faith in Christ and in His perfect sacrifice. Quit playing a game because without I AM you are all me (self), and none of God. The best image is Me + I AM. That way you will not have to worry about age because you will have eternal life.

"And God said unto Moses, I AM THAT I AM: and he said, Thus shalt thou say unto the children of Israel, I AM hath sent me unto you." - Exodus 3:14

"For all have sinned, and come short of the glory of God;" - Romans 3:23

"And have put on the new *man*, which is renewed in knowledge after the <u>image</u> of him that created him:" - Colossians 3:10

Israel

El (God) – Is - Real - Seal

Make no mistake about it; <u>Israel</u> has a special place in God's heart and in His plans. <u>Israel</u> is the "apple of God's eye." God has established an everlasting covenant with <u>Israel</u>, so His seal is on this nation. Israel is the center of the earth to God, and all nations on earth are located in reference to the small nation of <u>Israel</u>. Borders and destinies of nations are determined by God, based upon their stance concerning <u>Israel</u>.

Regrettably, Israel as a nation is still secular. The Jewish people were called back to the land in unbelief, but that will change. Already, there are many signs this is a spiritual transition period for Israel. Be a part of this process through prayer and support. Every true church should have passion for <u>Israel</u>, as well as connections to <u>Israel</u>. The nation was given its name because the God of Abraham, Isaac and Jacob is the one true and Living God. Make no mistake, El is real.

"And I will establish my covenant between me and thee and thy seed after thee in their generations for an everlasting covenant, to be a God unto thee, and to thy seed after thee." - Genesis 17:7

"For thus saith the LORD of hosts; After the glory hath he sent me unto the nations which spoiled you: for he that toucheth you toucheth the apple of his eye." - Zechariah 2:8

For more current information see *Israel In Prophecy* by John Walvoord published by Zondervan; *25 Messianic Signs In Israel Today* by Noah Hutchings published by Hearthstone Pub LTD; and/or *God's Promise and the Future of Israel* by Don Finto published by Regal Books.

J

Jerusalem

USA - Rule - Real

<u>Jerusalem</u> is located in a small nation, and it does not have a port, river or a major industry. So what is the big deal? Does it astonish you how important this city is to so many groups of people that represent billions of the world's population? It has important historical and spiritual significance to four large religious groups; Catholics, non-Catholic Christians, Jews and Muslims. There is a lot of emotion for this great city from the four religious groups cited above.

Abraham demonstrated his faith by bringing his son of promise, Isaac, to <u>Jerusalem</u> to offer the boy to God as a sacrifice. The Messiah or Christ had a real crucifixion and resurrection in <u>Jerusalem</u>. The Wailing Wall is all that is left exposed of the magnificent and Holy Temple, which was destroyed by a Roman army in 70 AD. The Muslim Dome of the Rock is located in <u>Jerusalem</u>, close to the Temple site. <u>Jerusalem</u> is called the City of David and is the capital city of Israel.

The Jewish people regained control of <u>Jerusalem</u> in 1967, and this is the first time the city has been under Jewish control since the 70 AD Roman conquest. There is a spiritual battle being waged between light and darkness, and <u>Jerusalem</u> has been, and will continue to be, very important in that battle. Pray for the peace of <u>Jerusalem</u>.

The United States of America (USA) has been very important for Israel and the Jewish people. President Truman played an essential role in passing of the UN resolution that chartered Israel as a nation in May 1948. The USA has provided the Jewish people with their longest stability and greatest prosperity of any nation. In other lands, persecution eventually begins and the Jewish residents have to flee. The reasons for Jewish acceptance are the Christian foundations in the USA, and the recognition of the heritage shared by Christians and Jews. If a religion is not able to flourish through a free choice environment, it is a worthless religion. If the USA foundations erode, the peace and prosperity that the Jews have enjoyed in the USA will erode as well.

There is a tremendous amount of Biblical history and prophecy regarding Israel and <u>Jerusalem</u>. Israel and <u>Jerusalem</u> are important in Eschatology, the study of end times. The Book of Revelation states that during the tribulation two witnesses will be killed in <u>Jerusalem</u>. Their dead bodies will be seen by many kindreds and tongues (languages) and nations. It would require television, internet, and satellite communications for that prophecy written over 1,900 years ago to take place.

Again, Israel, its capital of <u>Jerusalem</u>, and the Jewish people group are prominent throughout end time prophecy. When the "I am the Alpha and Omega" returns at the Battle of Armageddon, He will defeat the armies of the world assembled against Israel (really against Jesus) and led by the Antichrist. The Lord will then establish His rule, a thousand year kingdom, over the entire earth, and the capitol will be <u>Jerusalem</u>.

"And the children of Benjamin did not drive out the Jebusites that inhabited <u>Jerusalem</u>; but the Jebusites dwell with the children of Benjamin in <u>Jerusalem</u> unto this day." - Judges 1:21

"And these were born unto him in <u>Jerusalem</u>; Shimea, and Shobab, and Nathan, and Solomon, four, of Bathshua the daughter of Ammiel:" - 1 Chronicles 3:5

"O <u>Jerusalem</u>, <u>Jerusalem</u>, *thou* that killest the prophets, and stonest them which are sent unto thee, how often would I have gathered thy children together, even as a hen gathereth her chickens under *her* wings, and ye would not!" - Matthew 23:37

"For we wrestle not against flesh and blood, but against principalities, against powers, against the rulers of the darkness of this world, against spiritual wickedness in high *places*." - Ephesians 6:12

"And it shall come to pass in the last days, *that* the mountain of the LORD'S house shall be established in the top of the mountains, and shall be exalted above the hills; and all nations shall flow unto it. And many people shall go and say, Come ye, and let us go up to the mountain of the LORD, to the house of the God of Jacob; and he will teach us of his ways, and we will walk in his paths: for out of Zion shall go forth the law, and the word of the LORD from <u>Jerusalem</u>." - Isaiah 2:2-3

"And I John saw the holy city, new <u>Jerusalem</u>, coming down from God out of heaven, prepared as a bride adorned for her husband." - Revelation 21:2

Jesus

Use(s) – Us

The Lord is in the process of building the Kingdom of God by salvation and sanctification of those who believe. His method to accomplish this important work is to use those who became born again believers. The Lord, while seated at the right hand of the Father, uses believers as His body on earth. Believers are privileged to be useful to God. The Lord's organization is the local church where believers assemble together. Without faith in God through <u>Jesus Christ</u>, no one is able to please God.

When you receive <u>Jesus</u> you are sealed with the Holy

Spirit, saved, and called to serve God. The beneficial results from Christian service Biblically are identified as fruit. As Christians, there are many ways, big and small, that God uses us, to the benefit of family, brethren, church, community, nation, world, and ultimately the Kingdom of God.

"So we, *being* many, are one body in Christ, and every one members one of another." - Romans 12:5

"Wherefore, my brethren, ye also are become dead to the law by the body of Christ; that ye should be married to another, *even* to him who is raised from the dead, that we should bring forth fruit unto God." - Romans 7:4

"But without faith *it is* impossible to please *him*: for he that cometh to God must believe that he is, and *that* he is a rewarder of them that diligently seek him." - Hebrews 11:6

"And other fell on good ground, and did yield fruit that sprang up and increased; and brought forth, some thirty, and some sixty, and some an hundred." - Mark 4:8

"Verily, verily, I say unto you, He that believeth on me, the works that I do shall he do also; and greater *works* than these shall he do; because I go unto my Father." - John 14:12

Joyfulness

Enjoy/Joy- Soul - ful (full) – Luv (Ph. - Love)

True spirituality, sound doctrine, and a love for the Lord are accompanied by unspeakable joy. Joy is a delight (God is light) that seems to be beyond happiness. It makes your soul full and satisfies the deepest human need for unconditional love.

"And David spake to the chief of the Levites to appoint their brethren *to be* the singers with instruments of musik, psalteries and harps and cymbals, sounding, by lifting up the voice with joy." - 1 Chronicles 15:16

"Then the people rejoiced, for that they offered willingly, because with perfect heart they offered willingly to the LORD: and David the king also rejoiced with great joy." - 1 Chronicles 29:9

"Yet I will rejoice in the LORD, I will joy in the God of my salvation." - Habakkuk 3:18

"But the fruit of the Spirit is love, joy, peace, longsuffering, gentleness, goodness, faith," - Galatians 5:22

"Whom having not seen, ye love; in whom, though now ye see *him* not, yet believing, ye rejoice with joy unspeakable and full of glory:" - 1 Peter 1:8

Judgmental

El (God) – Meant – Mean

We should not be <u>judgmental</u> of others because that is not meant for our role or responsibility. God is able to love the sinner and hate the sin; however, humans have difficulty making that clear distinction.

John Newton was a slave ship captain, and in that position he would have been part of tremendous cruelty and injustice to many dark skinned victims of the slave trade. This man had been among the greatest of sinners, but he experienced Jesus and converted to Christianity. Afterwards, he worked against the slave trade and he wrote one of the greatest hymns ever written, *Amazing Grace*.

During his lengthy career in the slave trade, how easy it would have been for people to have been <u>judgmental</u> regarding this man or have been mean to him. A judgment that slavery was sinful and immoral would have a correct ethical position, but being <u>judgmental</u> of the sinner is not appropriate. We are all sinners and have all "come short of the glory of God." Every single person has the seeds for every sin, and these seeds can bring forth evil fruit.

"And he shall <u>judge</u> among the nations, and shall rebuke many people: and they shall beat their swords into plowshares, and their spears into pruninghooks: nation shall not lift up sword against nation, neither shall they learn war any more." - Isaiah 2:4

"Judge not, that ye be not judged. For with what judgment ye judge, ye shall be judged: and with what measure ye mete, it shall be measured to you again."- Matthew 7:1-2

"Judge not, and ye shall not be judged: condemn not, and ye shall not be condemned: forgive, and ye shall be forgiven:" - Luke 6:37

"But after thy hardness and impenitent heart treasurest up unto thyself wrath against the day of wrath and revelation of the righteous judgment of God;" - Romans 2:5

"But the heavens and the earth, which are now, by the same word are kept in store, reserved unto fire against the day of judgment and perdition of ungodly men." - 2 Peter 3:7

"And I saw a great white throne, and him that sat on it, from whose face the earth and the heaven fled away; and there was found no place for them. And I saw the dead, small and great, stand before God; and the books were opened: and another book was opened, which is *the book* of life: and the dead were judged out of those things which were written in the books, according to their works. And the sea gave up the dead which were in it; and death and hell delivered up the dead which were in them: and they were judged every man according to their works. And death and hell were cast into the lake of fire. This is the second death. And whosoever was

not found written in the book of life was cast into the lake of fire."
- Revelation 20:11-15

Justifies

Just - Jesus – Us

To be justified by God is to be accepted by God as righteous and to be free from any blame and penalty for sin. All have sinned and come short of God's required standard. So, who is justified, and how do you become justified? Simply put, Jesus justifies us. It is just by grace through faith in Jesus Christ. There is no work you can do to pay the penalty for sin. Jesus already paid the penalty for the sins of the whole world, but you need that payment personally applied to your sin. Believe. Just believe.

"Keep thee far from a false matter; and the innocent and righteous slay thou not: for I will not justify the wicked." - Exodus 23:7

"He (Jesus) shall see of the travail of his soul, *and* shall be satisfied: by his knowledge shall my righteous servant justify many; for he shall bear their iniquities." - Isaiah 53:11

"And the scripture, foreseeing that God would justify the heathen through faith, preached before the gospel unto Abraham, *saying*, In thee shall all nations be blessed." - Galatians 3:8

"For by grace are ye saved through faith; and that not of yourselves: *it is* the gift of God:" - Ephesians 2:8

K

Kingdom

Kin – God

The Bible states that when we accept Jesus, we inherit the <u>Kingdom</u> of God. We are also told that being born again we become brothers and sisters in Christ. That makes us spiritual kin to everyone who is in Christ. Those in the <u>Kingdom</u> of God are now our immediate family. Abraham is called the "father of faith", so those of faith in the God of Abraham, Isaac, and Jacob are spiritually kin to Abraham. Being in the family of God brings many special privileges, including access to God and eternal life.

In many cultures, there is a special value on family. People will go out of their way to make sure their kinfolk are safe and their basic needs are met. It should be no different with our Christian brothers and sisters. We should help, care for, encourage, and love our kin in Christ. This is what God commands. By being light that shines in darkness, Christians assist God in building His <u>Kingdom</u>.

Though it is not presently a visible <u>kingdom</u>, God is in the process of increasing His <u>kingdom</u> by adding believers from all over the world. Following the Battle of Armageddon, described in Revelation, the "Lamb of God", Jesus the Christ, will inherit the Davidic Throne and be King for a thousand years. This <u>Kingdom</u> will have rule and authority over all nations and will be located in Jerusalem.

"But seek first the <u>kingdom</u> of God, and his righteousness; and all these things shall be added unto you." - Matthew 6:33

"And he said unto them, When ye pray, say, Our Father which art in heaven, Hallowed be thy name. Thy <u>kingdom</u> come. Thy will be done, as in heaven, so in earth." - Luke 11:2

"And if children, then heirs; heirs of God, and joint-heirs with Christ; if so be that we suffer with *him*, that we may be also glorified together." - Romans 8:17

Knowledge

Now – Ledge

Knowledge, apart from humility through a relationship with God, can puff you up and make you prideful. Some theologians consider pride to be one of the worse sins. Many pursue knowledge alone, and neglect God. Are you a doctor, lawyer, professor, scientist, jet pilot, CEO, etc. that has knowledge which gives you advantages? Your knowledge may have made you a multi-millionaire or even built a $25 billion foundation, but I would not trade places with you if you do not know God. And I promise God is really worth knowing!

Knowledge changes, so it is just for now, and it only takes you so far until you end up at a ledge where you are not able to go any farther. I was sitting on an airplane beside a pharmacy student that was graduating in two months. I asked him about his field and how current the text books needed to be. He said last years book would be out of date. Then I asked him a hypothetical question: If a person graduated from pharmacy school twenty years ago and had not done any learning since . . . He interrupted and said his education would be worthless.

Eating fruit from the Tree of Knowledge is the only sin that Adam could have committed. This Tree of Knowledge was important to God. But why might God have forbidden something that does not appear that serious? Why would a Tree of Knowledge be so bad?   I think the tree represents a false and perilous pursuit. This tree apparently represents seeking knowledge apart from God. Is it any surprise that countless millions of people still seek their understanding by this method apart from God? Science means knowledge, so this tree could be called the "tree of science." Unfortunately this seems to be the Tree of Knowledge that so many think will advance mankind, and make humans the measure of all things instead of God, the Creator of this universe, and the Sovereign Supreme eternal being.

"And out of the ground made the LORD God to grow every tree that is pleasant to the sight, and good for food; the tree of life also in the midst of the garden, and the tree of <u>knowledge</u> of good and evil." - Genesis 2:9

"For what is a man profited, if he shall gain the whole world, and lose his own soul? Or what shall a man give in exchange for his soul? - Matthew 16:26

L

Learn(ing)

Earn

<u>Learning</u> is a gain of knowledge, and spiritual <u>learning</u> is identified as growth. New converts are called babes in Christ. All believers are referred to as children of God. Spiritual maturity develops from a complex combination that includes an increase in Bible knowledge and understanding, fellowship, answered prayer, service, giving and worship. This whole process is called sanctification. After you are saved, God begins to work in your life to build your faith and ability to bear spiritual fruit. What a privilege to be able to <u>learn</u> more and more about the Creator of the universe.

Education or <u>learning</u> usually improves your ability to earn more money and enjoy a higher standard of living. Spiritual <u>learning</u> also improves your ability to earn more in terms of eternal rewards. Those saved will not be judged for sin, but will be judged only to reveal their contributions to God's kingdom.

The reward he/she will receive will be based on the eternal good that they accomplish after being saved. He/she will not earn any heavenly reward until they have <u>learned</u> just enough to have saving faith in God. The most important things to <u>learn</u> are not mathematical skills, music, proper grammar, etc., but wisdom, principals for living, guidance, truth, and most importantly, more and more about the eternal Eloheim.

"But continue thou in the things which thou hast <u>learned</u> and hast been assured of, knowing of whom thou hast learned them; And that from a child thou hast known the Holy Scriptures, which are able to make thee wise unto salvation through faith which is in Christ Jesus. All scripture is given by inspiration of God, and is profitable for doctrine, for reproof, for correction, for instruction in righteousness: That the man of God may be perfect, thoroughly furnished unto all good works."- 2 Timothy 3:14-17

"But seek ye first the kingdom of God, and his righteousness; and all these things shall be added unto you." – Matthew 6:33

"And I, brethren, could not speak unto you as unto spiritual, but as unto carnal, *even* as unto babes in Christ." – 1 Corinthians 3:1

Letters

Lets - See - El (God) – Tel (ph. Tell) Rest – Settle

Letters in English language words let us see God's design. These word letters provide answers that settle many beliefs and issues. Sometimes they tell us the rest of the story, which could settle many issues, like evolution (evil notion).

"And it came to pass, that, when Abraham's servant heard their words, he worshipped the LORD, *bowing himself* to the earth." Genesis 24:52

"And ye shall be unto me a kingdom of priests, and an holy nation. These *are* the words which thou shalt speak unto the children of Israel." Exodus 19:6

Liberal

Libel – Lie – Rebel – El (God)

These, as a group, believe a lie and therefore make and say false assumptions regarding God. They rebel against the God that brought them into existence. Those that do not believe in God or oppose the light that came into the world actually hate God.

Harvard University was founded by John Harvard to prepare men for ministry, but today it is liberal. This pattern of godly men establishing and liberals taking over is seen frequently. Problems do seem to occur when faith and politics get too entwined. Liberals please do not be offended and keep an open mind. Years ago I had to make value changes and you may decide you need to reconsider some values and issues as well.

"Ye are of *your* father the devil, and the lusts of your father ye will do. He was a murderer from the beginning, and abode not in the truth, because there is no truth in him. When he speaketh a lie, he speaketh of his own: for he is a liar, and the father of it." - John 8:44

"God forbid that we should rebel against the LORD, and turn this day from following the LORD" - Joshua 22:29

Liberty

El (God) – Try

Freedom is found in truth. America became a nation of freedom and <u>liberty</u> because it was founded on Biblical principals. The correct fight is not to establish a state religion, but to establish freedom for all religion. If you have not already done so, I suggest that you try God and be set free. "It is impossible to enslave, mentally or socially, a Bible reading people. The principles of the Bible are the groundwork of human freedom." Horace Greeley

"The Spirit of the Lord GOD *is* upon me; because the LORD hath anointed me to preach good tidings unto the meek; he hath sent me to bind up the broken hearted, to proclaim <u>liberty</u> to the captives, and the opening of the prison to *them that are* bound;" – Is. 61:1

"And ye shall know the truth, and the truth shall make you free." - John 8:32

Life

File

What is the meaning of life? You have a <u>life</u> because God has a file on you and on everyone else. In your file, even the hairs on your head are numbered. Human <u>life</u> is sacred because mankind is made in the image of God. God gave you the breath of <u>life</u> and your human spirit and soul will always exist somewhere. There are only two options, heaven or hell. In heaven, you will experience the presence of God, and in hell, there is separation from God. You want to be sure that you have eternal <u>life</u>, which a person receives at the time of salvation. This guarantees ones eternal security. Once you have eternal <u>life</u>, there is no sin remembered against you. In the Bible the word remember means to act upon. In true salvation all of your sin is forgiven. This is not a license to freely commit sin, because God will chasten, or discipline you for continued sin, even to death if necessary.

"He that hath the Son hath <u>life</u>; *and* he that hath not the Son of God hath not <u>life</u>." - 1 John 5:12

For he that eateth and drinketh unworthily, eateth and drinketh damnation to himself, not discerning the Lord's body For this cause many *are* weak and sickly among you, and many sleep." – 1 Corinthians 11:29-30

Last

Salt

Salt is a preservative and a purifier. Christians are supposed to be salt and light in the world. Christians have the responsibility to preserve truth and purity, and to represent the true character of God. God is love, but God also executes judgment against evil. It is human nature to want to be first rather than <u>last</u>. But the inspired Bible teaches that it is far more important to be a servant to others, than to be first for ourselves.

"Let your speech *be* alway with grace, seasoned with salt, that ye may know how ye ought to answer every man." - Colossians 4:6

"Ye are the salt of the earth: but if the salt have lost his savour, wherewith shall it be salted? it is thenceforth good for nothing, but to be cast out, and to be trodden under foot of men." - Matthew 5:13

"Salt is good: but if the salt have lost its saltness, wherewith will ye season it? Have salt in yourselves, and be at peace one with another." - Mark 9:50

Live

Evil – Vile - Lie

Since Adam sinned, all mankind is born with a sin nature into a fallen world. All of creation is under the curse that came when Adam brought sin into the world. The sin of man is evident throughout history with wars, racism, crimes, greed, corruption, addictions, sexual immorality, idolatry, false religions, pride, etc. If you <u>live</u>, you have part of your nature that is sinful, evil, vile and satanic. If you say you have never told a lie, you just did. You are charged by God to overcome this fallen nature. You are not capable in your own power to achieve this. It is impossible for you to achieve it on your own. But God provided a way to overcome through Jesus. God is extraordinarily good! Even though there are those that lead apparent moral lives, and they think that they are

good, they are not good because only God is good. That is why you need God to obtain righteousness and overcome the world.
"Behold, I was shapen in iniquity; and in sin did my mother conceive me." - Psalm 51:5

"To open their eyes, *and* to turn *them* from darkness to light, and *from* the power of Satan unto God, that they may receive forgiveness of sins, and inheritance among them which are sanctified by faith that is in me." - Acts 26:18

"Nevertheless death reigned from Adam to Moses, even over them that had not sinned after the similitude of Adam's transgression, who is the figure of him that was to come." - Romans 5:14

"For as many as are of the works of the law are under a curse: for it is written, Cursed is every one who continueth not in all things that are written in the book of the law to do them." - Galatians 3:10

"Christ hath redeemed us from the curse of the law, being made a curse for us: for it is written, Cursed *is* every one that hangeth on a tree:" - Galatians 3:13

"Now the just shall <u>live</u> by faith: but if *any man* draw back, my soul shall have no pleasure in him." - Hebrews 10:38
"In this was manifested the love of God toward us, because that God sent his only begotten Son into the world, that we might <u>live</u> through him." - 1 John 4:9

M

Meekness

Knees – Seek(s)

The definition of the word meek may cause people to think that it is a flaw rather than a virtue. The Hebrew word for meek is *anaw*, meaning "in need, wretched, impoverished, and oppressed." When we hear the word meek, we think of weak, as in one who is easily brought to his knees; or one who is easy to trample over without much resistance. However, the definition of <u>meekness</u>, as seen in the Bible, is that of humility and kindness to our neighbors, and reverence for God. <u>Meekness</u> is a result of love, meaning it is an attribute of God. Some of the strongest people in the Bible are defined as being meek, like Moses, the Apostle Paul, and even the Lord Jesus.

<u>Meekness</u> is also a Fruit of the Spirit, and is the third characteristic that Jesus described in his teaching of the Beatitudes from his Sermon on the Mount. That should indicate how important this virtue is! He says the meek will be blessed and will inherit the earth. Why? Because <u>meekness</u> allows one to be prepared to do what Jesus commands, which is love your neighbor and love God. The meek don't seek revenge for insult or injury from those who wrong or oppress them. But instead they feel a sense of pity for them, and towards sinners in general, feeling inclined to love and help them with their character issues. Revenge is an attitude of get even, and it is prevalent and destructive. Jesus demonstrated this when He was on the cross, saying "Father, forgive them for they know not what they do." This is the true definition of <u>meekness</u> in action. He could have easily taken Himself down from the cross, but showed <u>meekness</u> by constraining His strength for our sake. Jesus reacted to insult, oppression, rejection, and condemnation with unconditional love for those who committed these things against Him.

The meek are also able to stay calm and are not quick to get angry with other people or with God. The meek humbly bow on their knees before God and willingly submit to Him. They will seek him and will be blessed for it. <u>Meekness</u> is also a cure for stress and anxiety, which allows room for joy to come in.

"Seek ye the Lord, all ye <u>meek</u> of the earth, who have kept His ordinances; Seek righteousness, Seek <u>meekness</u>: it may be you shall be hid in the day of the Lord's anger." - Zephaniah 2:3

The <u>meek</u> shall eat and be satisfied: they shall praise the Lord who seek him: your heart shall live for ever. - Psalm 22:26

"The <u>meek</u> shall also increase their joy in the Lord, and the poor among men shall rejoice in the Holy One of Israel. - Isaiah 29:19

"Blessed are the <u>meek</u>: for they shall inherit the earth." – Matt. 5:5

Mental

Lament – Mean – Tale – Man/Men

<u>Mental</u> pertains to the mind and intellect and all of man is in a fallen <u>mental</u> state due to the sin curse. Therefore to a greater or lesser degree everyone has some kind of mental condition. Sometimes, a person with <u>mental</u> problems from personal struggles will be mean to others. This is a type of misdirected anger. Sometimes they are actually angry with God. Satan likes to keep people in that condition because meanness, bitterness and hatred make you a victim of your own mind.

Sometimes people have <u>mental</u> problems that are so serious that they are categorized as pathological. Guilt is one emotion that can be the cause of a pathological condition producing extreme lament (grief, sorrow). The source of this guilt is not God, but is from a person's own mind. The guilt is based on a tale that they tell themselves. Forgiveness of self and of others is an important component of true spirituality. One-reason believers should be able and willing to forgive is because they were lost sinners that received the grace of forgiveness from a Holy God.

"For thus saith the LORD, Enter not into the house of mourning, neither go to lament nor bemoan them: for I have taken away my peace from this people, saith the LORD, *even* loving kindness and mercies." Jeremiah 16:5

"Seest thou a man diligent in his business? He shall stand before kings; he shall not stand before mean *men*." Proverbs 22:29 ¶

"To open their eyes, *and* to turn *them* from darkness to light, and *from* the power of Satan unto God, that they may receive forgiveness of sins, and inheritance among them which are sanctified by faith that is in me." - Acts 26:18

Mentor

One – On – One

A <u>mentor</u> usually is a person that is in a one-on-one relationship with another person, and he/she functions as a friend, teacher and counselor. I looked at this word because I was attending a conference and listening to a keynote speaker in Prince William County Virginia that was a renowned <u>mentor</u>. She did not know that the letters for one-on-one were in the word <u>mentor</u>. God deals and leads us one-on-one just like a mentor. God is the best mentor that you could have for guidance, counseling and comfort.

"The way of a fool *is* right in his own eyes: but he that hearkeneth unto counsel *is* wise." Proverbs 12:15

"Ointment and perfume rejoice the heart: so *doth* the sweetness of a man's friend by hearty counsel." Proverbs 27:9

Messiah

He - Is – I - Am – Same

From the time that man sinned in the Garden of Eden, God promised His people a <u>Messiah</u>; One who would save them and reign over them. When the time was just right, God acted on this plan. The <u>Messiah</u> came to Earth in the form of a child, being born as a created being from the womb of one He created. Jesus existed long before anything was created. He was and is and is to come because He is part of the Godhead, Father, Son and Holy Spirit. Everything was created by Him and for Him. He is I Am. The prophesied Jewish <u>Messiah</u> is the same as the gentle Jesus. The <u>Messiah</u> was rejected nationally by Israel; therefore God placed the Jews, except for a remnant, in spiritual blindness. This condition has lasted to this very day, but it is not permanent. The Jewish people have been in denial long enough, and they need to be true children of Abraham, "a friend of God" and the "father of faith." The "times of the Gentiles" will be brought to an end. This is not bad because the world will receive great blessings after Israel recognizes her <u>Messiah</u>. I see signs that God has already started the preparation for this transition of spiritual power from the Gentiles back to Israel. It is a privilege through prayer and giving to be part of this prophecy. It will happen with or without you. If you are on God's side you should gladly support Israel in ministry, particularly Messianic ministry, in Israel.

The Jewish people are amazed that Christians have taken a book they wrote (Torah) all over the world. Every true New Testament church in America, and the world, should have a passion for Israel. God separated the Jewish people for His purpose. Through them He produced prophets, the Old and New Testaments, the Apostles, the Church and most importantly the Jewish <u>Messiah</u>. The only Savior of the world, Jesus, was a Jew, while on earth. "And in none other is there salvation: for neither is there any other name under heaven, that is given among men, wherein we must be saved." (Acts 4:12) We have much to be thankful to Israel for, she gave us our Savior.

By God's grace we have been grafted into the kingdom inheritance. "The <u>Messiah</u> is "A light to lighten the Gentiles, and the glory of thy people Israel." (Luke 2:32) The <u>Messiah</u> is the "consolation of Israel." (Luke 2:25)

"And I will put enmity between thee and the woman, and between thy seed and her seed: he shall bruise thy head, and thou shalt bruise his heel." - Genesis 3:15

"Jesus said unto them, 'Verily, verily, I say unto you, Before Abraham was, I Am.'" - John 8:58

"He first findeth first his own brother Simon, and saith unto him, We have found the <u>Messiah</u> which is, being interpreted, the Christ." - John 1:41

Ministers

Resist – Sin (s) - Insist

Insist means to stand upon or follow diligently, and how appropriate this is for <u>ministers</u> that have a calling from God. Ministers should stand firmly upon Scripture and insist on everyone's need for salvation because all were separated from God by sin. First and foremost sin is an offense against a Holy God. Therefore <u>ministers</u>, as representatives of God, should resist sin. They should encourage people to have behavior that is based on what the Word of God says because there are moral absolutes.

Christian leaders should resist sin themselves, and they have a responsibility to correctly represent God's character to the best of their ability. People expect to see a high standard of morality set by the people who have been chosen by God to <u>minister</u> to them. When a spiritual leader sins, it may cause those who see this sin to be turned away from the church, or to think the sin is okay since a <u>minister</u> has committed it. That's why those who are in a position of power should resist sin, not only for themselves, but for the well being of others, the church, and the Kingdom.

"For after that in the wisdom of God the world by wisdom knew not God, it pleased God by the foolishness of preaching to save them that believe." - 1 Corinthians 1:21

"But now being made free from sin, and become servants to God, ye have your fruit unto holiness, and the end everlasting life" - Romans 6:22

Miracle

I – Am – Real – Clear – Claim – Reclaim

During the ministry of Jesus He performed many <u>miracles</u>, including those that fulfilled Messianic prophecy.   Jesus said, "He that hath seen me, hath seen the Father." Jesus verified his claim that He was the I Am in the Old Testament, and that He was real because of the many <u>miracles</u> He performed. When Jesus cast out a demon from the one who was both deaf and blind, it was clear that He was the expected Messiah. The miracles that Jesus did showed his authority over demons, death, health, nature, and physical laws. He changed wash water into fine wine and walked on the surface of water. His <u>miracles</u> over all domains demonstrated His authority and were a clear picture message to anyone wanting the real Messiah. In the future Jesus will miraculously reclaim the earth from Satan and establish His Kingdom.

"Insomuch that the multitude wondered, when they saw the dumb to speak, the maimed to be whole, the lame to walk, and the blind to see: and they glorified the God of Israel." - Matthew 15:31

"Then was brought unto him one possessed with a devil, blind, and dumb: and he healed him, insomuch that the blind and dumb both spake and saw." - Matthew 12:22

"And Jesus said unto them, I am the bread of life: he that cometh to me shall never hunger; and he that believeth on me shall never thirst." - John 6:35

"I said therefore unto you, that ye shall die in your sins: for if ye believe not that I am *he*, ye shall die in your sins." John 8:24

"He answered and said, Whether he be a sinner *or no*, I know not: one thing I know, that, whereas I was blind, now I see." - John 9:25

"For the man was above forty years old, on whom this <u>miracle</u> of healing was shewed." - Acts 4:22

"For the Lord himself shall descend from heaven with a shout, with the voice of the archangel, and with the trump of God: and the dead in Christ shall rise first:" – 1 Thessalonians 4:16

Miser

Ire – Mire – Is – Me

A <u>miser</u> is a covetous person who makes themselves <u>miser</u>able by fearing poverty. Their ire about money makes them angry and has them stuck in mire so they miss a lot of the happiness and joy that life offers. Generosity is good for the soul.

"Then the people rejoiced, for that they offered willingly, because with perfect heart they offered willingly to the LORD: and David the king also rejoiced with great joy." - 1 Chronicles 29:9

"Wherefore is light given to him that is in <u>misery</u> and life unto the bitter *in* soul;" - Job 3:20

Mockers

Some – Come – Mock – Rock (Jesus)

Jesus was mocked when He was with us, and there are plenty of people today that are <u>mockers</u> (express contempt or ridicule) of Christianity. They may not know it, but they are fulfilling Bible prophecy.

"How that they told you there should be <u>mockers</u> in the last time, who should walk after their own ungodly lusts." Jude 1:18

"As it is written, Behold, I lay in Sion a stumblingstone and rock of offence: and whosoever believeth on him shall not be ashamed." Romans 9:33

"And did all drink the same spiritual drink: for they drank of that spiritual Rock that followed them: and that Rock was Christ." 1 Corinthians 10:4

Music(k)

Sum – Us

<u>Music</u> has always been described as a sort of universal language because just about anyone can understand the sound of an orchestra, a jazz quartet, or a solo classical guitarist. Furthermore, those who have become "fluent" in the language are able to read it and speak it. As with any other language, music has dialects, which are called genres. Classical, Jazz, Rock, Country, Blues, Eastern Indian, Celtic, and Klezmer are just a few of the many genres of music heard throughout the world. Each one is distinctive to its native people (A product of the wonderful diversity that God has created among man), but each of these distinct styles share the same roots (Melody, Harmony and Rhythm), just as each nation shares a common ancestor, Adam. And just as each man can choose to reject or accept God, each style of music can be used to praise or curse Him. He has created <u>music</u> for us, not only to enjoy and to express our desire to create (Man can create because he has been made like his Creator), but He expects us to use it to glorify Him. King David, as well as other men in Israel's history, knew this intimately. These musicians wrote, sang, and played songs to

the Lord, giving back to Him with gifts and talents that were first given to them by God (See *Preeminence, Fruits*).

When studying the very basics of <u>music</u> (what is known as <u>Music</u> Theory), you can see God's fingerprints all over it. As seen in the Bible, God loves to use numbers and sums of numbers to point back to Him. <u>Music</u> is one of the most obvious cases in which we can see how individual numbers add up to create a sum that displays God's wisdom in creation. The following examples are meant only to show just that.

Three: There are three parts to <u>music</u>. Melody, a series of notes played in succession and variance of notes. Harmony, the relative notes to a melody that are pleasant to the ear, and are used to make up chords. Rhythm is the pattern within a song that governs the length of notes and gives the song its form.

Harmony, one of these three parts of <u>music</u>, is based on the number three. A basic chord is made up of three notes, or a triad, which starts with the root, adds the third, and finally the fifth. These intervals can be major, minor, augmented or diminished. Three is a number representative of Divine Perfection. The musical triad is another useful picture of the Godhead. The Holy Trinity is the Father, Son, and Holy Spirit; and these three are in such harmony that they are One God. There are many threes seen in scripture aside from the Trinity. Jesus rose on the third day. His ministry lasted three years. The Earth was separated from the water on the Third day of Creation. The Seraphim proclaim "Holy, Holy, Holy!" three times at God's throne. There are many other scriptural references to three, as well. Outside of scripture, three is a prominent number in the things around us, and people around us. There are three Human abilities (Thought, Word, and Deed). There are three parts of the universe (Time, Space, and Matter). As with the Godhead, they exist together as one, but they also each have three parts of their own. Time: Past, Present, Future. Matter: Solid, Liquid, Gas. Matter: Depth, Width, Length.

Seven: There are seven notes in a musical scale (Major, Minor, Dorian, Phrygian and Aeolian are all types of scales called Modes, each with seven notes). A seven note scale is full, but not complete. It is missing four notes to make it chromatic (a total of eleven notes), and even then, it is not yet perfectly complete. The number seven biblically represents completion or fullness and can be seen several places in Scripture; Seven days in a week, Seven parables in Matthew, Seven seals and Seven Trumpets in Revelation, Seven promises to the churches, and many other not-so-obvious Sevens and numbers divisible by seven.

Eight: An octave is the interval between ranges in <u>music</u>. Based on the seven note scale, when it is the end of a full scale, it notes the beginning of a new, but higher, range of notes, thus completing the scale. The number eight in the Bible represents New Beginnings. There were eight people on Noah's Ark, and circumcisions were performed on the eighth day. Eight is also synonymous with the number one, as seen in the example of the musical scale, and explains why this number is used for starting anew.

Eleven: There are eleven notes available in <u>music</u> (certain Eastern Indian genres uses a Carnatic scale, which includes microtones found slightly in between the twelve chromatic notes, making twenty-one available notes. Note that this number is divisible by seven). Played consecutively, they form a chromatic scale, with a twelfth note completing the scale (this note is the same note, eight, that completes a seven note scale). Eleven is the number of disorder and imperfection, and symbolizes something that is not yet full. Examples in Scripture include the state of the disciples after Judas committed suicide, leaving them incomplete at eleven. In Genesis, we see how Jacob's life becomes disorderly and somewhat chaotic after Joseph is sold into slavery, and the number of his children goes from a complete twelve to an incomplete eleven. Meanwhile, Joseph spends eleven years in the house of Potiphar, whose wife causes disorder for Joseph resulting in his inprisonment.

Twelve: There are twelve notes in a full chromatic scale, arranged in half-steps or semitones. The number twelve represents Perfection of Completion (In music, this is seen by filling in the missing four notes of a seven note scale and ending at the first note in the next octave, completing the chromatic, twelve note scale) , and also Perfection of Authority or Government. There are twelve months in a year, Twelve patriarchs, Twelve tribes of Israel, Twelve prophets of the Old Testament, Twelve legions of angels, Twelve Apostles, Twelve signs in the Hebrew Mazzorot (What eventually became the corrupted Zodiac, and the Twelve foundations of the New Jerusalem.

"And David spake to the chief of the Levites to appoint their brethren to be the singers with instruments of <u>music</u>, psalteries and harps and cymbals, sounding, by lifting up the voice with joy."- 1 Chronicles 15:16

"And the priests waited on their offices: the Levites also with instruments of <u>music</u> of the LORD, which David the king had made to praise the LORD, because his mercy *endureth* for ever, when David praised by their ministry; and the priests sounded trumpets before them, and all Israel stood." - 2 Chronicles 7:6

"I will praise Thee, O LORD, with my whole heart; I will shew forth all Thy marvelous works. I will be glad and rejoice in Thee: I will sing praise to Thy Name, O Thou Most High." - Psalm 9:1-2
"Sing unto the LORD; for He hath done excellent things: this is known in ALL the earth." - Isaiah 12:5

"And they sung as it were a new song before the throne, and before the four beasts, and the elders: and no man could learn that song but the hundred and forty and four thousand, which were redeemed from the earth." - Revelation 14:3

"He hath made the earth by his power, he hath established the world by his wisdom, and hath stretched out the heaven by his understanding."- Jeremiah 51:15

"For by Him were all things created, that are in heaven, and that are in earth, visible and invisible, whether they be thrones, or dominions, or principalities, or powers: all things were created by Him, and for Him. And He is before all things, and by him all things consist." - Colossians 1:16-17

N

Name

Man – Me

The word <u>name</u> contains man (woman) because everyone has a name, and their <u>name</u> is known by God. God has many <u>name</u>s. These <u>name</u>s are representative of qualities of God, and they help us to know more about God. Calling people by their name is a way of showing that you know them. People like to hear their <u>name</u>. Calling someone by their <u>name</u> also gives them honor and esteem. God values us so much that He has his own <u>name</u>s for each of us in heaven. God also likes for us to know His <u>names</u> because He desires for us to know Him intimately. It is not all about me as it is said today. It should always be more about God and less about me.

"And Adam called his wife's <u>name</u> Eve; because she was the mother of all living." - Genesis 3:20

"Then Peter said, Silver and gold have I none; but such as I have, that give I thee: In the <u>name</u> of Jesus Christ of Nazareth, rise up and walk." - Acts 3:6

"Him that overcometh will I make a pillar in the temple of my God, and he shall go no more out: and I will write upon him the name of my God, and the name of the city of my God, *which is* new Jerusalem, which cometh down out of heaven from my God: and *I will write upon him* my new name." - Revelation 3:12

Nations

Saint - Sin

The Bible teaches the priesthood of the believer, so that all true believers have access to God. All believers are classified as saints. There will be saints in heaven from every nation on earth. Everyone that is not saved will be "without excuse." There will be no defense that my <u>nation</u> did not hear about or believe the prophets, the Bible, Jesus and the gospel. Every <u>nation</u>, Continent, and Island from America to Zante has demonstrated sin and departing from God. <u>Nations</u> are made up of people and people sin. In the book of Revelation, only one of the seven churches that were named and described spiritually exist today. They were in Turkey; which is now primarily Muslim. When a <u>nations</u>' sin becomes full, God brings judgment. Unlike individuals, <u>nations</u> cannot be dealt with in eternity. Many believe that there are many <u>nations</u> today that are on a course for judgment and wrath. What do you think about your own <u>nation</u>?

"But in the fourth generation they shall come hither again: for the iniquity of the Amorites is not yet full." - Genesis 15:16

"if my people, which are called by my name, shall humble themselves, and pray, and seek my face, and turn from their wicked ways; then will I hear from heaven, and will forgive their sin, and will heal their land." - 2 Chronicles 7:14

"Ye also, as lively stones, are built up a spiritual house, a holy priesthood, to offer up spiritual sacrifices, acceptable to God by Jesus Christ." - 1 Peter 2:5

"Paul and Timothys, the servants of Jesus Christ, to all the saints in Christ Jesus that are at Philippi, with the bishops and deacons:" - Philippians 1:1

"And they sung a new song, saying, Thou art thou to take the book, and to open the seals thereof: for thou was slain, and hast redeemed us to God by thy blood out of every kindred, and tongue, and people, and <u>nation</u>:" - Revelation 5:9

Nature

Tune – Turn (return) – Art

<u>Nature</u> gives us a macro and micro glimpse into God's <u>nature</u>. I appreciate <u>nature</u>, the science and the art, but it is better to love the Creator than the created. Turn means to rotate or revolve around, and our planet earth certainly does both of those. Tune can mean to bring into harmony, and God has certainly fine tuned <u>nature</u> throughout the universe. Man fell out of tune with God through sin. Everyone has a need to turn to God, and return to peace and harmony with God. The whole creation is in a fallen condition because of sin. There is no paradise or Garden of Eden anywhere on earth. Man may build a castle or mansion, but the curse still affects <u>nature</u> and everything that is there.

"The heavens declare the glory of God; And the firmament showeth his handiwork." - Psalm 19:1

"I will praise thee; For I am fearfully *and* wonderfully made: marvelous are thy works; and *that* my soul knoweth right well." - Psalm 139:14

"And the peace of God, which passeth all understanding, shall guard your hearts and your thoughts in Christ Jesus." – Phil. 4:7

"For we know that the whole creation groaneth and travaileth in pain together until now." - Romans 8:22

Nothing

No - Thing

The Bible states in Genesis 1:1 that "God created the heaven and the earth." That verse is a summary statement and details follow. One of those details reveals that God made the creation out of <u>nothing</u>. God created the universe "ex-nilo," meaning that He used no thing, but spoke everything into existence. This is explained in chapter two of section three.

"By the word of the Lord were the heavens made, and all the host of them by the breath of his mouth." - Psalm 33:6

Numbers

Sum

What is the biggest <u>number</u> that you know? A google is 10^{99}; which is a one followed by ninety-nine zeros. A google is a sum that is greater than the <u>number</u> of stars in the universe, or the number of miles across the universe. The only thing I can think of that would be larger than 10^{99} is God's IQ.

"When thou takest the sum of the children of Israel after their number, then shall they give every man a ransom for his soul unto the LORD, when thou numberest them; that there be no plague among them, when thou numberest them." Exodus 30:12

O

Obedience

Be – Do – Bend

Why do you think that God would want us to practice obedience to His precepts and laws? He even says in the Bible that there is fun in sin for a season, so does He just want to take away our fun? God gave laws and moral values because He knows that obedience to His ways are best for strong families; which is the foundation for a strong society. Obedience is best for communities, best for individuals - both in the present and in eternity. And very importantly, obedience is necessary to properly reflect His image and reputation. Man was made in God's image, but when sin entered through Adam the natural man no longer reflected God's image.

When you have a spiritual birth (born again) you make the choice to "walk in the Spirit" practicing attributes of Christ. This includes obedience, because He was obedient unto death. You have the ability to reflect God's image through your life. This is not automatic, even for those that are saved. By being obedient to God, we let Him, through the power of His Spirit; show us how we should be and what we should do. By practicing obedience, we learn to bend to God's will because He knows what is best for us. Obedience is edified by faith, and rewarded by a growing and greater faith. When we have faith in God, we trust that He has the absolute best for us; and we know how to listen for His voice.

Obedience to God has a direct effect on just about everything in our lives. How would it be if murder was accepted in society and people could just kill anyone they felt like? Would you want to live in that environment? Hitler had a legal form of murder called genocide. Unfortunately, in America and many other nations, currently there is a legalized form of murder called abortion. All sin is an offense to God, but especially the shedding of innocent blood. This brings judgment and the wrath of God. All of the laws God gave and instructions for righteous are beneficial for everyone.

Obedience determines how much He can use us, and how much He blesses us here on Earth, and with eternal rewards. It can also affect current and future generations. Adam and Eve's disobedience to God in the Garden of Eden caused every person who lived after them to be cursed by sin. If we do not do what God tells us, we may miss out on a huge blessing He has in store for us. Or we may suffer even worse consequences. Reflecting our own image to the world instead of Christ's is pride, which God hates.

Because of our fallen, sinful nature we can never be completely <u>obedient</u> to God in our flesh. But we should still strive to do God's will, and be who He calls us to be (Like Christ/Godly). Even though we may mess up, we cannot mess up God's plan. God may have someone picked out for a specific, important purpose, but if they disobey, God may choose to use someone else. A perfect example is King Saul. He disobeyed God's command, which led to his death, and God chose David to be the great King of Israel and to be the ancestral line for the Messiah.

"Every one that is proud in heart is an abomination to the Lord:" - Proverbs 16:5

"Better is a little, with righteousness, than great revenues without right." - Proverbs 16-8

"But ye are not in the flesh but in the Spirit, if so be that the Spirit of God dwell in you. Now if any man hath not the Spirit of Christ, he is none of his." - Romans 8:9

"And being found in fashion as a man, he humbled himself, and become <u>obedient</u> unto death, even, the death of the cross." - Philippians 2:8

Oil

Lo (Ph: Low) - Il (Phonetically Ill)

Have you ever heard the statement that <u>oil</u> and water do not mix? That is true because <u>oil</u> is not water soluble, so it does not dissolve in water. The spiritual and the natural do not mix either. <u>Oil</u> was used in the Bible for anointing kings, priests and prophets. Jesus is all three and He was anointed with spikenard <u>oil</u>, which was very costly. I have anointing <u>oil</u> from Jerusalem that I order online from Abba Oil. The <u>oil</u> contains frankincense and myrrh. These were two of the gifts that the wise men brought to Jesus. I like to put on a little of this <u>oil</u> because I feel that the aroma will be pleasing to God.

In scripture <u>oil</u> can represent the Holy Spirit. I believe having the "<u>oil</u> of gladness" means to be indwelt by the Holy Spirit. The Bible account given by Jesus about the ten virgins has oil as an essential part of the story. Only five were wise because they had the <u>oil</u> they needed when the bridegroom came. You will feel ill if you are caught low on <u>oil</u> like the five foolish virgins, because one day Jesus, the bridegroom will return for His bride. "And thou shalt make it an oil of holy ointment, an ointment compound after the art of the apothecary: it shall be an holy anointing oil. And thou shalt anoint the tabernacle of the congregation therewith, and the ark of the testimony, And the table and all his vessels, and the candlestick and his vessels, and the altar of incense, And the altar of burnt offering with all his vessels, and the laver and his foot. And thou shalt sanctify them, that they may be most holy: whatsoever toucheth them shall be holy. And thou shalt anoint Aaron and his sons, and consecrate them, that they may minister unto me in the priest's office. And thou shalt speak unto the children of Israel, saying, This shall be an holy anointing oil unto me throughout your generations. Upon man's flesh shall it not be poured, neither shall ye make any other like it, after the composition of it: it is holy, and it shall be holy unto you. Whosoever compoundeth any like it, or whosoever putteth any of it upon a stranger, shall even be cut off from his people. And the LORD said unto Moses, Take unto thee sweet spices, stacte, and onycha, and galbanum; these sweet spices with pure frankincense: of each shall there be a like weight:And thou shalt make it a perfume, a confection after the art of the apothecary, tempered together, pure and holy: And thou shalt beat some of it very small, and put of it before the testimony in the tabernacle of the congregation, where I will meet with thee: it shall be unto you most holy. And as for the perfume which thou shalt make, ye shall not make to yourselves according to the composition thereof: it shall be unto thee holy for the LORD." Exodus 30:25-37

"Then Samuel took the horn of <u>oil</u>, and anointed him in the midst of his brethren: and the Spirit of the Lord came upon David from that day forward. So Samuel rose up, and went to Ramah." - 1 Samuel 16:13

"Thou lovest righteousness, and hated wickedness: therefore God, thy God, hath anointed thee with the <u>oil</u> of gladness above thy fellows." - Psalm 45:7

"Jesus answered, Verily, verily, I say unto thee, Except a man be born of water and of the Spirit, he cannot enter into the kingdom of God." - John 3:5

"But the natural man receiveth not the things of the Spirit of God: for they are foolishness unto him; neither can he know them, because they are spiritually discerned - 1 Corinthians 2:14

"Then shall the kingdom of heaven be likened unto ten virgins, which took their lamps, and went forth to meet the bridegroom. And five of them were wise, and five were foolish. They that were foolish took their lamps, and took no oil with them: But the wise took oil in their vessels with their lamps. While the bridegroom tarried, they all slumbered and slept. And at midnight there was a cry made, Behold, the bridegroom cometh; go ye out to meet him. Then all those virgins arose, and trimmed their lamps. And the foolish said unto the wise, Give us of your oil; for our lamps are gone out. But the wise answered, saying, Not so; lest there be not enough for us and you: but go ye rather to them that sell, and buy for yourselves. And while they went to buy, the bridegroom came; and they that were ready went in with him to the marriage: and the door was shut. Afterward came also the other virgins, saying, Lord, Lord, open to us. But he answered and said, Verily I say unto you, I know you not. Watch therefore, for ye know neither the day nor the hour wherein the Son of man cometh."– Matthew 25:1-13

Ordinary

Ordain(ed)

God has a knack for using, unexceptional, <u>ordinary</u> people for extraordinary purposes. Dwight L. Moody (1831-1899) was one of the greatest all time preachers in America. Mr. D. L. Moody was a shoe salesman with a third grade education. He spoke at Oxford University in England, and astonished the listeners that were present. One doesn't have to go to seminary, have a DD, or PhD to know God, or to be able to spread the news of the Gospel. All born again believers have faith, at least one spiritual gift, direct access to God through prayer, and the privilege of receiving understanding from the Holy Spirit. Believers can be instruments through which God communicates to others.

There is formal ordination where a person is established by a specific organization for ministry. D. L. Moody was told no when he first went through the ordination process. He was told that he did not have the necessary qualities for the ministry. G. Campbell Morgan (1863-1945), was one of England's greatest preachers, and he also was originally denied ordination and told he was not capable. Today, probably most or all of the Apostles would not look like good candidates for formal ordination.

Sometimes God just has fun with the standards for success that man values. Billy Sunday was a great baseball player. One day he was walking past a revival service, stopped and went in. The rest is history because he became the greatest evangelist in America during his day. The famous Ryman Auditorium in Nashville, Tennessee which is the original home of the Grand Ole Opry was built by a riverboat captain. He went to a tent revival with some of his men to cause a disruption. Instead, he had a conversion and declared that the preacher would not stay in a tent. He raised $150,000 and the Ryman was built to hold revival meetings. Seeking God and growing through His Word allows us to be ordained by God. This enables us to be witnesses to lost souls, and to participate in the building of the Kingdom of God.

But God hath chosen the foolish things of the world to confound the wise; and God hath chosen the weak things of the world to confound the things which are mighty;" - 1 Corinthians 1:27

"Now also when I am old and grayheaded, O God, forsake me not; until I have shewed thy strength unto *this* generation, *and* thy power to every one *that* is to come." - Psalm 71:18

P

Parables

Able – Real – Pearls – Pare - Par

Wisdom does not come as a result of man's searching; it is a gift from God. Wisdom does not need to explain every question. But it leads to a reverent awe of God and believing in the "Word." Wisdom is gifts of pearls from God. <u>Parables</u> are earthly stories that contain parallels to heaven. In the Bible, Jesus usually spoke to the multitudes in <u>parables</u>. Why <u>parables</u>? These <u>parables</u> contained pearls; fictional illustrations that had real truths hidden in them. Just as pearls are hidden inside of the shell, the valuable truths Jesus taught are hidden within these ordinary parables.

These truths were not for everyone to understand. Jesus had to pare, or remove the mystery for His disciples to be able to understand the meaning of the parable. The Bible provides us with the meaning of the <u>parables,</u> which puts us on par with the disciples that Jesus personally taught. Parables contain pearls of wisdom and truth brought to us by Jesus. Though most of the parables in the Bible don't paint a picture of life in the 21st century, they have major value and truth that still applies today.

"All these things spake Jesus unto the multitude in parables; and without a parable spake he not unto them:" - Matthew 13:34

"And the disciples came, and said unto him, Why speakest thou unto them in parables? He answered and said unto them, Because it is given unto you to know the mysteries of the kingdom of heaven, but to them it is not given. For whosoever hath, to him shall be given, and he shall have more abundance: but whosoever hath not, from him shall be taken away even that he hath.
 Therefore speak I to them in parables: because they seeing see not; and hearing they hear not, neither do they understand. And in them is fulfilled the prophecy of Esaias, which saith, By hearing ye shall hear, and shall not understand; and seeing ye shall see, and shall not perceive:" - Matthew 13:10-14

"And unto man he said, Behold, the fear of the Lord, that is wisdom; and to depart from evil is understanding." - Job 28:28

"And these are they which are sown on good ground; such as hear the word, and receive *it*, and bring forth fruit, some thirtyfold, some sixty, and some an hundred." - Mark 4:20

Parents

Nest - Pear (Ph. - Pair) – Rent – Part

<u>Parents</u> naturally play a vital role in the proper raising of children. Marriage is the first institution God established and this writer believes the creation ideal is the traditional nuclear family of a married man and wife pair. The issue is not about individual rights, but about what is best for society and children. All societies have recognized these vital societal responsibilities.
Both the father and mother must do their part to teach their

children about God as they raise them. Exposing the children to the teachings of Scripture and sharing their own experiences with God should be regularly done. Children are supposed to grow up and leave the nest because the <u>parents</u> only have them temporarily. They belong to God, not the <u>parents</u> who only rent them. Just as it is customary with anything that you rent, you are accountable for how you take care of something that is not your own.

Statistics show that what children become as adults is determined more by who the parents are than by what they do for the children. These children could ultimately have families of their own, and produce your grandchildren. They carry on your name; and the greatest impact that you will make is determined by who you are. Are you a godly father, mother, and family?

"Train up a child in the way he should go: and when he is old, he will not depart from it." - Proverbs 22:6

"But Jesus called them *unto him*, and said, Suffer little children to come unto me, and forbid them not: for of such is the kingdom of God." - Luke 18:16

"Children, obey your <u>parents</u> in the Lord: for this is right. Honour thy father and mother; which is the first commandment with promise; That it may be well with thee, and thou mayest live long on the earth. And, ye fathers, provoke not your children to wrath: but bring them up in the nurture and admonition of the Lord." - Ephesians 6:1-4

"The aged women likewise, that they be in behaviour as becometh holiness, not false accusers, not given to much wine, teachers of good things; That they may teach the young women to be sober, to love their husbands, to love their children, To be discreet, chaste, keepers at home, good, obedient to their own husbands, that the word of God be not blasphemed." - Titus 2:3-5

Passion

Son – No – Sin - Pain – SOS – Sion – Pass - On

Passion can be an intense emotional drive and is quite the opposite of lukewarm; which describes the church at Laodicea in the third chapter of Revelation. What you have a passion for you pass-on to others. This book was written out of passion.

The Son of God was a sacrifice for the sins of the world on a cross in Sion (Jerusalem). He had no sin, but he suffered extreme pain because mankind was in distress without any remedy for sin. He answered the SOS call and provided the perfect help that was needed. The agony, pain and suffering of the Messiah (Son) during the crucifixion is referred to as the Passion.

"To whom also he shewed himself alive after his passion by many infallible proofs, being seen of them forty days, and speaking of the things pertaining to the kingdom of God." Acts 1:3

"And unto the angel of the church of the Laodiceans write; These things saith the Amen, the faithful and true witness, the beginning of the creation of God; I know thy works, that thou art neither cold nor hot: I would thou wert cold or hot. So then because thou art lukewarm, and neither cold nor hot. I will spue thee out of my mouth." Revelation 3:14-16

Patience

Pace – Peace –Pain

In the book of Acts, The Apostle Paul compared the Christian life to a race, and Jesus is the prize. There are no placements in this race, and you don't run to compete with each other. You run to finish the race. In Hebrews 12, it says you should run the race with patience, keeping your eyes on Jesus.

Though the definition of <u>patience</u> has been obscured over the years to simply mean "waiting" without complaining, that's only part of what the word means. If you look in a dictionary, you will see that <u>patience</u> is defined as the ability to bear pain or trials without complaining. It is shown by having faith that God will deliver you, and your ability to wait for God's timing as opposed to your own timing.

Today's culture is time segmented and has a lot of urgency. Things happen so fast, and many people are so busy. Rushing here and there and having too much on our plate has not only become normal, but has almost become a mark of status. People should be keeping themselves connected to God at all times. There is even fast food for people who need a quick bite to eat while they're on lunch break, just so they can get back to their work at the office.

Worship services have also become affected by this culture. Some want to go to church and complain if the service doesn't end at a specific time. We hurry through the service so we can beat the Methodists to the buffet, and get home to catch the kickoff of the NFL game. The Christian life should not be about rushing through the race to the finish line. If we do that, we will wear ourselves out, just as in a real race. Runners in a long race have to pace themselves and only sprint near the end. We should pace ourselves because the Christian run is life long. It is not a sprint; it is a marathon. We must finish well. In God's time, the finish line will come, and we will eventually arrive and cross it.

"Know ye not that they who run in a race run all, but one receiveth the prize? So run, that you may obtain. And every man that striveth for the mastery is temperate in all things. Now they *do it* to obtain a corruptible crown; but we an incorruptible. I therefore so run, not as uncertainly; so fight I, not as one that beateth the air: But I keep under my body, and bring *it* into subjection: lest that by any means, when I have preached to others, I myself should be a castaway." - 1 Corinthians 9:24-27

"Rest in the Lord, and wait patiently for him."- Psalm 37:7a

"For our conversation is in heaven; from whence also we look for the Saviour, the Lord Jesus Christ:" - Philippians 3:20

"In your <u>patience</u> possess ye your souls." - Luke 21:19

Pattern

Repeat – Part

Once on a mission trip to Rio de Janeiro I glued and nailed wooden boards together that had been cut on a jig (<u>pattern</u>) and made fifteen church pews. The <u>pattern</u> was made by a master carpenter from East Tennessee, and since the members of the mission team had his pattern we could cut boards correctly and work without his continued assistance.

Jesus who also worked as a carpenter is presented in four Gospels (good news) instead of one and some parts are repeated for a type of pattern. The word pattern repeats many times throughout the Bible as do many other words. The main pattern throughout the Holy Bible from Genesis to Revelation is the salvation of man through God's only begotten Son, the redeemer and Lamb of God.

"According to all that I shew thee, *after* the <u>pattern</u> of the tabernacle, and the <u>pattern</u> of all the instruments thereof, even so shall ye make *it*." Exodus 25:9

"Howbeit for this cause I obtained mercy, that in me first Jesus Christ might shew forth all longsuffering, for a <u>pattern</u> to them which should hereafter believe on him to life everlasting." 1 Timothy 1:16

"In all things shewing thyself a <u>pattern</u> of good works: in doctrine *shewing* uncorruptness, gravity, sincerity," Titus 2:7

Perish

Ripe – Pie – His – Ship - Rise

Perish means to be destroyed or come to nothing. I have to agree with the renowned minister Henry Blackaby when he said, "There is something so deep about the word perish that probably only God understands it." He based that remark on God's knowledge of what happens to lost souls after death that is never reversed. Henry asked, if we saw what God saw what would we do? Would we pray day and night?"

Apparently, the lost are in an everlasting state of perishing. The Bible descriptions of perish includes torment, outer darkness, and separation from God. That darkness would not even include the light produced by one fire fly (lightning bug). Light from an insect is miraculous not evolution. If you think that an insect that can make light was by evolution you are probably on course to experience the horror of this outer darkness.

The Bible does state that the broad way leads to destruction (Mt. 7:13), and since the word perish is used in reference to the lost it provides the opportunity to examine the duration of hell. Is mankind immortal or is immortality a gift from God? Those that are saved will receive a new glorified body, and I believe that is when we become immortal. Thus immortality is a gift from God.

A big question is will the lost experience eternal punishing or eternal punishment? The eternal punishing theology was supported and systematized by Augustine around 400 AD. His views on heaven were influenced by Greek philosophy and do not come close to being Biblically correct. He did get some things right, but if he got it wrong about heaven I have to be suspect of his view about hell. But certainly there are scriptures that appear to support that position (Isaiah 66:24, Mathew 25:46, Rev. 14:9-11 and 20:10). However, the view of eternal punishing does not seem consistent with God's character (love, merciful, just, etc.). The letters in punishment spell "IN TIME," so I suspect that punishing (torment) is not in eternity, but is limited to time. I am not taking a definitive position on this, but I would like you to consider that possibly the lost are sent to hell, and their status is to <u>perish</u>.

Years ago I would buy grapes and berries that had started to decay at a discount and use them to make wine. I would not have wanted to eat them, but they made excellent wine. It is interesting to me that some wines are very valuable and might cost hundreds of dollars a bottle. If wine gets contaminated by bacteria it perishes and turns it into vinegar. The first miracle of Jesus was to make quality wine out of wash water. Wine is an extremely complex substance containing two hundred compounds. I believe he could have turned that wine into grapes. God is able to deal with and love a ripe humanity and a rotten humanity. Mortal has the letters for the word rot.

We are all sinners that need to be rescued from God's wrath. Have you heard the term space ship earth? Planet earth is His ship and he did rise from the dead to save those that believe He is the real Son of God. Those that do not accept the free gift of salvation by grace through faith will be sent to hell. Hell is not a roundtrip ticket. Hell is a one way ticket with no second chance.

Those souls that are saved will rise again to immortality, eternal life, heaven and a grand future beyond the imagination. Whatever "to perish" does mean, it is not good and I want life and not the second death. I believe that hell is a place of torment and separation from access to God, but why go there when God has provided by grace through faith a free "ticket" to paradise.

"For God so loved the world, that he gave his only begotten Son, that whosoever believeth in him should not <u>perish</u>, but have everlasting life." - John 3:16

"For this corruptible must put on incorruption, and this mortal *must* put on immortality. So when this corruptible shall have put on incorruption, and this mortal shall have put on immortality, **then** (author's emphasis) shall be brought to pass the saying that is written, Death is swallowed up in victory." - 1 Corinthians 15:53

"And death and hell were cast into the lake of fire. This is the second death." – Revelation 20:14

Persecution

Person – Rescue – See – Son – Rest - Rise

Persecution for religious beliefs or practices has been one of the prominent causes of persecution and goes all the way back to Cain, a son of Adam and Eve, killing his brother Abel. Even Rabbi Saul, who became the Apostle Paul after seeing the person of the Son, was involved in the pursuit, persecution and stoning of Christian believers. It seems that those doing the persecuting are the one's that are on the wrong spiritual side. Real truth stands the test of questioning without the need of force or persecution. The true God supports freedom and liberty. If your religion uses legalism, guilt or fear for control you need a new religion!

Christian believers have been rescued from the wrath of God by the Son and are able to rest in the blessed assurance of having eternal security. Jesus was the first fruits of the resurrection, but all believers will be raised from the dead.

"Who shall separate us from the love of Christ? *shall* tribulation, or distress, or persecution, or famine, or nakedness, or peril, or sword?" Romans 8:35

"Yea, and all that will live godly in Christ Jesus shall suffer persecution." 2 Timothy 3:12

Perseverance

Race – Pace – Peace – Serve - Reverence - Verse

In the race of the Christian life that Paul talks about in Philippians, you not only need patience to reach the finish line, but perseverance as well. These two virtues go hand-in-hand and work together to get you the prize. Many times, Christians running the race may stumble due to sin, suffering, or complacency. You become discouraged and stop running, thinking that the finish line is too far away. Or you think that you can run the race without God's guidance; or that you simply don't deserve the prize because of failures. However, these things shouldn't keep you from finishing the race. If you keep your eye on the prize all the way to the end, you may stumble, but you will be able to get back up and keep running. Again, you should pace yourselves so that you don't get worn out. But when you do get tired, you should rest in God and have peace in Him. When you suffer from the aches and pain that running such a long, hard race often causes you to have, you should trust God to heal you so that you may continue to run.

Your sins don't disqualify you from the race. You are born a sinner, yet you are still able to enter the race at any time. God doesn't do background checks to see if you have any felonies, divorce, or other offenses in the past and not allow you to enter the race. Your past has been forgiven by the blood of Jesus. And you can run with joy, knowing that, if born again, you can serve him, no matter what sins you have committed or will commit in the future. This provides you a liberty in Christ; however this liberty is not for you to freely sin, but it is liberty.

Thinking that you can win the race without God's help is a sure fire way to stumble. But even then, you won't be disqualified. He will find a way to fix your eyes on the prize again and stay fixed on it to the end. In many children's sports, they tell the kids to "Believe in yourself!" This philosophy may work for kids playing tee-ball, but in the Christian race, you should believe in God and should show reverence for his sovereignty, power and love. To rely on yourself is a mistake because you are imperfect, weak, and sinful. Trust God to guide you and give you strength to complete His race to the end. Keep your eyes on the prize of Jesus, the Author and Finisher of your faith!

"I have fought the good fight, I have finished the course, I have kept the faith:" – 2 Timothy 4:7

"No servant can serve two masters: for either he will hate the one, and love the other; or else he will hold to one, and despise the other. Ye cannot serve God and mammon." - Luke 16:13

"Praying always with all prayer and supplication in the Spirit, and watching thereunto with all perseverance and supplication for all saints;" - Ephesians 6:18

"And the peace of God, which passeth all understanding, shall keep your hearts and minds through Jesus Christ." - Philippians 4:7

Philosophy

Phil (Ph: Full) – Los (Ph: loss)

Philosophy is defined as the love and pursuit of wisdom by intellectual means, and a view of reality based on logical reasoning and speculation. Man's wisdom is foolishness to God, and any philosophy without God is vain and lacking real wisdom. Many eastern religions are based on philosophical thought (Buddhism, Taoism, etc.), which are full of loss. This is because they do not know the saving grace of Jesus Christ; who is the one and only way to God the Father. "Without the shedding of blood there is no remission of sin."

The speculative philosophy of the Greeks opened up the minds of many to ideas on nature, creation, government, morality and ethics. And while they attempted to provide solutions and answers to all of these ideals; they were still full of loss because they are from man and not from God.

When this writer took a philosophy class in college, the Professor wrote on a paper, "You are an original thinker." Actually, I was a Christian thinker with some advantages over secular thinkers. I knew that man's wisdom was inferior to God's wisdom revealed in his Word. Without Christ, there is loss, but with Him we are full and complete. Philosophy usually represents the pursuit of knowledge apart from God, which is what caused man to sin in the Garden of Eden in the beginning. And millions are still eating that fruit from the "Tree of Knowledge" to this day.

"Beware lest any man spoil you through <u>philosophy</u> and vain deceit, after the tradition of men, after the rudiments of the world, and not after Christ."- Colossians 2:8

Praise

Raise – Praer (Phonetically: Prayer)

When you give people honest <u>praise</u> you exhort them or raise them emotionally. Sometimes if you have to deal with a negative issue it is wise to make a "praise sandwich." You start with <u>praise</u> and end with <u>praise</u>. In <u>praise</u> of someone you are expressing value for something about them.

Authentic Christians are able to genuinely <u>praise</u> the Creator God because they know God through the Scripture and through a personal relationship. They are able to make honest statements of <u>praise</u>. The <u>praise</u> of God usually is in the beginning of prayer and is a prerequisite to real worship of the Almighty, Living and Holy God. The <u>praise</u> of God is a benefit to them, and it raises them and adds effectiveness to their prayer time.

"Enter into his gates with thanksgiving, *and* into his courts with <u>praise</u>: be thankful unto him, *and* bless his name." - Psalm 100:4

Prayers

Repay(s) – Ear – Prepare (Use letter e twice) - Reap

<u>Prayer</u> is a privilege that gives believers direct access to the throne and the ear of God. The New Testament teaches the priesthood of the believer, so all authentic Christians do not need to go through anyone or anything else to address God. <u>Prayer</u> gives

believers direct and immediate access to the infinite, eternal, omnipotent, and holy God.

Prayer is an excellent way to prepare for a war or battle. George Washington believed in prayer and established the Chaplin Service for the US Military. Christians are in spiritual warfare, so prayer should be a prerequisite for battle.

Jesus is the High Priest, and He is the intercessor with God the Father. Prayer may be individual or corporate, like a church prayer group or prayer service. For corporate prayer guidance, I recommend *And The Place Was Shaken* or *Walking With God* by Dr. John Franklin. I have seen many answered prayers from both individual and corporate prayer.

Christians should pray daily because prayer is a way to repay God for His grace toward you. Those who pray know how to lean on God. God loves and esteems faithful prayer. Prayer should not just be for a life emergency, but rather a way of life. Prayer has two blessings because the person praying will reap a reward and it blesses those who are prayed for. Prayer also helps the person praying to experience calmness, tranquility and peacefulness.

The prayer of a hypocrite does not get the reward. A hypocrite would be praying for recognition, not for contact with God. This would be a pretense. I have experienced amazing answers and accomplishments through prayer. Christians should love the privilege of prayer, and pray in faith with the expectation of receiving answers.

"The Lord *is* far from the wicked; But he heareth the prayer of the righteous." - Proverbs 15:29

"And when thou prayest, thou shalt not be as the hypocrites *are*:
for they love to pray standing in the synagogues and in the corners
of the streets, that they may be seen of men. Verily I say unto you,
They have their reward." - Matthew 6:5

"For this cause we also, since the day we heard *it*, do not cease to pray for you, and to desire that ye might be filled with the knowledge of his will in all wisdom and spiritual understanding;" - Colossians 1:9

"Let us therefore come boldly unto the throne of grace, that we may obtain mercy, and find grace to help in time of need." - Hebrews 4:16

Provision

Vision - Son - Poor

Provision is an arrangement to meet needs. God is the Creator and the sustainer of the universe. All provision, both physical and spiritual, comes from God. There are common provisions and grace like rain and sunlight that benefits everyone. You should have the vision to see that it is God that provides. The gift of salvation is a provision made by God, and Christ was "the Lamb that was slain before the foundation of the world."

Yes, God had made a provision to free mankind from the penalty of sin before He created Adam and Eve. Most people have a natural interest in wanting to live and have concern regarding death. Jesus defeated death, and this victory is offered as a free gift to all who will believe in the Son of God by faith. Those who are "poor in spirit" and have no hope, except in the provision of God, will be blessed citizens of the Kingdom.

"And he said, Hear now my words: If there be a prophet among you, *I* the LORD will make myself known unto him in a vision, *and* will speak unto him in a dream." - Numbers 12:6

"Cast thy burden upon the Lord, and he will sustain thee: he shall never suffer the righteous to be moved." - Psalm 55:22

"Then thou spakest in vision to thy holy one, and saidst, I have laid help upon *one that is* mighty; I have exalted *one* chosen out of the people." - Psalm 89:19

"Where there is no vision, the people cast off restraint; But he that keepeth the law, happy is he." - Proverbs 29:18

"Blessed are the poor in spirit: for theirs is the kingdom of heaven." - Matthew 5:3

"And as they came down from the mountain, Jesus charged them, saying, Tell the vision to no man, until the Son of man be risen again from the dead." - Matthew 17:9

"But put ye on the Lord Jesus Christ, and make not <u>provision</u> for the flesh, to *fulfil* the lusts *thereof.*" - Romans 13:14

"And deliver them who through fear of death were all their lifetime subject to bondage." - Hebrews 2:15

"Death is swallowed up in victory. O death, where is thy sting? O grave, where is thy victory?" - 1 Corinthians 15:54-55

Preachers

Hear – Shape - Reach

<u>Preachers</u> are people who are supposed to be called and ordained by God to reach lost souls and lead them to God the Father through the Lord Jesus Christ. They have spiritual gifts to supernaturally equip them to hear from God and deliver inspired messages. This is not theory; I have personally witnessed this happen on multiple occasions. Ministers carefully shape messages from God with the aid of the Holy Spirit and Scripture. This allows their message to be understood and applied to the heart of those who hear it.

"For seeing that in the wisdom of God the world through its wisdom knew not God, it was God's good pleasure through the foolishness of the <u>preaching</u> to save them that believe." –
1 Corinthians 1:21

"Jesus saith unto him, I am the way, and the truth, and the life: no one cometh unto the Father, but by me." - John 14:6

"and how shall they <u>preach</u>, except they be sent? even as it is written, How beautiful are the feet of them that bring glad tidings of good things!" - Romans 10:15

Preeminence

Prime - Mine - Ripen

God is preeminent, meaning He is superior to everything and everyone. Because of this, He should be the prime focus of our worship, adoration, servitude, love, and sacrifice. All of these actions are forms of giving of ourselves, because anything we have received comes from God in the first place. God said to Job, "Who has first given to Me that I should repay him? Everything under Heaven is mine." God doesn't need these things from us since, as stated, everything already belongs to Him. But He delights in us giving back to Him through worship, love and service. Not only that, worshiping and serving God is for our own good.   God designed it that way.

Jesus commands us to love God with everything that we are. We come to an understanding of true love by giving back to God. And since God is fully love, we come to understand and know Him better as well. In return we are blessed. When we receive the Holy Spirit as new believers, He brings us the Fruit of Love. Love brings forth all the other Fruits of the Spirit because they are a result of love in action. So when we learn to love God fully and give him priority and worship, we mature like fruit that will ripen on a tree. As these fruits from our life ripen, the sweeter the fruits are that we will have to give back to God. It becomes a cycle that draws us closer to God. Jesus also commands us to love our neighbors as we love ourselves. We learn to do this by loving God. As the Fruits of the Spirit ripen, it becomes easier and easier to follow this command.

"And you shall love the Lord thy God with all your heart, and with all your soul, and with all your mind, and with all your strength: this is the first commandment. And the second is this. You shall love your neighbour as yourself. There is none other commandment greater than these." - Mark 12:30-31

"But the <u>fruit</u> of the Spirit is love, joy, peace, longsuffering, kindness, goodness, faithfulness," - Galatians 5:22

"And he is the head of the body, the church: who is the beginning, the firstborn from the dead; that in all things he might have the <u>preeminence</u>." - Colossians 1:18

Pulpit

Pul (*Pull*) – Pit

"Hey, Preacher! Get up there and pull them out of the pit, Brother!"

"He brought me up also out of an horrible pit, out of the miry clay; and set my feet upon a rock, and established my goings."– Ps. 40:2

"preach the word; be urgent in season, out of season; reprove, rebuke, exhort, with all longsuffering and teaching." - Timothy 4:2

Q

Qualified

Life – I – Lied - Die

You are not qualified to obtain righteousness on your own merit. No matter what you do, you are not deserving of God's love. Everything you receive from God is by grace because you are not deserving of it. If you are <u>qualified</u> you are worthy, and in heaven there will be a great voice saying, "Worthy is the Lamb." The Lamb laid down His life for us. Is your voice saying, "Worthy is the Lamb?" If not, consider asking yourself, "Why not?"

"And the Lord God formed man of the dust of the ground, and breathed into his nostrils the breath of life; and man became a living soul." - Genesis 2:7

"He said unto him, I *am* a prophet also as thou *art*; and an angel spake unto me by the word of the Lord, saying, Bring him back with thee into thy house, that he may eat bread and drink water. *But* he lied unto him." - 1 Kings 13:18

"Say unto them, *As* I live, saith the Lord GOD, I have no pleasure in the death of the wicked; but that the wicked turn from his way and live: turn ye, turn ye from your evil ways; for why will ye die, O house of Israel?"- Ezekiel 33:11

"Saying with a loud voice, Worthy is the Lamb that was slain to receive power, and riches, and wisdom, and strength, and honour, and glory, and blessing.." - Revelation 5:12

"For if, when we were enemies, we were reconciled to God by the death of his Son, much more, being reconciled, we shall be saved by his life." - Romans 5:10

R

Rapture

Reap – Up

The Bible states in 1 Thessalonians in the end times those who that are in Christ will be caught up to meet Him in the clouds. First, He will take up those who are "dead in Christ," meaning those who are saved, but have died physically. Next, He will take up those who are still alive and in Him. Christians are like a crop that has grown from seeds of faith. The end times will find the believers ripe and ready for harvest. Jesus will reap the harvest of the earth during the <u>rapture</u>.

The exact day or hour of the <u>rapture</u> is unknown. However, believers are supposed to recognize signs, just as we recognize seasons, as to when the time is near. The hope of His glorious return at any time, should remind believers to not get too attached to the things of this world. The possessions of this earthly life are temporary and insignificant compared to the eternity to come. One clue that the end is approaching is that in 1948 Israel was reestablished as a nation. The dispersion of the Jewish people and their return was prophesied in Jeremiah about 2,500 years ago. This important prophecy was fulfilled in exact detail and needed to take place before the end would come.

Israel is of special importance to God's end time plans for this planet. God weighs nations in the balances based on their treatment of this small unique nation. No nation or individual has any right to divide land that was given by God to this nation for an everlasting inheritance. If you are not a friend of Israel, you are probably not in a very good spiritual position for the Lord's return.

"For this we say unto you by the word of the Lord, that we which are alive *and* remain unto the coming of the Lord shall not prevent them which are asleep. For the Lord himself shall descend from heaven with a shout, with the voice of the archangel, and with the trump of God: and the dead in Christ shall rise first: Then we which are alive and remain shall be caught up together with them in the clouds, to meet the Lord in the air: and so shall we ever be with the Lord."-1 Thessalonians 4:15-17

"Hear the word of the LORD, O ye nations, and declare *it* in the isles afar off, and say, He that scattered Israel will gather him, and keep him, as a shepherd *doth* his flock." - Jeremiah 31:10
"And I looked, and behold a white cloud, and upon the cloud *one* sat like unto the Son of man, having on his head a golden crown, and in his hand a sharp sickle. And another angel came out of the temple, crying with a loud voice to him that sat on the cloud, Thrust in thy sickle, and reap: for the time is come for thee to reap; for the harvest of the earth is ripe. And he that sat on the cloud thrust in his sickle on the earth; and the earth was reaped." – Revelation 14:14-16

Reasonable

Able – Son – Reason

The reason we are able to be reconciled with God the Father is because the Son is able to provide for our justification.

"I beseech you therefore, brethren, by the mercies of God,
that ye present your bodies a living sacrifice, holy,
acceptable unto God, *which is* your <u>reasonable</u> service."–Rom.12:1

"For if, when we were enemies, we were reconciled to God
by the death of his Son, much more, being reconciled, we
shall be saved by his life." - Romans 5:10

Rebellion

El (God) - Lion

Rebellion is resistance or defiance of authority. And since God is the supreme authority, defying God is the supreme rebellion. When Jesus Christ returns for His second advent, He will be the Lion of Judah. Rebellion will not fare very well, because He will rule with a rod of iron. There might still be sin, but there will not be any organized system of sin.

Satan led a rebellion in heaven, and one third of the angels followed him. The devil is in a spiritual battle with God, and he has brought tremendous death, destruction, and lies to this planet. The Devil is involved in rebellion on planet earth, and is looking for followers to devour. He has two very different approaches because Lucifer is both an "angel of light" and a "roaring lion."

His work and influence is very different depending on which of these two traits are in use. Hatred and persecution of Christians would clearly be the roaring lion. The angel of light would be more subtle, and could manifest in numerous ways. I along with many serious students of the Bible, share the opinion that modern translations of the Bible fit this category. Satan could not eliminate the Bible even though he tried that throughout history. I have observed that a flood of copyrighted translations that omit important verses and change the meaning of dozens of verses, are well accepted.

Finally, this rebellious angel of enormous influence and power on planet earth will eventually be removed by the Lion of Judah and the King of Kings. Satan will be cast into the lake of fire and will no longer be the prince of this world. Please, Lord Jesus come quickly and establish your rightful throne on earth!

"An evil *man* seeketh only rebellion: therefore a cruel messenger shall be sent against him." - Proverbs 17:11

"Therefore thus saith the LORD; Behold, I will cast thee from off the face of the earth: this year thou shalt die, because thou hast taught <u>rebellion</u> against the LORD." - Jeremiah 28:16

"Hear, O heavens, and give ear, O earth: for the LORD hath spoken, I have nourished and brought up children, and they have rebelled against me." - Isaiah 1:2

"And no marvel; for Satan himself is transformed into an angel of light." – 2 Corinthians 11:14

"Be sober, be vigilant; because your adversary the devil, as a

roaring lion, walketh about, seeking whom he may devour:" –
1 Peter 5:8

Reconcile

One - Circle

To <u>reconcile</u> is to make compatible or bring into harmony. Who better to <u>reconcile</u> us to God the Father, than the Son of God who brought the universe into existence! In Christ, whether Gentile or Jew, we are all made "one new man." By believing, we become a part of the family of faith. When we are <u>reconciled</u> unto God we are one faith, connected with God for eternity like a circle that has no end. Our love for God and God's love for us will be expressed in the presence of God in Heaven for eternity.

"And, having made peace through the blood of his cross, by him to <u>reconcile</u> all things unto himself; by him, *I say*, whether *they be* things in earth, or things in heaven." - Colossians 1:20

Redeem

Reed (Ph. - Read) – Me

The Bible is a priceless account of God's <u>redeeming</u> love. He promised redemption to Adam and Eve. He <u>redeemed</u> the people of Israel from slavery in Egypt. Eventually, the Abrahamic Covenant to bless all nations was fulfilled through Jesus the Messiah. Scripture is God's inspired written Word and it is the truth that reveals the true God. The God of Abraham, Isaac and Jacob is the true and living God.

Jesus is truth and in the Gospel of John, He is identified as the Word. Faith, the key to salvation, comes from hearing the Word of God. Every Christian, from the newly born-again, to the most seasoned minister, needs the Holy Bible for correction, instruction, and guidance. Redemption is God's greatest gift, and it is received through a faith that comes from hearing the Word of God. The Bible is God's written word, and it is calling, "I am God's Word - read me, hear me in your heart, and love me!"

"So then faith *cometh* by hearing, and hearing by the word of God." - Romans 10:17

"For by grace are ye saved through faith; and that not of yourselves, *it is* the gift of God; Not by works lest any man should boast." - Ephesians 2:8-9

Reliant

Learn – Earn – El (God)

The more you learn about God the more you will rely on God. People can disappoint you, but God is completely reliable; so you can completely trust in God. The Bible teaches that God has some remarkable qualities that contribute to our being <u>reliant</u> on Him. God is unchangeable, all knowing, all powerful, merciful, gracious, and loving. Once you find God, He will earn your confidence and you will learn to love Him.

"Were not the Ethiopians and the Lubims a huge host, with very many chariots and horsemen? yet, because thou didst rely on the LORD, he delivered them into thine hand." - 2 Chronicles 16:8

"The God of my rock; in him will I trust: *he is* my shield, and the horn of my salvation, my high tower, and my refuge, my saviour; thou savest me from violence." - 2 Samuel 22:3

"The LORD *is* good, a strong hold in the day of trouble; and he knoweth them that trust in him." - Nahum 1:7

Religion

Lion – Legion – Lie – Gone

Uniting publicly with a Christian church is a profession of your faith or <u>religion</u>. Sometimes an individual will unite with a church for a reason other than being an authentic believer. The church should only be for authentic Christians that profess faith in Jesus Christ, so a non-Christian should have to lie to gain membership. However, legions of churches are liberal and have gone so far from the faith that they will even allow various types of non-believers to join. This policy is not Biblically correct, and should not be found in new Testament Christian churches.

There is also a legion of false <u>religions</u> that are always works based, and will not lead you to saving faith. The first murder when Cain killed Able was over <u>religion</u>. <u>Religion</u> can be abused and misused. It can become more about business and money than about God. Do not let the failure of men through <u>religion</u> confuse you about God. Today, with many things that are done in the name of some <u>religion</u> or "deity", I understand why there are atheists that think all <u>religion</u> should be banned.

Jesus Christ, the Lion of Judah, is the head of the Christian church. True believers are the actual church: these are the body of Christ on earth. The church is the divine established institution for Christianity. The church has and does suffer persecution, has many divisions or denominations, and is certainly not perfect. In the book of Revelation, we find that churches had problems going back to the first century. Still, it is important for believers to assemble with and fellowship with other believers, and to support local churches. Some ritual and formal structure is necessary; however, I prefer a church that is more relational with God and less "religious." The Bible states that the church will prevail, and it has for twenty centuries because it is a supernatural institution.

Recently, I asked God what was His biggest fault with the church today? I got an immediate answer; which was a lack of passion. This seems to be the same as "lukewarm" in the church at Laodicea, the end of the age church as described in the book of Revelation. This means we need **passion driven churches** and individuals with passion in the churches! What is your spiritual passion; what is the passion of your church? If you do not know the answers you might have a problem.

"How is it that ye do not understand that I spake *it* not to you concerning bread, that ye should beware of the leaven of the Pharisees and of the Sadducees?" - Matthew 16: 11

"And I say also unto thee, That thou art Peter, and upon this rock I will build my church; and the gates of hell shall not prevail against it." - Matthew 16:18

"I know thy works, that thou art neither cold nor hot: I would thou wert cold or hot. So then because thou art lukewarm, and neither cold nor hot, I will spue thee out of my mouth." – Rev. 3:15-16

Remain

Name – Near – Man – I am

During His first advent on earth Jesus did not have any title, property, wealth, or military victories. He was not a king or a conqueror. What He was is what He is, and that is the Christ, the

Messiah, the only begotten Son of God. He is the King of Kings and Lord of Lords, and His name is above every name. No person that has ever lived has had more influence on events, and on the history of this planet than Jesus Christ.

How did a man of such low estate have such influence and have thousands of millions believe in Him? It is only because He is exactly who He says that He is. Jesus is I am that I am. Jesus was God that became a man, so that He could be the atonement for the sins of the world. He is, and will always <u>remain</u> the second person of the eternal Godhead.

"Take my yoke upon you, and learn of me; for I am meek and lowly in heart: and ye shall find rest unto your souls. For my yoke *is* easy, and my burden is light." - Matthew 11:29-30

"Wherefore God also hath highly exalted him, and given him a name which is above every name:" - Philippians 2:9

"Let us draw near with a true heart in full assurance of faith, having our hearts sprinkled from an evil conscience, and our bodies washed with pure water." - Hebrews 10:22

"Who is a liar but he that denieth that Jesus is the Christ? He is an-ti-christ, that denieth the Father and the Son. Whosoever denieth the Son, the same hath not the Father: [*but*] *he that acknowledgeth the Son hath the father also*. He is antichrist, that denieth the Father and the Son. Whosoever denieth the Son, the same hath not the Father: *(but) he that acknowledgeth the Son hath the Father also*. Let that therefore abide in you, which ye have heard from the beginning. If that which ye have heard from the beginning shall <u>remain</u> in you, ye also shall continue in the Son, and in the Father."
- 1 John 2:22-24

Resurrection

Risen – Sure – Erect

Jesus had risen after three days and three nights in the tomb. The risen Saviour is a claim that is unique to Christianity. Because of the tremendous evidence for the <u>resurrection</u> of Jesus, believers have a blessed assurance and hope they also will be raised from the grave. Christians will physically stand erect before God in new incorruptible and glorified bodies.

"For unto you is born this day in the city of David a Saviour, which is Christ the Lord." - Luke 2:11

"Jesus said unto her, I am the <u>resurrection,</u> and the life: he that believeth in me, though he were dead, yet shall he live:" - Jn. 11:25

"In a moment, in the twinkling of an eye, at the last trump: for the trumpet shall sound, and the dead shall be raised incorruptible, and we shall be changed." - 1 Corinthians 15:52

Revelations

Alert – Listen – See – Israel – Seal - Veil

The last chapter in the Book of Daniel, in the Old Testament, prophesies that near the end of time there will be a tremendous increase in knowledge and in transportation. In the last fifty years knowledge has increased by more than it had in the previous 5,000 years. Transportation went from horse & buggy to automobiles, airplanes, jet airplanes and space in just a few generations. This alone is a major announcement relating to the twentieth and twenty-first Centuries. A number of other biblical prophecies have been fulfilled since I was born. This is an exciting spiritual time when prophecy events and time are intersecting.

Conditions that are described as being present as the end nears are observable now. These include, but are not limited to, the increase of earthquakes and wars. One in five nations presently is involved at some level in war. There is war that is unseen, but it is above the earthly wars. There is spiritual warfare between light and darkness, between God and Satan. This battle will increase as the end nears, and it will have tremendous effects on planet earth. Israel is prominent in end time events, and is a key to understanding the "signs of the times." As a nation, Israel, is still secular and not accepting of Jesus, their Messiah. But that will change and all of God's purposes for Israel will be fulfilled.

<u>Revelation</u>, the last Book of the Bible, is an amazing picture of end times events, and of the tribulation that will affect the entire planet. It is a book that reveals a victorious Jesus Christ. I would summarize Revelation in two words: "Jesus wins." There is a lot of encouragement and hope for believers; but a grim picture for spiritual powers, nations, false religion, and individuals on the wrong side of the battle. There is no neutrality; everyone is on one side or the other.

<u>Revelation</u>, written by the Apostle John provides an alert. This alert provides believers with an understanding for preparation and appropriate response. John is able to see the future and witness seven seals opened by the "Lamb of God." It would be wise to listen to the prophets, especially the prophecy of John as the end approaches. Are you ready for the Lord's return? If your answer is no, the Lord would love an opportunity to help you become ready. "Ask and ye shall receive."

"All ye inhabitants of the world, and dwellers on the earth, see ye, when he lifteth up an ensign on the mountains; and when he bloweth a trumpet, hear ye" - Isaiah 18:3

"And they that be wise shall shine as the brightness of the firmament; and they that turn many to righteousness as the stars for ever and ever. But thou, O Daniel, shut up the words, and seal the book, *even* to the time of the end: many shall run to and fro, and knowledge shall be increased." - Daniel 12:3-4

"The <u>Revelation</u> of Jesus Christ, which God gave unto him, to shew unto his servants things which must shortly come to pass;

and he sent and signified *it* by his angel unto his servant John:" - Revelation 1:1

Reward

Ward - War - Draw

God's word does promise a reward to believers for laboring together with God to build on the foundation that was laid: which is Jesus Christ. <u>Reward</u> is one of four motivations for Christian service (the other three are gratitude, compulsion and fear). God wants to draw us near and have us follow Him. The advantage for doing this is a richer spiritual life now, and a <u>reward</u> in heaven. Believers are supposed to be more concerned about the kingdom of God than building treasure on earth. You cannot take your treasure here with you when you die, but you can "pay it forward." That way you can build up a <u>reward</u> in heaven. Those that do not think that heaven would interest them have no idea of the treasures and <u>rewards</u> that will be received by the faithful because we are under God's protection and care. No one of us deserves God's love, and no one can earn God's love. His priceless unconditional love is given by grace. For our sins to be completely forgiven and for us to be allowed to spend eternity in heaven in God's presence; is far more than any of us merit. So, even though I like the privilege of building up a treasure on the other side, I know this too is by God's marvelous grace.

I know how excited I was to be saved. Heavenly <u>rewards</u> were the farthest thing from my mind. However, as the years go by and I am aware of spiritual contributions, I think more about <u>rewards</u>. It will be interesting in heaven to see how God's accounting system works when it comes to <u>rewards</u>. I feel that there are many ways to earn eternal rewards, and I know that prayer is one of them. I believe a prayer partnership with God is very powerful. The more you know God the more you appreciate God. And I want to know God. Little knowledge of God usually produces little interest in God.

I believe that <u>rewards</u> could include positions, titles, mansions, travel, and personal transportation vehicles to use on streets of gold. However, I believe that the greatest <u>reward</u> would be to be close to God, like the twenty-four elders sitting around the throne of God. I see that as the ultimate <u>reward</u>. The <u>reward</u> of heaven is great beyond our understanding. Unfortunately many trade eternity for this brief time in a sinful world. It is so sad that many sell the opportunity for an eternal inheritance cheaply: really cheap. It is far better to be poor on earth and rich in heaven, than vice-versa.

Spiritual warfare is a reality, and there is no neutrality with God. Being a soldier and fighting in this war on God's side will bring a <u>reward</u>. The other option will bring a <u>reward</u> that you definitely would not want. Instructing individuals in becoming human bombs, or being a suicide bomb participant is the wrong side of the war. Fighting against Christianity in America or any other nation is the wrong side of the war. Persecuting Christians is the wrong side of the war. Trying to divide or eliminate Israel is the wrong side of the war. If you are on the wrong side you need to repent – change your mind and ask for God's forgiveness.

"The LORD recompense thy work, and a full <u>reward</u> be given thee of the LORD God of Israel, under whose wings thou art come to trust." - Ruth 2:12

"Behold, the Lord GOD will come with strong *hand*, and his arm shall rule for him: behold, his <u>reward</u> *is* with him, and his work before him." - Isaiah 40:10

"He that receiveth a prophet in the name of a prophet shall receive a prophet's <u>reward</u>; and he that receiveth a righteous man in the name of a righteous man shall receive a righteous man's <u>reward</u>." - Matthew 10:41

"Rejoice ye in that day, and leap for joy: for, behold, your <u>reward</u> *is* great in heaven:" - Luke 6:23

"For where your treasure is, there will your heart be also." - Luke 12:34

"And round about the throne *were* four and twenty seats: and upon the seats I saw four and twenty elders sitting, clothed in white raiment; and they had on their heads crowns of gold." - Revelation 4:4

Righteousness

Right - In - His – Sight

Righteousness involves restoring or setting right. So how is this done between mankind and God?   No person on earth is righteous before God in their natural condition. All are sinners and unable to meet God's standard for righteousness. Many think, without a Scriptural basis, that if they do enough good then God will accept them. Good works is not the method to obtain righteousness before God. Without righteousness no one can be in God's glorified presence. So, if not by works, how does anyone become righteous? Justification or righteousness has to be imputed to you by God, and it is not done by works or by divine clemency.

There is one way to God, and anyone trying to come by any other method is rejecting God's salvation plan. You are saved by believing in God's perfect Passover Lamb, Jesus the Christ. Salvation or righteousness is a gift that you receive through faith. To enter heaven you will have to be right in His sight.

"And he believed in the LORD; and he counted it to him for righteousness." - Genesis 15:6

"There is a way that seemeth right unto a man, but the end thereof *are* the ways of death." - Proverbs 16:25

"Jesus saith unto him, I am the way, the truth, and the life: no man cometh unto the Father, but by me." - John 14:6

"Even as David also describeth the blessedness of the man, unto whom God imputeth <u>righteousness</u> without works," - Romans 4:6

"What shall we say then? That the Gentiles, which followed not after <u>righteousness</u>, have attained to <u>righteousness</u>, even the <u>righteousness</u> which is of faith." - Romans 9:30

"For by grace are ye saved through faith; and that not of yourselves: *it is* the gift of God:" - Ephesians 2:8

S

Saints

Ain't - Stain – Sin

The New Testament Scriptures reveal that all believers in this present age are <u>saints</u>. To be a saint means to be set apart to God. Sometimes people who are believers do not behave like they are a pure and godly <u>saint</u>. This does not change their position of sainthood if he/she are true believers. A <u>saint</u> ain't got any stain from sin because they are clean by the covenant sacrifice of Jesus.

"He will keep the feet of his <u>saints,</u> and the wicked shall be silent in darkness; for by strength shall no man prevail." - 1 Samuel 2:9

"Gather my <u>saints</u> together unto me; those that have made a covenant with me by sacrifice." - Psalms 50:5

"Unto the church of God which is at Corinth, to them that are sanctified in Christ Jesus, called *to be* <u>saints,</u> with all that in every place call upon the name of Jesus Christ our Lord, both theirs and ours:" - 1 Corinthians 1:2

"Paul and Timotheus, the servants of Jesus Christ, to all the <u>saints</u> in Christ Jesus which are at Philippi, with the bishops and deacons:" - Philippians 1:1

"And he gave some, apostles; and some, prophets; and some, evangelists; and some, pastors and teachers; For the perfecting of the <u>saints,</u> for the work of the ministry, for the edifying of the body of Christ:" - Ephesians 4:11-12

"When he shall come to be glorified in his <u>saints,</u> and to be admired in all them that believe (because our testimony among you was believed) in that day." - 2 Thessalonians 1:10

"And Enoch also, the seventh from Adam, prophesied of these, saying, Behold, the Lord cometh with ten thousands of his <u>saints,</u>" - Jude 1:14

Salvation

Lavations (washings) - Lost – Sin – Son - Nails - Stain –– Slain

Our graceful and merciful God loved us so much that He sent His only son for our <u>salvation</u>. We who were stained with sin drove nails into the hands and feet of the one who was blameless. He that was slain is the blameless Passover Lamb, and the covenant sacrifice. That is why there is a new covenant and a New Testament. We are in a lost condition without that sacrifice applied to us. He forgives us for the sin against Him and our sins are washed away.

We are able to enter into the presence of God and to personally know Him. The more we know God, the more we want to know God. Those who know God little have little interest in knowing God. This is a benefit and the purpose of <u>salvation,</u> not only that we will be able to live eternally after death, but that we will be able to live eternally with God. After <u>salvation</u> there is opportunity to know more and more about God through a process called sanctification. Because of the magnitude and complexity of God, the saved will need eternity to get to know Him fully. God wants us to deeply know Him.

"The LORD liveth; and blessed *be* my rock; and exalted be the God of the rock of my <u>salvation</u>." - 2 Samuel 22:47
"Jesus answered them, Verily, verily, I say unto you, Whosoever committeth sin is the servant of sin. And the servant abideth not in the house for ever: *but* the Son abideth ever. If the Son therefore shall make you free, ye shall be free indeed." - John 8:34-36

"But God commendeth his love toward us, in that, while we were yet sinners, Christ died for us." - Romans 5:8

"For the grace of God that bringeth <u>salvation</u> hath appeared to all men" - Titus 2:11

"How shall we escape, if we neglect so great <u>salvation</u>; which at the first began to be spoken by the Lord, and was confirmed unto us by them that heard *him*;" - Hebrews 2:3

Sanctified

Saint - Set– Aside – Distance

The blood of Jesus washes away all of our sins, making us clean. The word <u>sanctified</u> as seen in the Old Testament comes from the Hebrew word Qadash, meaning to make clean. By Jesus' sacrifice for us, we have been made Holy in God's sight and set aside to be used by Him for His purposes. Though no one but Jesus was ever perfect or will ever be perfect in the flesh on this side of death, we should still strive for that Christ like perfection.

Believers are <u>sanctified</u> by Christ's blood. This means that we will be continually going through a sanctification process to make us more spiritual. This means that we are to distance ourselves from the world because being too attracted to the world removes us from God's leading. There are spiritual expectations of saints, and to serve the Living God is advantageous, but it is impossible to win in a fight against God. If a saint does not distance himself/herself enough from the world you can be sure that God knows how to gain the person's attention.

" To open their eyes, *and* to turn *them* from darkness to light, and from the power of Satan unto God, that they may receive forgiveness of sins, and inheritance among them which are sanctified by faith that is in me."- Acts 26:18

"And such were some of you: but ye are washed, but ye are <u>sanctified,</u> and you are justified in the name of the Lord Jesus, and by the Spirit of our God." - 1 Corinthians 6:11

"Ye adulterers and adulteresses, know ye not that the friendship of the world is enmity with God? whosoever therefore will be a friend of the world is the enemy of God." - James 4:4

Sanctuary

Satan

A <u>sanctuary</u> is a place set aside to worship God. This would include Christian churches, but it especially applies to the Jewish Temple at Jerusalem. The last Temple there was destroyed by the Roman Army in 70 AD. Jesus prophesied the destruction of the Temple. According to Scripture, it must be rebuilt because it will be defiled by the anti-Christ (empowered by Satan) in the great tribulation three and one-half years before the Battle of Armageddon. This event is called the "abomination of desolation." Satan is always trying to enter or influence the worship in the <u>sanctuary</u>. Satan desires to "be like the most High" and receive worship.

"I (Satan) will ascend above the heights of the clouds; I will be like the most High." - Isaiah 14:14

"But when ye shall see the abomination of desolation, spoken of by Daniel the prophet, standing where it ought not, (let him that readeth understand,) then let them that be in Judaea flee to the mountains:" - Mark 13:14

Scripture

Ure (Ph. - Your) – Script – Cite – Picture - Pure

The Holy Bible is God's written word and it is your script. The script has some things that are the same for everyone and it has others that are just for you. It is about God's will and plan for you. Just as ignorance of the law is not a legal excuse, neither are you excused if you do not know your script. You are responsible to search the <u>Scriptures</u> and respond as it gives guidance to your life. Biblical <u>scripture</u> is a vital part of a growing and maturing Christian life.

God's word was written by the Holy Spirit through forty men over a period of about 1,500 years. It is a priceless and timeless book that is absolutely astonishing. The Bible accurately reveals the true God.

Ravi Zacharias states in *The Case For faith*, "If the resurrection of Jesus is true then all other faith systems cannot be true." Ravi suggests another approach, "That of looking at the four fundamental questions every religion seeks to answer: <u>Origin</u>, <u>meaning</u>, <u>morality</u>, and <u>destiny</u>." I agree with Ravi, "That only the answers of Jesus correspond to reality." The Bible gives consistent, logical explanations, and also includes hundreds of accurate prophecies. Hundreds of Biblical prophecies about the future have proven to be accurate because God knows the future.

<u>Scripture</u> is the best source of revelation about a complex and mysterious God. Fortunately, God has removed much of the mystery about Him for those that read <u>Scripture</u> in prayer for

understanding. <u>Scripture</u> paints a marvelous picture for us of God's attributes and character. Through the written word God reveals Himself in the Son. We should use the Bible to become more godly and Christ-like, so that the Bible becomes a picture of our lives as well.

The Bible is truth, and once you find real truth you would not give it up because it is a precious treasure. Believers should be prepared to cite the Bible as their authoritative source for truth and absolute values. If the Bible says it, then that settles it. Our responsibility is not to interpret <u>Scripture</u>, but rather to understand it and find the script that God has for us within the contents of verses in the Bible.

"And beginning at Moses and all the prophets, he expounded unto them in all the <u>scriptures</u> the things concerning himself." - Luke 24:27

"Jesus saith unto him, Have I been so long time with you, and yet hast thou not known me, Philip? he that hath <u>seen</u> <u>me</u> hath seen the Father; and how sayest thou *then*, Shew us the Father?" - John 14:9

"He that rejecteth me, and receiveth not my words, hath one that judgeth him: the word that I have spoken, the same shall judge him in the last day." John 12:48

Secular

Curse – Use - Lure

<u>Secular</u> means those things that are not spiritual or sacred. Whether or not a person is spiritual or secular makes a big difference in his/her view of reality. Do you have a Christian world view, or a <u>secular</u> world view? Many believers see <u>secular</u>ists as having an incorrect view of reality and walking in darkness. Those lacking true spirituality are at a disadvantage because things like the origin of life, the meaning of life, their

purpose, and destiny are viewed incorrectly. They would not even realize that because of sin the whole world is under a curse, and that everyone has a fallen nature. Yes, a person's view of the world affects their life, and the lives of others in many ways. An example would be research that shows Christians give more to all types of charity than non-Christians.

Some organizations exist to advance God's purposes and kingdom, and unfortunately others exist for exclusively contrary <u>secular</u> goals. Many secularists are known as <u>secular</u> humanists. This means they think that man is the measure of all things. They start from the assumption there is no real god, so they have their own gods. The Pharaoh of Egypt resisted God and the last of the plagues killed the entire first born population, including his son. Pharaoh was linked to the sun god.

If your god is the sun, the moon or any god other than the God of the Bible you might not be <u>secular</u>, but still have a serious spiritual problem. Like Pharaoh, all <u>secular</u> persons eventually lose their fight against the Almighty.

Worldly, <u>secular</u> things may not necessarily be bad in and of themselves. Yet, they can lure us away from godly thoughts and behavior. The world has many temptations, and is always trying to encroach on or replace the spiritual realm. Worldly attractions have no use to us spiritually, and can even end up being a curse. If you love this world too much you will be more <u>secular</u> than spiritual, and the spiritual is superior to the physical.

God is a spirit and should be worshipped in spirit and in truth. Christians are in the world, but not of the world. We are merely pilgrims that are passing through because our citizenship is actually in heaven in the presence of God.

"He that giveth unto the poor shall not lack: but he that hideth his eyes shall have many a curse." - Proverbs 28:27

"Then the magicians said unto <u>Pharaoh</u>, This *is* the finger of God: and Pharaoh's heart was hardened, and he hearkened not unto them; as the LORD had said." - Exodus 8:19

"But I say unto you, Love your enemies, bless them that curse you, do good to them that hate you, and pray for them which despitefully use you, and persecute you;" - Matthew 5:44

"Ye are of *your* father the devil, and the lusts of your father ye will do. He was a <u>murderer</u> from the beginning, and abode not in the truth, because there is no truth in him. When he speaketh a lie, he speaketh of his own: for he is a liar, and the father of it."-John 8:44

"And lead us not into temptation, but deliver us from evil: For thine is the kingdom, and the power, and the glory, for ever. Amen." - Matthew 6:13

"In whom the god of this world hath blinded the minds of them which believe not, lest the light of the glorious gospel of Christ, who is the image of God, should shine unto them." - 2 Cor. 4:4

"Charge them that are rich in this world, that they be not highminded, nor trust in uncertain riches, but in the living God, who giveth us richly all things to enjoy;" - 1 Timothy 6:17

"Teaching us that, denying ungodliness and worldly lusts, we should live soberly, righteously, and godly, in this present world;" - Titus 2:12

"God *is* a Spirit: and they that <u>worship</u> him must worship *him* in spirit and in truth." - John 4:24

"Love not the <u>world</u>, neither the things *that are* in the world. If any man love the world, the love of the Father is not in him." - 1 John 2:15

Serpent

Repent – See - Step - Tree

In the Garden of Eden, Satan used the serpent to deceive Eve into eating the fruit of the Tree of Knowledge of Good and Evil. Satan told her "your eyes shall be opened and ye shall be as gods, knowing good and evil." After she and Adam ate the fruit, they could see that they were naked, and they were ashamed. Public nakedness is a sin because sin is passed on through the genitals through reproduction. Since the serpent did this, God cursed the serpent, saying he would crawl on his belly and eat dust.

The seed of Eve would step on and bruise his head, and he would bruise his heel (Genesis 3:15). This verse in Genesis was prophesying the outcome of battle between God and Satan. The bruise to Satan's head, and bruise the seed of woman's heel was carried out on a tree in Jerusalem that was used to make a cross.

He also cursed the woman with labor pains, and her husband would continue his role to rule over her. Eve was deceived and disobedient, and Adam willfully sinned. Man's role to be the head of the family would continue and a desire or urge against this would reside with women. Relationship distortions would continue to occur and sadly, as we see, in some cases the man's rule would result in tyranny. (Genesis 3:16) Man has the responsibility to be the spiritual head of his family and to love his wife sacrificially. Many men do not fulfill those responsibilities.

God cursed the man with ground that would be hard to cultivate and would bring forth thorns. The sin carried a death sentence. Spiritual separation from God and physical death – they would return to dust. Because they were tempted in the garden by the <u>Serpent</u>, we now have sin, and we must strive to repent from choosing evil and get back in good standing with God. If anyone does not think that mankind generally needs to change their mind about evil, just look at world events today.

"Christ hath redeemed us from the curse of the law, being made a curse for us: for it is written, Cursed *is* every one that hangeth on a tree:" - Galatians 3:13

"How that they told you there should be mockers in the last time, who should walk after their own ungodly lusts." Jude 1:18

"Neither repented they of their murders, nor of their sorceries, nor of their fornication, nor of their thefts." Revelation 9:21

Sinai

As – I – Sin

God spoke on Mount Sinai and gave the law, the famous Ten Commandments to the people of Israel. The law presented an ideal and a standard that no person ever kept, except Jesus Christ, and He fulfilled the law. The law is a schoolmaster to show that you cannot be saved by keeping it or by your own works. The law is a curse and has never provided salvation. Fortunately, Christians are under the law of Christ and the Ten Commandments have been summarized as two. "And he (Jesus) answering said, Thou shalt love the Lord thy God with all thy heart, and with all thy soul, and with all thy strength, and with all thy mind; and thy neighbour as thyself." Luke 10:27

"And be ready against the third day: for the third day the LORD will come down in the sight of all the people upon Mount Sinai." Exodus 19:11

"For neither they themselves who are circumcised keep the law; but desire to have you circumcised, that they may glory in your flesh." Galatians 6:13

"And Moses said unto the people, Fear not: for God is come to prove you, and that his fear may be before your faces, that ye sin not." Exodus 20:20

Sinner

Risen

The Greek philosophers thought that the body was bad; and at death the spirit, which was good, was freed from the body. They believed that after death you would remain as a spirit thereafter. Spirits lacking a body are very weak. The Hindu religion teaches that you are reincarnated after you die, and the womb, sweet or sour, that you enter is based on your deeds in this life. This very judgmental pagan works-based belief system allows for extreme social injustice. There are 260 million Dalits, or untouchables, in India that live in abject poverty. How convenient this belief system is for those in the higher classes.

Well, what is the truth about existence after death? Jesus Christ had a physical resurrection three days (72 hours) after His death and burial. Believers will also receive a new physical resurrection body. This body will be incorruptible and will be glorified. Our lives in our current body are temporary because of sin. God will not allow immortality in a sinful body. As Christians and sinners, our hope is in the risen Savior—Jesus Christ.

"And as they came down from the mountain, he charged them that they should tell no man what things they had seen, till the Son of man were risen from the dead." - Mark 9:9

Song

Son

The Bible says a lot about <u>song</u>. <u>Song</u> and the new <u>song</u> is about the Son, the Lord Jesus Christ. There is nothing more important to sing about here or in heaven than the Son. The Son got the victory when on Calvary He said, "It is finished." The 144,000 that sing in heaven before the very throne of God are all Jewish. They are twelve thousand from each of the twelve tribes of Israel. If you thought God was finished with Israel or that the church replaced Israel you had better read the Bible again.

"And he hath put a new <u>song</u> in my mouth, *even* praise unto our God: many shall see *it*, and fear, and shall trust in the LORD." - Psalm 40:3

"O sing unto the LORD a new <u>song</u>; for he hath done marvelous things: his right hand, and his holy arm, hath gotten him the victory." - Psalm 98:1

"And they sung a new <u>song</u>, saying, Thou art worthy to take the book, and to open the seals thereof: for thou wast slain, and hast redeemed us to God by thy blood out of every kindred, and tongue, and people, and nation;" - Revelation 5:9

"And they sung as it were a new <u>song</u> before the throne, and before the four beasts, and the elders: and no man could learn that <u>song</u> but the hundred *and* forty *and* four thousand, which were redeemed from the earth." - Revelation 14:3

"And I heard the number of them which were sealed: *and there were* sealed an hundred *and* forty *and* four thousand of all the tribes of the children of Israel. Of the tribe of Juda *were* sealed twelve thousand. Of the tribe of Reuben *were* sealed twelve thousand. Of the tribe of Gad *were* sealed twelve thousand. Of the tribe of Aser *were* sealed twelve thousand. Of the tribe of Napthali *were* sealed twelve thousand. Of the tribe of Manasseh *were* sealed twelve thousand. Of the tribe of Simeon *were* sealed twelve thousand. Of the tribe of Levi *were* sealed twelve thousand. Of the tribe of Issachar *were* sealed twelve thousand. Of the tribe of Zebulun *were* sealed twelve thousand. Of the tribe of Joseph *were* sealed twelve thousand. Of the tribe of Benjamin *were* sealed twelve thousand." - Revelation 7:4-8

Sound

Son – Sun

Where could this enormous universe have come from? Modern science supports that it did not always exist but rather had a beginning. Could God speak everything into existence? The claim made by God in His Bible is, that everything was spoken into existence by Almighty God. Where there is speaking there is <u>sound</u>. Scripture is clear that God alone is responsible for all that exists. This means that the Son spoke the universe into existence. There is more information about this topic in Chapter two of Section One.

"In the beginning God created the heaven and the earth." – Gen.1:1

"All things were made by him (Son); and without him was not any thing made that was made." - John 1:3

"For by him were all things created, that are in heaven, and that are in earth, visible and invisible, whether *they be* thrones, or dominions, or principalities, or powers: all things were created by him, and for him: And he is before all things, and by him all things consist." - Colossians 1:16-17

"For this they willingly are ignorant of, that by the word of God the heavens were of old, and the earth standing out of the water and in the water:" - 2 Peter 3:5

"In a moment, in the twinkling of an eye, at the last trump: for the trumpet shall <u>sound</u>, and the dead shall be raised incorruptible, and we shall be changed." - 1 Corinthians 15:52

Spirit

Tips – Stir

Jesus Christ not only gives us the gift of salvation, but also the gift of the Holy <u>Spirit</u> that He called the Comforter. Both Jesus and the Holy <u>Spirit</u> are gifts from the Father, and they are one with Him. At the time of salvation believers are sealed with the Holy <u>Spirit,</u> and He remains with them forever. The Holy <u>Spirit</u> inside of us makes our body a temple, and gives us 24/7 access to God the Father. The presence of the Comforter also gives God a means in which to communicate with us, to teach us, and to guide us. Learn to listen to the Holy <u>Spirit</u> because He is the mind of God and conveys His purposes.. The <u>Spirit</u> not only guides us in our walk, and conveys God's thoughts to us, but He gives us tips for the Christian life. He teaches us how to walk, how to talk, and how to be like Christ.

When God wants us to listen He will stir the <u>Spirit</u> up, so we will take notice. This can be accomplished through reading Scripture and coming across a verse that applies to a situation we are facing at the time, through prayer and God's answer to that prayer, or through a sudden thought that makes us stop and listen closely for direction. Personal experiences in our walk with God improve our ability to discern that God is speaking to us. I personally have found that a whisper is serious and important. Sometimes a dream will have a spiritual message, but it could be missed if you do not ponder the dream seeking the message. The importance of the Holy <u>Spirit</u> is often underrated, but it's important to know that He is vital to our growing relationship with God.

"The <u>Spirit</u> of the Lord *is* upon me, because he hath anointed me to preach the gospel to the poor; he hath sent me to heal the brokenhearted, to preach deliverance to the captives, and recovering of sight to the blind, to set at liberty them that are bruised," - Luke 4:18

"If ye then, being evil, know how to give good gifts unto your children: how much more shall *your* heavenly Father give the Holy <u>Spirit</u> to them that ask him? - Luke 11:13

"But when they shall lead *you*, and deliver you up, take no thought beforehand what ye shall speak, neither do ye premeditate: but whatsoever shall be given you in that hour, that speak ye: for it is not ye that speak, but the Holy Ghost." - Mark 13:11

"Jesus answered, Verily, verily, I say unto thee, Except a man be born of water and *of* the <u>Spirit</u>, he cannot enter into the kingdom of God. That which is born of the flesh is flesh; and that which is born of the <u>Spirit</u> is <u>spirit</u>." - John 3:5-6

"And I will pray the Father, and he shall give you another Comforter, that he may abide with you for ever;" - John 14:16

"But when the Comforter is come, whom I will send unto you from the Father, *even* the <u>Spirit</u> of truth, which proceedeth from the Father, he shall testify of me:" - John 15:26

"And it shall come to pass in the last days, saith God, I will pour out of my <u>Spirit</u> upon all flesh: and your sons and your daughters shall prophesy, and your young men shall see visions, and your old men shall dream dreams:" - Acts 2:17

"God *is* a <u>Spirit</u>: and they that worship him must worship *him* in spirit and in truth." - John 4:24

"Wherefore I put thee in remembrance that thou stir up the gift of God, which is in thee by the putting on of my hands. For God hath not given us the <u>spirit</u> of fear; but of power, and of love, and of a sound mind." - 2 Timothy 1:6-7

Stars

Art

Stars are small points of light in the night heaven. The stars have provided much inspiration for poets, painters and other artists. The Republic of Israel is represented by the Star of David, which literally is the Shield of David. The American flag contains one <u>star</u> for every state, which makes a total of fifty.

How many stars are there? On a clear night around 1,000 to 1,500 stars are visible to the naked eye. The Bible was criticized for many years for stating that the stars were for number like the sand on the sea shore (not countable). On April 19, 2008 I learned that science has now counted seventy sextillion stars. (Note: million, billion, trillion, quadrillion, quintillion, *sextillion*, septillion, etc. - 1,000 quintillion = 1 *sextillion*). Science is getting a lot closer, but its scientists still have not counted all of the <u>stars</u>. God not only knows the exact number of the <u>stars</u>, but he also knows the name of every <u>star</u>.

"He telleth the number of the <u>stars</u>; he calleth them all by *their* names." Psalm 147:4

"And he brought him forth abroad, and said, Look now toward heaven, and tell the <u>stars</u>, if thou be able to number them: and he said unto him, So shall thy seed be." Genesis 15:5

"That in blessing I will bless thee, and in multiplying I will multiply thy seed as the <u>stars</u> of the heaven, and as the sand which *is* upon the sea shore; and thy seed shall possess the gate of his enemies;" Genesis 22:17

"And ye shall be left few in number, whereas ye were as the <u>stars</u> of heaven for multitude; because thou wouldest not obey the voice of the LORD thy God." Deuteronomy 28:62

"And there shall be signs in the sun, and in the moon, and in the stars; and upon the earth distress of nations, with perplexity; the sea and the waves roaring;" Luke 21:25

"And the fourth angel sounded, and the third part of the sun was smitten, and the third part of the moon, and the third part of the stars; so as the third part of them was darkened, and the day shone not for a third part of it, and the night likewise." Revelation 8:12

Study

Duty - Us

The most important duty for us regarding learning is to study the Word of God. Early public education in America included verses from the Bible as an integral part of classroom teaching. Even the alphabet was learned by tying each letter to a Bible verse. "In Adam's fall, we sinned all." If a person with a Doctor of Philosophy degree did not study the Bible, I believe by God's standard, they would be considered a learning failure.

The freedom of religion amendment in the Bill of Rights of the U.S. Constitution was a restriction on Congress preventing the government from interfering with religion. Now we are told that it restricts us by separating church and state. Since the founding Fathers clearly intended only to restrict government, a blatant lie is being told to the American people.

"Having the understanding darkened, being alienated from the life of God through the ignorance that is in them, because of the blindness of their heart:" - Ephesians 4:18

"Study to shew thyself approved unto God, a workman that needeth not to be ashamed, rightly dividing the word of truth." – 2 Timothy 2:15

Suffering

Fire – Urn – Rise – Us – Use - Sin – Refine -

After the fall of mankind in the Garden of Eden many changes occurred that cause <u>suffering</u>. There are diseases (sad in the word), disasters, wars, accidents, famines, aging, death, and many difficulties and challenges. I am persuaded that in this life everyone has to deal with adversity to some degree or another. We are not in a perfect world – that is reserved for the next life in heaven. A huge amount of <u>suffering</u> has its origin in sin and man's inhumanity to man. <u>Suffering</u> provides opportunities for character building, and can help us grow stronger by overcoming unfavorable situations. Sometimes <u>suffering</u> brings repentance and turning to God. A contrite heart and a broken spirit could be just what you need. Better to suffer a little while here than be in the eternal fire. The Father's purging is to produce more fruit and make our joy full. John 15:2-11

God allows <u>suffering</u> to happen. The book of Job is the "instruction manual" for dealing with <u>suffering</u>. Satan stated that the only reason Job feared and respected God was because of all the blessings that he enjoyed. Satan stated that Job would curse God if he lost his processions and blessings. God allowed Satan to bring severe <u>suffering</u> unto Job. Satan destroyed everything that was dear to Job, including physical sufferings, bringing him close to death. However, Job never turned from God, and later God blessed Job with even more than he had before. God's victory over Satan through Job was very important because that is an accusation that Satan can no longer use against any of us.

I recently saw a book in an airport book store that said that the Bible cannot explain <u>suffering</u>. I disagree, but I will say that unspiritual people do not have the ability to properly understand suffering. Moses chose to suffer affliction with the people of God rather than the pleasure of sin for a season. That is your Bible answer. The man who wrote the first five books of the Bible chose <u>suffering</u> with God over the Palace of Egypt. There are two ff's in the words difference and suffering. God is the difference because without God suffering could not be explained. Without God suffering would not make any sense. The scripture even tells believers to suffer for his sake.

So how does this apply in our lives today? How do we deal with suffering? It's simple. We maintain strong faith in God, realizing that he is the Supreme power in the universe, and God will not bring us more suffering than we can endure. Suffering is an opportunity for us to build character. If we have faith during times of suffering, God will use it to shape and mold us into what He wants us to be in order for Him to use us for Kingdom purposes. He is the Potter, and we are the clay. He may want to shape you into a beautiful urn, so as you grow in your spiritual walk, He will mold you into the perfect piece of pottery for his purposes. Satan may bring the fire of suffering, but God will use that for His good. Like a kiln which a potter uses to harden the clay, making the urn tougher than it was when it was only soft clay. Furthermore, when a potter wants to make a piece of pottery more beautiful, he will add a coat of glaze and fire it again. Trusting God throughout our hard times will make us even more beautiful each time. God will refine you like silver and gold. God will use this process to build godly character.

Jesus' suffering is a prime example by which to handle hard times that Satan may bring upon us. He was tortured and beaten and nailed to a cross on Calvary Hill in Jerusalem. Satan probably celebrated thinking that he had taken care of that problem. Though Satan thought he was victorious, what he didn't know that just three days later Jesus would rise and be victorious over death. As it turned out the crucifixion of Christ was the most important victory for God and us that will ever occur. Jesus trusted His Father, and once again the Sovereign God prevailed over the evil purposes of Satan. When we put our trust in God and our faith in Jesus, no amount of suffering can ultimately defeat us, even to the point of death, because we will rise to live eternally.

"If I must needs glory, I will glory of the things which concern mine infirmities." - 2 Corinthians 11:30

"Take, my brethren, the prophets, who have spoken in the name of the Lord, for an example of <u>suffering</u> affliction, and of patience." - James 5:10

"Even as Sodom and Gomorrah, and the cities about them in like manner, giving themselves over to fornication, and going after strange flesh, are set forth for an example, <u>suffering</u> the vengeance of eternal fire." - Jude 1:7

"And I will bring the third part through the fire, and will refine them as silver is refined, and will try them as gold is tried: they shall call on my name, and I will hear them: I will say, It *is* my people: and they shall say, The LORD *is* my God." – Zech. 13:9

T

Temptations

Eat – Sin - Potent – Pain – Test - Point– Son

<u>Temptations</u> are anything that allure or entice us into immorality or sin. Satan is called in Scripture "the Tempter," and no doubt this adversary is potent in his efforts to lead us into <u>temptations</u>. Satan, as a serpent, tempted Eve to eat the fruit God had forbidden; and Adam willfully followed Eve and ate as well. This was the original sin for mankind, and from that moment sin and pain entered the world to become a reality of life. Other sources of <u>temptations</u>, besides Satan, include attractions of this world and pride, greed, envy, flesh, lust, etc.

When I was a young teenage boy an older female second cousin invited me to go to the drive-in theater. This cousin had a reputation of being very "wild", and no doubt immorality would have been planned for the evening. My parents were usually lenient on my choices of activities, but this time my father was very adamant that I could not go. This shows us another side of temptation: God providing me a way out of temptation. The heavenly Father is also in the business of keeping us from temptations or evil. This protection may have happened in our lives many times without us even knowing it.

God is also in the business, not of tempting us, but of testing us. David passed a major test by not killing King Saul when he had the opportunity. He would not kill God's anointed. This test demonstrated something very important – God was more important to David than being King. I know that I had this same test many years ago. So I suspect that this type of test, God being first, might be a common one for God to use. Do you know of any spiritual tests that you might have passed or failed?

God sent His Son, who was also tempted by Satan, to set us free from the bondage of sin. And though sinless, He bore the pain of the cross for our sakes. The Holy Spirit, who dwells in the body of believers, will lead and point us away from temptation and sin. The reality is that even those who are born again still have a sin nature and are not sinless. Believers should agree with God that righteousness should be preferred over sin. Believers are subject to being chastened by God when they sin. Also, God established the church, which gives us other believers to keep us accountable and encouraged so that we are able to better resist temptations. Christians should make the effort to restore a fellow believer who has been tempted to sin, but a warning in Galatians says to be watchful in such cases, *"Lest thou also be tempted."*

"Now the serpent was more subtil than any beast of the field which the LORD God had made. And he said unto the woman, Yea, hath God said, Ye shall not eat of every tree of the garden?
And the woman said unto the serpent, We may eat of the fruit of

the trees of the garden: But of the fruit of the tree which *is* in the midst of the garden, God hath said, Ye shall not eat of it, neither shall ye touch it, lest ye die. And the serpent said unto the woman, Ye shall not surely die: For God doth know that in the day ye eat thereof, then your eyes shall be opened, and ye shall be as gods, knowing good and evil. And when the woman saw that the tree *was* good for food, and that it *was* pleasant to the eyes, and a tree to be desired to make *one* wise, she took of the fruit thereof, and did eat, and gave also unto her husband with her; and he did eat.

 And the eyes of them both were opened, and they knew that they *were* naked; and they sewed fig leaves together, and made themselves aprons. And they heard the voice of the LORD God walking in the garden in the cool of the day: and Adam and his wife hid themselves from the presence of the LORD God amongst the trees of the garden. And the LORD God called unto Adam, and said unto him, Where *art* thou? And he said, I heard thy voice in the garden, and I was afraid, because I *was* naked; and I hidmyself.

 And he said, Who told thee that thou *wast* naked? Hast thou eaten of the tree, whereof I commanded thee that thou shouldest not eat?

 And the man said, The woman whom thou gavest *to be* with me, she gave me of the tree, and I did eat. And the LORD God said unto the woman, What *is* this *that* thou hast done? And the woman said, The serpent beguiled me, and I did eat." - Genesis 3:1-13

"Then was Jesus led up of the Spirit into the wilderness to be tempted of the devil. And when He had fasted forty days and forty nights, He was afterward an hungred. And when the tempter came to Him, He said, If Thou be the Son of God, command that these stones be made bread. But He answered and said, It is written, Man shall not live by bread alone, but by every word that proceedeth out of the mouth of God. Then the devil taketh Him up into the holy city, and setteth Him on a pinnacle of the temple, And saith unto Him, If Thou be the Son of God, cast thyself down: for it is written, He shall give his angels charge concerning thee: and in their hands they shall bear thee up, lest at any time thou dash thy foot against a stone. Jesus said unto him, It is written again, Thou shalt not tempt the Lord thy God. Again, the devil taketh Him up into an exceeding high mountain, and sheweth Him all the kingdoms of the world, and the glory of them; And saith unto Him, All these things will I give Thee, if Thou wilt fall down and worship me. Then saith Jesus unto him, Get thee hence, Satan: for it is written, Thou shalt worship the Lord thy God, and him only shalt thou serve. Then the devil leaveth Him, and, behold, angels came and ministered unto Him." - Matthew 4:1-11

"Behold, this day thine eyes have seen how that the LORD had delivered thee to day into mine hand in the cave: and *some* bade *me* kill thee: but *mine eye* spared thee; and I said, I will not put forth mine hand against my lord; for he *is* the LORD'S anointed." - 1 Samuel 24:10

"And it shall come to pass, if ye shall hearken diligently unto my commandments which I command you this day, to love the LORD your God, and to serve him with all your heart and with all your soul," - Deuteronomy 11:13

"And lead us not into <u>temptation,</u> but deliver us from evil: For thine is the kingdom, and the power, and the glory, for ever. Amen." - Matthew 6:13

"For all that *is* in the world, the lust of the flesh, and the lust of the eyes, and the pride of life, is not of the Father, but is of the world." - 1 John 2:16

"Watch and pray, that ye enter not into <u>temptation</u>: the spirit indeed *is* willing, but the flesh *is* weak." - Matthew 26:41

"Brethren, if a man be overtaken in a fault, ye which are spiritual, restore such an one in the spirit of meekness; considering thyself, lest thou also be tempted." - Galations 6:1

"Blessed *is* the man that endureth <u>temptation</u>: for when he is tried, he shall receive the crown of life, which the Lord hath promised to them that love him." - James 1:12

Temperance

Act - Repent –Trap - Tame

Christianity is a faith that primarily teaches moderation rather than abstinence. Temperance is defined as moderation and self-restraint in actions, thoughts, and emotions. Examples of moderation could include eating, drinking, spending, amusement, etc. The supernatural Fruit of the Spirit gives one the potential to have self control; yet it's the Spirit Himself who points a heart and mind away from wrongful desires and emotions. This part of the Fruit of the Spirit is a book-end of sorts (the other being love) which holds the Fruit as a whole together. It's difficult to have love, joy, peace, longsuffering, kindness, goodness, faithfulness and gentleness without <u>temperance</u>. And likewise, it is impossible to have any of these without love. If <u>temperance</u> is completely accomplished by self, it would fail because self is flesh and flesh is weak.

Before salvation, and before the Spirit, we are left vulnerable to sin because <u>temperance</u> does not come naturally. Individuals without the Spirit are in a trap, unable to get out of the habits of excess: ill emotions, unclean thoughts, and a bad temper. The Holy Spirit will tame the heart and soul so that we are better able to control them. Even still, we are unable to control everything our flesh desires, and we must repent (examine our thoughts and actions and see beneficial changes) daily.

"But the fruit of the Spirit is love, joy, peace, longsuffering, gentleness, goodness, faith, Meekness, <u>temperance</u>: against such there is no law." - Galatians 5:22-23

Testament

Meant - Test - Man – Ten

In the Bible, <u>testament</u> is another word for covenant. Biblically, a covenant is a solemn promise by God to man, usually containing requirements for man to fulfill. The covenant requiring males to be circumcised on their eighth day is an example of this type of covenant. God is always faithful, but God knows that man is a covenant breaker. Fortunately, there are covenants that God will keep regardless of what man does or does not do. An example, God made a covenant with Noah that the rainbow would be a sign that the earth would never be destroyed by water again. More importantly, the covenant of salvation by grace through faith has no test that will reverse this covenant once it has been received by saving faith.

Many covenants are meant to test man. God tested Abraham with the sacrifice of his son Isaac. In which, Abraham was ready to faithfully follow through until the angel of the Lord stopped him. Abraham called the place Jehovahjireh and the angel of the Lord made a covenant with Abraham that in his seed all the nations of the earth would be blessed. Later, God allowed the nations that Joshua had not driven out of the Land to remain and to test Israel, to see whether they would keep God's commands and ways in the midst of turmoil.

In both Old and New <u>Testaments,</u> faith in God was the test, and salvation has always come by faith. "Abraham's faith was counted for righteousness." The Law of Moses, the Ten Commandments (or Torah), was a standard of righteousness that God gave to the Jewish people. Man is imperfect, has a sin nature, and no individual has ever met this standard, with the exception of Jesus. Man is not able to obtain salvation from good works or from the law. God's requirement to be justified by the law is 100% compliance. If you make 99.9% then you still have failed. The law is the schoolmaster showing that man is indeed a sinner in need of God's grace.

Jesus came as both God and man, God incarnate, and fulfilled the precepts and law of God. He demonstrated the proper balance between faith, law, and works. God wants His Word in our heart and His law written on our hearts. Through our faith we live in a relationship with God. And obedience should flow from a renewed heart and spirit which, is why it is written "The just shall live by faith." Galatians 3:11

"This *is* my covenant, which ye shall keep, between me and you and thy seed after thee; Every man child among you shall be circumcised." - Genesis 17:10

"And it came to pass after these things, that God did tempt Abraham, and said unto him, Abraham: and he said, Behold, here I am. And he said, Take now thy son, thine only son Isaac, whom thou lovest, and get thee into the land of Moriah; and offer him there for a burnt offering upon one of the mountains which I will tell thee of." - Genesis 22:1-2

And said, By myself have I sworn, saith the LORD, for because thou hast done this thing, and hast not withheld thy son, thine only *son*: That in blessing I will bless thee, and in multiplying I will multiply thy seed as the stars of the heaven, and as the sand which *is* upon the sea shore; and thy seed shall possess the gate of his enemies; And in thy seed shall all the nations of the earth be blessed; because thou hast obeyed my voice." - Genesis 22:16-18

"Then said the LORD unto Moses, Behold, I will rain bread from heaven for you; and the people shall go out and gather a certain rate every day, that I may prove them, whether they will walk in my law, or no." - Exodus 16:4

"The fining pot is for silver, and the furnace for gold: but the LORD trieth the hearts." - Proverbs 17:3

"That whosoever believeth in him should not perish, but have eternal life." - John 3:15

"But that no man is justified by the law in the sight of God, *it is* evident: for, The just shall live by <u>faith</u>." - Galatians 3:11

"For by grace are ye saved through faith; and that not of yourselves: *it is* the gift of God:" - Ephesians 2:8

Thankfulness

El (God) – Fault – Sent - Fast – Knelt

To be truly thankful you need a heart that is grateful. All of mankind should be grateful to the Creator God who gave life, but this is not always the case. God is love and those many souls who know and love the true God have a supreme reason to be grateful because their sins have been forgiven at a great cost. God sent His son to the Roman cross in Jerusalem.

Those born of God have many reasons to be thankful and should have knelt many times to express genuine gratitude to the God they love. An important expression to God of humility, thankfulness and perhaps a special need is a spiritual fast.

The judgment of God is terrible, but it is less than what is deserved and this is an important reason to express thankfulness.

"Enter into his gates with thanksgiving, *and* into his courts with praise: be thankful unto him, *and* bless his name." – Psalm 100:4

"And Jehoshaphat feared, and set himself to seek the LORD, and proclaimed a fast throughout all Judah." - 2 Chronicles 20:3

"Now when Daniel knew that the writing was signed, he went into his house; and his windows being open in his chamber toward Jerusalem, he kneeled upon his knees three times a day, and prayed, and gave thanks before his God, as he did aforetime." – Daniel 6:10

"And let the peace of God rule in your hearts, to the which also ye are called in one body; and be ye thankful. - Colossians 3:15

"Then said Pilate to the chief priests and *to* the people, I find no fault in this man." - Luke 23:4

"For men shall be lovers of their own selves, covetous, boasters, proud, blasphemers, disobedient to parents, unthankful, unholy" – 2 Timothy 3:2

Time

Mite – Tie – Me

Sixty seconds from now, a minute will have passed, and in sixty minutes, an hour will have done the same. What can you accomplish in an hour, or a day? How many years did you wait for something you prayed for before God answered that prayer? How much longer before Jesus returns to reign? We, as humans, wonder these things because we live in time and space. It drives our lives because we have schedules and deadlines. We have become trained to the tune of *"Westminster Quarters"* and to whatever number of bell chimes follows telling us it's time to do something important. We hurry and hurry because time is fleeting, and we can't get time back once it's gone. And it's been this way since man learned how to measure minutes, hours, and days.

But God works outside of the limits of <u>time</u> and space. A century is but a mite to Him, and eternity has no calendar. God created time for us even though He may not need to measure time. He knew in all his wisdom that, however much we tend to give too much value to it, we would need it. It's important for us to know seasons for crops and harvest, days of the week for worship, work, and rest, and days of the year for feasts and Biblical holy days; which are mostly ignored today by churches.

Though God exists outside of <u>time</u> and space, He works inside <u>time</u> for us to be able to understand Him. His creation process took six days, and He gave Himself a seventh for rest. Do you think the Sovereign God of the Universe needed six days to create all that exists? Or does a God who is all powerful need a day of rest? It's clearly not for Him that He did it this way. He did it to establish the week as a period of time for you and me. His wisdom provided for only six days of work at a time before a day of rest and spiritual renewal. He showed us what the seventh day is for Shabbat (שבת). Shabbat is rooted in the Hebrew word shavat, meaning to rest, cease, or stop working; and where we also get the word Sabbatical, which is a needed time off from work. Shabbat is a day that God created for us to rest, but how many Christians keep the day for what it was intended? Shabbat is the day to rest and to worship the Creator of the Universe.

God also chooses specific timing to do His works, to show us His sovereignty and wisdom, and to usually tie events together so that we see it as no coincidence. This is easy to see when studying the fulfillment of the Old Testament by Jesus' renewed covenant of the latter testament Scriptures. For example, the nativity story that we all know as "Christmas" did not happen on the 25th of December. This date has no value whatsoever to the story of the Messiah. He was born during the Biblical feast of Sukkot (סכות) also called "Feast of Tabernacles", "Feast of Nations", and "Season of Our Joy." While Christmas (Christ Mass) was set up by Constantine to be concurrent with the pagan observance of the winter solstice, this was not the true day of Christ's birth. The true timing God chose in bringing his Son into the world, during Sukkot, holds much more significance and ties in perfectly with Jewish tradition seen in the Old Testament, which was set up by God Himself. John 1:14 chooses the Greek word Skenoo, which means "Tabernacle", thus Jesus came to Tabernacle with us during the Feast of Tabernacles. In the Nativity account of Luke, we see in chapter 2 verse 10, *And the angel said unto them, Fear not: for, behold, I bring you good tidings of Great Joy which shall be to All.*" This ties in correctly with Sukkot being called "Season of our Joy" and "Feast of Nations." Galatians describes the nativity story as occurring in "fullness of <u>time</u>", which God knew to be the correct <u>time</u> even before the universe was brought into existence.

Spiritual awareness is required for one to see and understand the timing of God. An event in a believer's life that is a clear act of the Father, done in His perfect timing, may seem like but a coincidence to an unbeliever. But a believer, seeing with spiritual eyes, will realize that God was involved and that He is glorified. This writer has literally had more personal experiences of this type with our God than I could count.

"Six days thou shalt do thy work, and on the seventh day thou shalt rest: that thine ox and thine ass may rest, and the son of thy handmaid, and the stranger, may be refreshed." - Exodus 23:12

"Now I say, That the Heir, as long as He is a child, differeth nothing from a servant, though He be Lord of all; But is under tutors and governors until the time appointed of the Father. Even so we, when we were children, were in bondage under the elements of the world: But when the fulness of the Time was come, God sent forth His Son, made of a woman, made under the law, To redeem them that were under the law, that we might receive the adoption of sons. And because ye are sons, God hath sent forth the Spirit of his Son into your hearts, crying, Abba, Father. Wherefore thou art no more a servant, but a son; and if a son, then an heir of God through Christ." - Galatians 4:1-7

"To every thing there is a season, and a time to every purpose under the heaven" - Ecclesiastes 3:1

"When they therefore were come together, they asked of Him, saying, Lord, wilt thou at this time restore again the kingdom to Israel? And He said unto them, It is not for you to know the times or the seasons, which the Father hath put in his own power. But ye shall receive power, after that the Holy Ghost is come upon you: and ye shall be witnesses unto me both in Jerusalem, and in all Judaea, and in Samaria, and unto the uttermost part of the earth. Acts 1:6-8

And, Thou, Lord, in the beginning hast laid the foundation of the earth; and the heavens are the works of thine hands: They shall perish; but thou remainest; and they all shall wax old as doth a garment; And as a vesture shalt thou fold them up, and they shall be changed: but thou art the same, and thy years shall not fail." - Hebrews 1:10-12

"Blessed be the LORD, God of Israel, from everlasting to everlasting. Amen and Amen." - Psalm 41:13

Transgressions

Atone – Risen – Season – Sin – Sinners – Son

Transgressions are the violation of a law or command. From a theological standpoint, this means any command that God gives, which when broken down all fall under the Ten Commandments or laws of Moses (Torah). These ten are changed to two by Jesus, but these are inclusive in that the ten fall under the two commands that Jesus gave (Love God, and Love your Neighbor). The Bible proclaims that we are all sinners, and fall short of the standard that a Holy God requires to be righteous.

Yes, all of us are all born into sin and deserve nothing more than eternity apart from God for our transgressions, since God requires perfect righteousness. Self-righteousness gets us nowhere as far as heaven is concerned. Fortunately, He is a gracious and loving God that wants us to enter an eternal relationship with Him. He is aware that no man can live without breaking His commands. Therefore, He sent His Son to die for our sins. The blood of Jesus is the only sacrifice that can atone for our transgressions against Him. Just as He was raised from the grave after taking our sins upon Himself, those who are covered by His blood will also rise to live eternally with God on high. A sinner's righteousness is only possible when God the Father sees the righteousness of His Son that has been imputed to them.

Though sins are forgiven, and believers have a changed heart and the Holy Spirit to lead away from the inclination to sin; we still have a sin nature in our flesh. Sin will take you deeper than you wanted to go, last longer than you wanted, and have a cost greater than you wanted to pay.

"For all have sinned, and come short of the glory of God;" - Romans 3:23

"Remember not the sins of my youth, nor my <u>transgressions:</u> according to thy mercy remember thou me for thy goodness' sake, O LORD." - Psalm 25:7

"Wash me thoroughly from mine iniquity, and cleanse me from my sin. For I acknowledge my <u>Transgressions</u>: and my sin is ever before me. Against thee, thee only, have I sinned, and done this evil in thy sight: that thou mightest be justified when thou speakest, and be clear when thou judgest." - Psalm 51:2-4

"But He was wounded for our <u>Transgressions</u>, He was bruised for our iniquities: the chastisement of our peace was upon Him; and with His stripes we are healed." - Isaiah 53:5

"For when we were yet without strength, in due time Christ died for the ungodly. For scarcely for a righteous man will one die: yet peradventure for a good man some would even dare to die. But God commendeth his love toward us, in that, while we were yet sinners, Christ died for us. Much more then, being now justified by his blood, we shall be saved from wrath through him. For if, when we were enemies, we were reconciled to God by the death of his Son, much more, being reconciled, we shall be saved by his life. And not only so, but we also joy in God through our Lord Jesus Christ, by whom we have now received the atonement. Wherefore, as by one man sin entered into the world, and death by sin; and so death passed upon all men, for that all have sinned: (For until the law sin was in the world: but sin is not imputed when there is no law. Nevertheless death reigned from Adam to Moses, even over them that had not sinned after the similitude of Adam's transgression, who is the figure of him that was to come. But not as the offence, so also is the free gift. For if through the offence of one many be dead, much more the grace of God, and the gift by grace, which is by one man, Jesus Christ, hath abounded unto many. And not as it was by one that sinned, so is the gift: for the judgment was by one to condemnation, but the free gift is of many offences unto justification. For if by one man's offence death reigned by one; much more they which receive abundance of grace and of the gift of righteousness shall reign in life by one, Jesus Christ.) Therefore as by the offence of one judgment came upon all men to condemnation; even so by the righteousness of one the free gift came upon all men unto justification of life. For as by one man's disobedience many were made sinners, so by the obedience of one shall many be made righteous. Moreover the law entered, that the offence might abound. But where Sin abounded, grace did much more abound: That as sin hath reigned unto death, even so might grace reign through righteousness unto eternal life by Jesus Christ our Lord." - Romans 5:6-21

Truths

Trust – Hurts - Ruth

God wants you to trust in His _truth_ and experience His goodness. God's word is filled with His _truths_. But we live in a world full of people who try to discredit these _truths_ with ridiculous theories and ideas. There has been a seemingly annual attack recently on Christian beliefs by the over-hyping of Gnostic accounts, such as The Gospel of Judas and fictional works like _The Da Vinci Code_, as well as attempts by a movie producer to try and prove that Jesus and His family are in a tomb in the suburbs of Jerusalem. These fallacies contradict Scripture and mislead individuals away from the sound _truths_ that God revealed to us in His holy scriptures.

In order to defend ourselves from being caught up in the lies of the world, we must study Scripture and learn how the Bible works and fits together as a whole. Even our modern church is filled with subtle lies that have become part of our Christian 'tradition', such as Christmas and Easter (see "Time"). While some of these may seem like "white lies" and are essentially harmless, the <u>truth</u> is much more powerful and meaningful. Bible prophecy states there will be a Christian falling away or apostasy in the end times. Do not make the mistake of judging God by the behavior of professing Christians or the state of Christianity. The sacrifice of truth and sound doctrine to avoid controversy and to produce fast growing mega churches is a questionable modern trend. People might let you down, but the rock of our salvation is faithful, trustworthy, unchanging, caring, and a constant source of strength.

It is not essential for salvation for one to know that Passover was the correct time when Jesus was crucified, and that He died on a Wednesday and not on "Good" Friday. The important thing has always been that He died for our sins, and physically rose again to claim victory over death. This is the one great <u>truth</u> that causes millions of people to put their faith in Jesus. He is the <u>truth</u>, and we must trust in Him to receive eternal life.

There is something about <u>truth</u> that once you find it you never let it go. The best secular life does not compare to the priceless experience of <u>truth</u>. Ruth was a Gentile woman that put her trust in the God of Israel as her God. Boaz became her kinsman redeemer, and she was grafted into the lineage that produced Jesus Christ: the kinsman redeemer for the whole human race. Ruth found <u>truth</u>. God is always presenting new <u>truths</u> to His children.

There is an old saying, "The <u>Truth</u> hurts." But, actually true <u>truth</u> will set you free. God has complete freedom, as He chose to create the universe. Mankind was made in God's image, and likeness and freedom is one of those characteristics we should have in common with God. If you are in bondage to sin and are under the curse of death you are not really free. God has a great plan for you that involves the <u>truth</u> in His Word.

"He shall cover thee with His feathers, and under His wings shalt thou Trust: His <u>Truth</u> shall be thy shield and buckler." - Psalm 91:4

"Come unto me, all *ye* that labour and are heavy laden, and I will give you rest." - Matthew 11:28

"And ye shall know the <u>truth</u>, and the <u>truth</u> shall make you free." - John 8:32

"Jesus saith unto him, I am the way, the <u>truth</u>, and the life: no man cometh unto the Father, but by me." - John 14:6

"Pilate therefore said unto him, Art thou a king then? Jesus answered, Thou sayest that I am a king. To this end was I born, and for this cause came I into the world, that I should bear witness unto the <u>truth</u>. Every one that is of the <u>truth</u> heareth my voice." - John 18: 37

U

Understand

Stand - Under

God's ways are not man's ways, and God's thoughts are higher than man's thoughts. Compared to God and apart from God, all men lack the understanding of that which is really important. Man cannot reach up to God; God had to come down to man. To really <u>understand</u> yourself and life you have to stand under the God that created you.

"All this, said David, the LORD made me understand in writing by his hand upon me, even all the works of this pattern." - 1 Chr.28:19

"The LORD looked down from heaven upon the children of men, to see if there were any that did <u>understand</u>, *and* seek God." - Psalm 14:2

"Who can <u>understand</u> *his* errors? cleanse thou me from secret *faults*." - Psalm 19:12

"Many shall be purified, and made white, and tried; but the wicked shall do wickedly: and none of the wicked shall <u>understand</u>; but the wise shall <u>understand</u>." - Daniel 12:10

"And in them is fulfilled the prophecy of Esaias, which saith, By hearing ye shall hear, and shall not <u>understand</u>; and seeing ye shall see, and shall not perceive:" - Matthew 13:14

Universe

Uni (one/first) - Verse – Sun - Rise

I have one word for those that promote evolution, which is an *evil notion*, and that word is <u>universe</u>. The <u>universe</u> exists because of one verse, and it is the first verse in the Bible. This first Bible verse is a summary statement, and what follows are many specific details.

This verse answers one of two main questions, "From where did everything originate?" By plainly stating that matter did have a beginning evolution is not only false, but it is evil. Those that promote this feeble theory would be better served to seek God and eternal life.

Fortunately, there have been evolutionists that did see the light and have become strong defenders of the Genesis creation account. One such well-known scientist that comes to mind is the published author Dr. Henry Morris (10/6/1918 – 2/25/2006). His doctorate in paleontology provided an academic evolution background. He became a creation apologetics (defender) author. If you do not believe this author, please read a book or two written by the late Dr. Henry Morris.

Scientists state that our sun is a star and one of the trillions of stars in the <u>universe</u>. However, this theory of stars may not be correct because Scripture states that the sun and stars were made separately. Planet earth has the sun for the day because the Son of God is the spiritual light of the world. Just as we can count on the **sun** to always rise, so are we able to count on the risen Son of God for strength and salvation.

"In the beginning God (Elohim) created the heaven and the earth." - Genesis 1:1

"And this is the condemnation, that light is come into the world, and men loved darkness rather than light, because their deeds were evil." - John 3:19

"Then spake Jesus again unto them, saying, I am the light of the world: he that followeth me shall not walk in darkness, but shall have the light of life." - John 8:12

V

Veil

Evil – Lie – Live

<u>Veil</u>s are used to cover, conceal, protect, or separate. What is being covered can be evil, or can be good. In "Song of Solomon", for example, the writer tells his beloved how, "your

eyes behind your <u>veil</u> are like doves" and "your temples behind your <u>veil</u> are like the halves of pomegranates" thus focusing on the beauty that is hidden behind the <u>veil</u> and yet to be uncovered. "Song of Solomon" is a book that parallels the love relationship with the Messiah and his bride, the church.

The Holy of Holies, which was located in the Temple, was separated by a thick <u>veil</u>. The privilege of entering and being where God was present was only allowed once a year, and only by the High Priest. The priest had to follow procedures and take special care to be "clean" before entering, or he would be struck dead. At the end of Jesus' crucifixion, the <u>veil</u> in the temple was torn from top to bottom. This demonstrates that God is now accessible for all those who believe in salvation through Jesus.

Through Jesus' sacrifice, it is now possible to enter the presence of God and live not worrying about being struck down; because His blood has covered (Psalm 85:2) or taken away our sins and made us righteous in the sight of the Father. When Christ comes to dwell in our hearts following salvation, He gives us direct spiritual access to the throne of God the Father. Christ is the High Priest who is an intercessor between us and the Father.

There is a similar <u>veil</u> that covers the eyes of Israel, as well. 2 Corinthians speaks of a <u>veil</u> that represents a blindness covering the eyes and hearts of the Jewish people when the Old Covenant is read. And the Apostle Paul (Rabi Saul) refers back to Moses, who wore a <u>veil</u> over his face to keep the Israelites from seeing the glory of God shining from his face. According to the book of Romans, this <u>veil</u> has been used to cover the eyes of Israel for the sake of the Gentiles. However, God promises the <u>veil</u> will be lifted once the fullness of the Gentiles has come; and the people of Israel will know their Messiah.

A remnant has always been saved. But nationally, Israel, is still in unbelief and spiritual blindness. It is important to the whole world for Israel to recognize the Messiah and to be as "the servant of God", and then that nation will spiritually lead the world. Thankfully, I see signs that are encouraging that this is close to happening. Israel, the only covenant nation on earth, is of extreme importance to God. This little nation, by God's grace, has produced the Prophets, the Messiah, the Apostles, the entire Bible and the Church. Stay tuned, there is a lot more to come from Israel.

Just as the Bible uses <u>veils</u> to cover a beautiful thing, it can also be used to cover something evil. False prophets and false teachers can <u>veil</u> the truth with lies. Ezekiel writes of false prophets and prophetesses within the land who lie to the people of Israel. They say that the words they speak are from God. The Lord tells Ezekiel that their <u>veils</u> will be ripped from their faces, and that the people will be saved from their trickery.

"Seeing then that we have such hope, we use great plainness of speech: And not as Moses, which put a <u>veil</u> over his face, that the children of Israel could not stedfastly look to the end of that which is abolished: But their minds were blinded: for until this day remaineth the same <u>veil</u> untaken away in the reading of the old testament; which <u>veil</u> is done away in Christ. But even unto this day, when Moses is read, the <u>veil</u> is upon their heart. Nevertheless when it shall turn to the Lord, the <u>veil</u> shall be taken away." - 2 Corinthians 3:12-16

"For I would not, brethren, that ye should be ignorant of this mystery, lest ye should be wise in your own conceits; that blindness in part is happened to Israel, until the fullness of the Gentiles be come in. And so all Israel shall be saved: as it is written, THERE SHALL COME OUT OF ZION THE DELIVERER, AND SHALL TURN AWAY UNGODLINESS FROM JACOB: FOR THIS IS MY COVENANT UNTO THEM, WHEN I SHALL TAKE AWAY THEIR SINS." – Rom. 11:25-27

"To wit, the prophets of Israel which prophesy concerning Jerusalem, and which see visions of peace for her, and there is no peace, saith the Lord GOD. Likewise, thou son of man, set thy face against the daughters of thy people, which prophesy out of their own heart; and prophesy thou against them, And say, Thus saith the Lord GOD; Woe to the women that sew pillows to all armholes, and make kerchiefs (<u>veils</u>) upon the head of every stature to hunt souls! Will ye hunt the souls of my people, and will ye save the souls alive that come unto you? And will ye pollute me among my people for handfuls of barley and for pieces of bread, to slay the souls that should not die, and to save the souls alive that should not live, by your lying to my people that hear your lies? Wherefore thus saith the Lord God; Behold, I am against your pillows, wherewith ye there hunt the souls to make them fly, and I will tear them from your arms, and will let the souls go, even the souls that ye hunt to make them fly. Your kerchiefs (veils) also will I tear, and deliver my people out of your hand, and they shall be no more in your hand to be hunted; and ye shall know that I am the LORD. Because with lies ye have made the heart of the righteous sad, whom I have not made sad; and strengthened the hands of the wicked, that he should not return from his wicked way, by promising him life: Therefore ye shall see no more vanity, nor divine divinations: for I will deliver my people out of your hand: and ye shall know that I am the LORD." - Ezekiel 13:16-23

Verse

Serve

Jesus explained to His disciples that to be great meant to have a heart to serve others, and to esteem others as greater than ourselves. Jesus left the glory of heaven and came to earth, as the meek and lowly Lamb of God. Have you personally gotten to know this servant of God that thought it not wrong to be equal with God?

"Take my yoke upon you, and learn of me; for I am meek and lowly in heart: and ye shall find rest unto your souls." – Matt.11:29

"The next day John seeth Jesus coming unto him, and saith, Behold the Lamb of God, which taketh away the sin of the world." - John 1:29

"Let nothing *be done* through strife or vainglory; but in lowliness of mind let each esteem other better than themselves." - Philippians 2:3

"Who, being in the form of God, thought it not robbery to be equal with God:" - Philippians 2:6

Vessel

See – El (God) – Eve – Lees (dregs or sediment)

A vessel is made to hold or contain something and is always distinct from what it contains. An example would be a coffee cup that has been filled with coffee. The coffee and the cup are two different things. Eve was a human vessel that was deceived and enticed to eat from the Tree of Knowledge, which was forbidden by God.

Your body is a vessel that contains a spirit and you, your spirit, will either have a destiny of wrath or of honor. A vessel having honor pleasing to God must see/recognize the true God. Many vessels of clay (people) settle for the lees of life instead of the abundant life found with God. Any life without God is the dregs.

"Surely your turning of things upside down shall be esteemed as the potter's clay: for shall the work say of him that made it, He made me not? or shall the thing framed say of him that framed it, He had no understanding?" Isaiah 29:16

"Woe unto him that striveth with his Maker! *Let* the potsherd *strive* with the potsherds of the earth. Shall the clay say to him that fashioneth it, What makest thou? or thy work, He hath no hands?" Isaiah 45:9

"O house of Israel, cannot I do with you as this potter? saith the LORD. Behold, as the clay *is* in the potter's hand, so *are* ye in mine hand, O house of Israel." Jeremiah 18:6

"Moab hath been at ease from his youth, and he hath settled on his lees, and hath not been emptied from <u>vessel</u> to <u>vessel</u>, neither hath he gone into captivity: therefore his taste remained in him, and his scent is not changed." Jeremiah 48:11

"Thou shalt break them with a rod of iron; thou shalt dash them in pieces like a potter's vessel." Psalm 2:9

"Israel is swallowed up: now shall they be among the Gentiles as a <u>vessel</u> wherein *is* no pleasure." Hosea 8:8

"But the Lord said unto him, Go thy way: for he is a chosen <u>vessel</u> unto me, to bear my name before the Gentiles, and kings, and the children of Israel:" Acts 9:15

"But I fear, lest by any means, as the serpent beguiled Eve through his subtilty, so your minds should be corrupted from the simplicity that is in Christ." 2 Corinthians 11:3

"If a man therefore purge himself from these, he shall be a <u>vessel</u> unto honour, sanctified, and meet for the master's use, *and* prepared unto every good work." 2 Timothy 2:21

Victory

City – Cry

The greatest <u>victory</u> that ever took place or ever will take place happened in a city. It happens to be the city that God views as the center of the world. That city is Jerusalem. And the <u>victory</u> was over sin, death, and hell when Christ gave out the cry "It is finished." Faith in Him as the Saviour through His sacrifice on the cross is our <u>victory</u>.

"The words of the Preacher, the son of David, king in Jerusalem." - Ecclesiastes 1:1

"Then the moon shall be confounded, and the sun ashamed, when the LORD of hosts shall reign in mount Zion, and in Jerusalem, and before his ancients gloriously." - Isaiah 24:23
"When Jesus therefore had received the vinegar, he said, It is finished: and he bowed his head, and gave up the ghost." - John 19:30

"O death, where *is* thy sting? O grave, where *is* thy <u>victory</u>?" - 1 Corinthians 15:55

"For whatsoever is born of God overcometh the world: and this is the <u>victory</u> that overcometh the world, *even* our faith." - 1 John 5:4

"Him that overcometh will I make a pillar in the temple of my God, and he shall go no more out: and I will write upon him the name of my God, and the name of the city of my God, *which is* new Jerusalem, which cometh down out of heaven from my God: and *I will write upon him* my new name." - Revelation 3:12

Vile

Live

One of the biggest roadblocks for the spiritually lost are doubts that they can never truly be saved because of a sinful past. But it's clear from reading the Gospels of the New Testament writers that anyone can be saved from sin. We are all sinners, and fall short of the glory of God, says the Bible. Jesus made himself a sacrifice, so that His blood would atone for our sins forever. One could be a <u>vile</u> sinner, spending most of his life as a murderer, thief, adulterer, idolater, and enemy of God. He could suddenly find the grace of God that will let him live eternally, forgiven and clean. But there's more to it than just saying that you believe. One has to truly believe in his/her heart that Jesus died for his/her sins.

So how does a new believer really know they are saved? Because when they truly believe, their heart and actions change. They start to live what they believe. The first century believers had a desire for Bible study and gave generously. Also, the commandments of God are no longer a burden, and love (for God, others, and self) comes more naturally, thanks to the guidance of the Holy Spirit.

Paul is a perfect example of a <u>vile</u> sinner who was persecuting Christians, including murdering some of them. He found the grace of God through Jesus on the road to Damascus. He zealously persecuted believers, yet he became a chosen Apostle and one of the greatest writers of the New Testament. Though a former Pharisee (trained in the Torah or law), Paul became the one to take the gospel to the Gentiles. This Jewish man became a man of faith in Jesus, and is one whom Christians around the world learn from and admire. "The Vilest offender who truly believes, That moment, from Jesus, a pardon receives."

"Purge me with hyssop, and I shall be clean: wash me, and I shall be whiter than snow." – Psalm 51:7

"For the <u>vile</u> person will speak villany, and his heart will work iniquity, to practice hypocrisy, and to utter error against the LORD, to make empty the soul of the hungry, and he will cause the drink of the thirsty to fail." - Isaiah 32:6

"Who shall change our <u>vile</u> body, that it may be fashioned like unto his glorious body, according to the working whereby he is able even to subdue all things unto himself." - Philippians 3:21

Vision

I & I (phonetically - two eyes) – Son – Is – Sion (Zion) – On

Jesus healed a man that had been blind from birth. When the former blind man was questioned by religious leaders he said, "I was blind, now I see." Everyone that is born again is able to make that same statement. Spiritually we need to see the Son with our two eyes. See Jesus and say, "Yes!"

The Son's <u>vision</u> is on Zion; which is the Apple of God's eye. Israel and Jerusalem are central to God's ultimate plan for redemption and the establishment of His Kingdom on earth. All Christians should share this <u>vision</u> and support Israel, especially they should support Messianic (Jesus is the Messiah) Ministry.

"If ye had known me, ye should have known my Father also: and from henceforth ye know him, and have seen him." - John 14:7

"If I had not done among them the works which none other man did, they had not had sin: but now have they both seen and hated both me and my Father." - John 15:24

W

Weather

Water – Awe – Wet – Earth – War – Wrath - Heat

Two thirds of planet earth is covered by water, which includes oceans, seas, rivers and lakes. Even though there are still some deserts, the Earth has been blessed to be a very wet planet. Ever since I took ninth grade science, I have been in awe of water because it has some amazing characteristics. It is actually lighter than air, so why is it mostly in the form of a liquid (on Earth it is also in solid and vapor form)? It is a dipolar molecule, so the molecules are attracted to each other and bond together. If water (H_2O) did not have this quality, it would not be in liquid or solid form. Also, water has the very unusual characteristic of expanding when it freezes instead of contracting. If it did not do this then ice would go to the bottom of lakes and rivers, and they would eventually freeze solid. Without water having these two special characteristics it would mean that this wonderful planet Earth would not be able to support life. This was by design, not accident. We should all be in awe of God who designed and created this amazing planet.

Our physical bodies are two-thirds water. Water is important spiritually as well as physically, because of the rainbow, water baptism, and Jesus saying that He is the Living Water. The rainbow is a sign of a covenant God made with Noah that the world would not be destroyed by water again. Baptism by immersion is symbolic of being buried with Christ and risen as He was buried and raised from the dead. And "living water" is symbolic of receiving salvation and spiritual blessings from Jesus that will flow from you to others.

The Dead Sea has water flowing into it, but there is no way for water to flow out. It is in a desert area and the trench is probably the deepest on earth. At the northern end the water is 1,200 feet deep. The high temperatures there cause rapid evaporation that leaves minerals making the water seven times denser than ocean water. That is why it is highly concentrated with minerals and it is poisonous to drink. These Dead Sea minerals have economic value. Christians are not supposed to be stagnant like the Dead Sea, but rather have a spiritual flow like the river that brought the water to the Garden of Eden because Jesus is "Living water" that quinces spiritual thirst.

Weather can have a wide range of characteristics anywhere from calm and benign, to a tornado or hurricane. These changes in weather can have a huge impact including the outcome of a battle or war. The first battle of the American Revolutionary war was at Harlem Heights, New York. General Washington had his forces in the hills and there was no way to retreat. A tremendous storm of unusual strength and duration hit the area. The British general, not knowing the artillery capacity of the American colonists, made a decision during this storm to leave and go to Nova Scotia. The historian, James Flexner, said that had the storm not arrived and the battle continued the American Continental Army would have been easily defeated. I see evidence of the intervention of God on behalf of Washington and his army, throughout this eight year war that ended British rule in America.

God is able to use <u>weather</u> to bring wrath and judgment. Hurricane Katrina, that did such extensive damage to New Orleans and the Gulf coast area, was God's justifiable wrath against America. Several days before this "natural" disaster occurred, I told my wife that God would soon be bringing a disaster to America. I based this on the heavy influence by the United States on Israel to give up the Gaza Strip (gauze –wound, strip – take away). I knew that this would happen because Scripture gives a serious warning against anyone dividing the land of Israel. The Prime Minister's name was the clue – Sharon (share own). I sent a letter to the Prime Minister nine months before the pullout stating that I knew it would take place.

I had been very involved with the Gaza issue for about a year before Hurricane Katrina hit. I knew that this hurricane was not going to be typical because it was going to bring God's wrath and judgment. God was fully justified to demonstrate His displeasure with our country. Gaza was the main issue, but New Orleans had a very immoral parade scheduled for Monday. This city had a long reputation for crime and sin. Also, by hitting the Gulf Coast and affecting the price of oil, this disaster was felt throughout the entire country. It was a judgment on America and a message for Americans. It was a time for salvation through judgment, but most churches and individuals missed the message and opportunity.

On Saturday night, the hurricane was a category five and headed straight for New Orleans. I am sure that many people were praying. I did an intercessory prayer stating that God's wrath was justified, but I asked for mercy anyway. I knew a lot about this situation since I had been involved for a year, and felt that I was in a position to make an effective prayer. After praying, I sensed that God was going to do something, but I did not know what. This was especially puzzling since I knew that God's judgment was an appropriate response for the Gaza giveaway. When I got up on Sunday morning I turned on the television and the very first thing I heard was, "The meteorologists are scratching their heads because a puff of warm air changed Hurricane Katrina from a 5 to a 4, and caused it to hit below New Orleans." Well, I knew where that air had come from. This hurricane caused the greatest disaster in the history of America, and yet there was mercy because the death toll could have been tens of thousands higher. People's prayers were heard and answered. Make no mistake God can bring judgment through the <u>weather</u>.

What about all the fuss over global warming? Is <u>weather</u> controlled by God or can man have an influence? *USA Today* had an article by Susan Page stating that a poll taken in 46 countries and Palestinian territories identified environmental problems such as increasing global warming as the world's greatest threat. The only problem here is that the earth's temperature (heat) is directly related to Sun spot activity. When Sun spots increase, the temperature goes up, and when they decrease temperature goes down. The correct answer is that God, not man, controls the weather on planet earth. Planet has plan in the word and control of the weather was part of that plan!

"And a river went out of Eden to water the garden; and from thence it was parted, and became into four heads." - Genesis 2:10

"And said unto me, Behold, I will make thee fruitful, and multiply thee, and I will make of thee a multitude of people; and will give this land to thy seed after thee *for* an everlasting possession." - Genesis 48:4

"Be strong and of a good courage: for unto this people shalt thou divide for an inheritance the land, which I sware unto their fathers to give them." - Joshua 1:6

"Riches profit not in the day of wrath: but righteousness delivereth from death." - Proverbs 11:4

"Jesus answered and said unto her, If thou knewest the gift of God, and who it is that saith to thee, Give me to drink; thou wouldest have asked of him, and he would have given thee living water. - John 4:10

"He that believeth on me, as the scripture hath said, out of his belly shall flow rivers of living water." - John 7:38

"And he arose, and rebuked the wind, and said unto the sea, Peace, be still. And the wind ceased, and there was a great calm." - Mark 4:39

"For the wrath of God is revealed from heaven against all ungodliness and unrighteousness of men, who hold the truth in unrighteousness;" - Romans 1:18

"This is he that came by water and blood, *even* Jesus Christ; not by water only, but by water and blood. And it is the Spirit that beareth witness, because the Spirit is truth." - 1 John 5:6

"And he said unto me, It is done. I am Alpha and Omega, the beginning and the end. I will give unto him that is athirst of the fountain of the water of life freely." - Revelation 21:6

"And the Spirit and the bride say, Come. And let him that heareth say, Come. And let him that is athirst come. And whosoever will, let him take the water of life freely." - Revelation 22:17

Well

El (God) - We

 We are never really <u>well</u> without God.

"If thou doest <u>well</u>, shalt thou not be accepted? and if thou doest not <u>well</u>, sin lieth at the door. And unto thee *shall be* his desire, and thou shalt rule over him." - Genesis 4:7

"Let the elders that rule <u>well</u> be counted worthy of double honour, especially they who labour in the word and doctrine." - 1 Tim. 5:17

Wickedness

Sick – Die – Sin – Wide

Because man has a sin nature, <u>wickedness</u> is wide spread on the earth. Many choose the wide way that leads them to destruction. Many get sick and die because of the <u>wickedness</u> of man. Many like to say that man is basically good, but that both contradicts scripture and observed history.

"And GOD saw that the <u>wickedness</u> of man *was* great in the earth, and *that* every imagination of the thoughts of his heart *was* only evil continually." - Genesis 6:5

"The soul that sinneth, it shall die. The son shall not bear the iniquity of the father, neither shall the father bear the iniquity of the son: the righteousness of the righteous shall be upon him, and the <u>wickedness</u> of the wicked shall be upon him." - Ezekiel 18:20

"Again, when the wicked *man* turneth away from his <u>wickedness</u> that he hath committed, and doeth that which is lawful and right, he shall save his soul alive." - Ezekiel 18:27

"Enter ye in at the strait gate: for *wide is* the gate, and broad *is* the way, that leadeth to destruction, and many there be which go in thereat:" - Matthew 7:13

Wisdom

Sow - Dim - Sounds like *"We Is Dumb"*

Reading Scripture will allow the Spirit to sow seeds of wisdom within us, so that we may (1 Corinthians 2:4) bear fruit to further the Kingdom. However, if your wisdom comes from the things of the world, you'll be just another dim wit! Man's knowledge compared to God's is foolishness, so wisdom that is from man and not from Scripture is flawed. God is all knowing, and real wisdom is from God. Ken Alpren, a Messianic Congregation leader stated, "Wisdom is making right choices based on eternal values." Without God we is dumb!

"Folly *is* joy to *him that is* destitute of wisdom: but a man of understanding walketh uprightly." - Proverbs 15:21

"And when he was come into his own country, he taught them in their synagogue, insomuch that they were astonished, and said, Whence hath this *man* this wisdom, and *these* mighty works?" - Matthew 13:54

"For Christ sent me not to baptize, but to preach the gospel: not with wisdom of words, lest the cross of Christ should be made of none effect. For the preaching of the cross is to them that perish foolishness; but unto us which are saved it is the power of God. For it is written, 'I WILL DESTROY THE WISDOM OF THE WISE, AND WILL BRING TO NOTHING THE UNDERSTANDING OF THE PRUDENT.' Where is the wise? Where is the scribe? Where is the disputer of this world? hath not God made foolish the wisdom of this world? For after that in the wisdom of God, the world by wisdom knew not God, it pleased God by the foolishness of preaching to save them that believe."- 1 Corinthians 1:17-21

"And my speech and my preaching *was* not with enticing words of man's <u>wisdom</u>, but in demonstration of the Spirit and of power:" - 1 Corinthians 2:4

Withstand

Stand – With

Crisis and suffering are a part of life, and spiritual warfare is ever present in the world around us. No one, even Jesus Christ, was immune from it. But when we stand with God, we can <u>withstand</u> trials. There might still be pain and hurt. But there will also be a special joy and peace that only the Holy Spirit can provide, giving us a huge advantage in tough situations.

God is our armor of defense, and our sword of offense. He protects us from evil, and He fights it off as well. It would be unwise for a man to run into battle in just his boxers, waving a plastic sword. Without God, that is what people do. And without His word we have no defense, we have no sword, and we will never withstand the attacks of the offender.

"And said, O LORD God of our fathers, *art* not thou God in heaven? and rulest *not* thou over all the kingdoms of the heathen? and in thine hand *is there not* power and might, so that none is able to <u>withstand</u> thee?" - 2 Chronicles 20:6

" For we wrestle not against flesh and blood, but against principalities, against powers, against the rulers of the darkness of this world, against spiritual wickedness in high *places*.
 Wherefore take unto you the whole armour of God, that ye may be able to withstand in the evil day, and having done all, to stand.
 Stand therefore, having your loins girt about with truth, and having on the breastplate of righteousness; And your feet shod with the preparation of the gospel of peace; Above all, taking the shield of faith, wherewith ye shall be able to quench all the fiery darts of the wicked. And take the helmet of salvation, and the

sword of the Spirit, which is the word of God: Praying always
with all prayer and supplication in the Spirit, and watching
thereunto with all perseverance and supplication for all saints;" –
Ephesians 6:12-18

"And the peace of God, which passeth all understanding, shall
keep your hearts and minds through Christ Jesus." - Philippians 4:7

Witness

News – New – Sent - Win

As Christians, it is our duty to lead the lost to a new life in
Christ. We become a <u>witness</u> to others of the gospel or good news.
When a Christian plants a seed of faith in a lost person's soul, the
hope is for that seed to grow into a vine rooted in Christ, which
will someday bear the fruit that carries the very same seed by
which they were saved. The common term used by professing
Christians who lead others to Christ is to win souls to Jesus. Jesus'
disciples were the first witnesses. They were sent by Jesus to tell
the world of the good news of His death, burial, and resurrection.
Likewise, we as Christians are sent by God to share the good news
and to win souls for Jesus.

"And Pharaoh sent, and called for Moses and Aaron, and said unto
them, I have sinned this time: the LORD *is* righteous, and I and my
people *are* wicked." - Exodus 9:27

"And this gospel of the kingdom shall be preached in all the world
for a <u>witness</u> unto all nations; and then shall the end come." -
Matthew 24:14
"And these are they which are sown on good ground; such as hear
the word, and receive *it*, and bring forth fruit, some thirtyfold,
some sixty, and some an hundred." - Mark 4:20

"I am the true vine, and my Father is the husbandman. Every
229

branch in me that beareth not fruit, he purgeth it, that it may bring forth more fruit" - John 15:1-2

"And they said, Cornelius the centurion, a just man, and one that feareth God, and of good report among all the nation of the Jews, was warned from God by an holy angel to send for thee into his house, and to hear words of thee." - Acts 10:22

"And how shall they preach, except they be sent? as it is written, How beautiful are the feet of them that preach the gospel of peace, and bring glad tidings of good things!" - Romans 10:15

"And sent Timothy, our brother, and minister of God, and our fellow labourer in the gospel of Christ, to establish you, and to comfort you concerning your faith:" - 1 Thessalonians 3:2

"Remember that Jesus Christ of the seed of David was raised from the dead according to my gospel:" - 2 Timothy 2:8

Words

Dor (Ph. - Door) – Sword – Sow - Rod

Jesus, the second person of the Godhead, is called the <u>Word</u>. This tells me that <u>words</u> are probably rather significant to God. The Holy Bible is the inspired, inerrant <u>Word</u> of God; and Scripture says that God will preserve His Word to all generations.

Today, there are many translations or versions of the Bible, but I prefer the King James Version (KJV) for several reasons. Firstly, it definitely meets the requirement of being powerful and sharper than a two edged sword, which indicates an anointing on the writers. This translation and the writing of Shakespeare are the highest quality writing ever produced in the English language. Secondly, it has proven itself effective over a long period of time – several centuries. Thirdly, the KJV is in the public domain (no copywriter royalties or permission to use is needed,) and it is not influenced by Wall Street. Fourthly, it is translated primarily from the Textus Receptus manuscript. I am suspect of later discovered manuscripts, like Alexandrian, used for "modern" translations. And lastly, I have found the word choices by the KJV translation scholars to be reliable and best when tested by Gmail.

For those that think the KJV is too hard to read, please understand that it starts at the fifth grade reading level with Genesis, and ends at the eighth grade level with Revelation. Centuries have proven that people best understand the Bible in their common language; therefore I do not feel that knowledge of Latin, Greek or Hebrew is at all necessary for Biblical understanding. I realize that knowledge of these languages may benefit Christian scholars; but I am convinced that for most of us foreign language is not necessary and can even be confusing. When Governor Pilate put "KING OF THE JEWS" in three languages on the sign on the cross, it was so that everyone could read it in their own language. When someone tells you what the Greek means, they usually have made a choice based on their own bias. I have confidence in the KJV, to provide the understanding to convert the soul, and to provide the instruction that will bring a close personal relationship with God. Amen.

Jesus taught a parable about a sower who went out to sow his seed. The seed is the <u>Word</u> of God and all believers should sow this seed. When the <u>Word</u> of God lands on good ground (hearts) and is kept, it brings forth fruit for the Kingdom.

There will be a "second coming" of Jesus Christ, and it will be quite different from His coming as a Lamb to be sacrificed for our sins. He will establish His earthly Kingdom and rule the nations with a rod of iron from Jerusalem. Christians are supposed to "watch and pray" for His coming, and not be taken by surprise. Many will not be expecting it, or be prepared when the Lord returns.

When will this event occur? No man knows the day or hour; however Christians are supposed to see the signs that will be evidence that this could happen soon. It could not have happened until after Israel was a nation once again. That happened in May

1948, and was the fulfillment of a 2,500 year old prophecy. These signs of His coming are very evident today, so I believe that this could happen in the lifetime of most that are living today. Are you watching and praying? Are you expectant of His coming?

"So shall my <u>word</u> be that goeth forth out of my mouth: it shall not return unto me void, but it shall accomplish that which I please, and it shall prosper *in the thing* whereto I sent it." - Isaiah 55:11

"And I will make them one nation in the land upon the mountains of Israel; and one king shall be king to them all: and they shall be no more two nations, neither shall they be divided into two kingdoms any more at all:" - Ezekiel 37:22

"Verily, verily, I say unto you, He that entereth not by the door into the sheepfold, but climbeth up some other way, the same is a thief and a robber. But he that entereth in by the door is the shepherd of the sheep." - John 10:1-2

"I am the door: by me if any man enter in, he shall be saved, and shall go in and out, and find pasture." - John 10:9

"Now the parable is this: The seed is the <u>word</u> of God." - Luke 8:11

"Heaven and earth shall pass away: but my <u>words</u> shall not pass away." - Luke 21:33

"And a superscription also was written over him in letters of Greek, and Latin, and Hebrew, THIS IS THE KING OF THE JEWS." - Luke 23:38

"Behold, I stand at the door, and knock: if any man hear my voice, and open the door, I will come in to him, and will sup with him, and he with me." - Revelation 3:20

"And I will scatter you among the heathen, and will draw out a sword after you: and your land shall be desolate, and your cities waste." - Leviticus 26:33

"For the word of God *is* quick, and powerful, and sharper than any two edged sword, piercing even to the dividing asunder of soul and spirit, and of the joints and marrow, and *is* a discerner of the thoughts and intents of the heart." - Hebrews 4:12
"And he had in his right hand seven stars: and out of his mouth went a sharp two-edged sword: and his countenance *was* as the sun shineth in his strength." - Revelation 1:16

"Thou shalt break them with a rod of iron; thou shalt dash them in pieces like a potter's vessel." - Psalm 2:9

"Yea, though I walk through the valley of the shadow of death, I will fear no evil: for thou *art* with me; thy rod and thy staff they comfort me." - Psalm 23:4

"That then the LORD thy God will turn thy captivity, and have compassion upon thee, and will return and gather thee from all the nations, whither the LORD thy God hath scattered thee." - Deuteronomy 30:3

"Then shall the kingdom of heaven be likened unto ten virgins, which took their lamps, and went forth to meet the bridegroom. And five of them were wise, and five *were* foolish. They that *were* foolish took their lamps, and took no oil with them: But the wise took oil in their vessels with their lamps. While the bridegroom tarried, they all slumbered and slept. And at midnight there was a cry made, Behold, the bridegroom cometh; go ye out to meet him. Then all those virgins arose, and trimmed their lamps. And the foolish said unto the wise, Give us of your oil; for our lamps are gone out. But the wise answered, saying, *Not so*; lest there be not enough for us and you: but go ye rather to them that sell, and buy for yourselves. And while they went to buy, the bridegroom came;

and they that were ready went in with him to the marriage: and the door was shut. Afterward came also the other virgins, saying, Lord, Lord, open to us. But he answered and said, Verily I say unto you, I know you not. Watch therefore, for ye know neither the day nor the hour wherein the Son of man cometh." - Matthew 25:1-13

"Watch ye therefore, and pray always, that ye may be accounted worthy to escape all these things that shall come to pass, and to stand before the Son of man." - Luke 21:36

"And out of his mouth goeth a sharp sword, that with it he should smite the nations: and he shall rule them with a rod of iron: and he treadeth the winepress of the fierceness and wrath of Almighty God." - Revelation 19:15

World

Lord – Word

The reason we are allowed to live in this <u>world</u> is because it has the Lord in it and the Word. The Lord Jesus Christ came and lived a sinless life in an imperfect <u>world</u>. He faced the temptations that we face, and set the example for us to follow. We also have truth revealed in the Word of God. But is that enough? There's the blood of Jesus that takes away our sins. There's the Word of God, which is the foundation of faith, and it provides instruction in righteousness and a blessed hope.

In this <u>world</u> we face disappointments, disease, death, suffering, war, crime, lies, false religions, greed, corruption, temptations, injustice and evil. The Bible says that we are in the world, but not of the world. We are not supposed to love this <u>world</u> and are not to expect to be accepted by the <u>world</u>. Today, the majority of the media organizations would be an example.

This is the same <u>world</u> that rejected its Creator, Jesus Christ. The <u>world</u> is worldly and not friendly to the things of God. Born again believers are just pilgrims here because we are citizens of heaven. As authentic Christians, we are aware that we only live in this <u>world</u> temporarily and that our permanent address is with God in heaven.

All those that have the spiritual birth are sealed with the Holy Spirit at that time of regeneration. The Holy Spirit is key to being able to follow the Lord, and to love and understand the word; so that we can be on Earth and not be so <u>world</u>ly. He is the link between the two, enabling us to be more like the Lord and understanding the word. Living a spirit filled life in relationship with God is a far superior experience to an ordinary secular life. A spiritual life will help us get the best out of our time in this <u>world</u>.

The Bible states "For where your treasure is, there will your heart be also." (Matthew 6:21) We can not "take it with us" when we die, but we can "pay it forward." In heaven there are no sins on our record, but there is record of works that will determine a reward. Why would anyone place their focus on building up temporary wealth, when an eternal treasure is a promise? I think a reasonable accumulation of wealth in this <u>world</u> is prudent, but our love should be for God and not for money. We should want to have far greater asset value on the other side than on this side. Where is your heart and treasure?

One problem is that wealth tends to make wealthy people "self reliant." They might trust more in their own resources instead of on God. I truly would not trade places with a billionaire if they were not born again. God owns everything, and that is why you are not allowed to take anything with you at death. It stays here because it is not actually yours. Certainly there are individuals that have great wealth that are also spiritual and not worldly. They would understand that money and material processions are temporal and not eternal.

The most important commandments in the Bible are "Love the Lord God with all your heart, soul, mind, and strength" and "Love your neighbor as yourself." Unfortunately, most of the inhabitants of this <u>world</u> are not going to value or practice those ideal absolutes. Scripture reveals that conditions in the <u>world</u> will get worse and worse before the end comes, and the Lord returns.

The end times events and conditions are observable today. Many prophecies have been fulfilled since I was born in 1943.

This once great nation was founded on Christian beliefs, laws, and principles. America showed the world the economic benefits of freedom along a large middle class. America was a leader in spreading the Gospel around the globe. Today, America is slipping more and more away from God. Now this nation produces eighty percent of the <u>world's</u> pornography and has the distinction of spreading it around the globe. Pornography does not even have a "sin" tax like tobacco and alcohol. Are our leaders asleep? There have been fifty million "legal" abortions in America making this land polluted with innocent blood. The disregard for the sanctity of human life is the <u>world</u>, and a violation a God's will. In World War II, seventy-five percent of all the children in Britain were in Sunday School. Today, only four percent of the people in Britain go to church. Britain is the mother and America is the daughter. And we are not far behind in abandoning God and slipping further into worldly materialism and decadence.

"And shed innocent blood, *even* the blood of their sons and of their daughters, whom they sacrificed unto the idols of Canaan: and the land was polluted with blood." - Psalm 106:38

"Their feet run to evil, and they make haste to shed innocent blood: their thoughts *are* thoughts of iniquity; wasting and destruction *are* in their paths." - Isaiah 59:7

"And that which fell among thorns are they, which, when they have heard, go forth, and are choked with cares and riches and pleasures of *this* life, and bring no fruit to perfection." - Luke 8:14
"And he answering said, Thou shalt love the Lord thy God with all thy heart, and with all thy soul, and with all thy strength, and with all thy mind; and thy neighbour as thyself." - Luke 10:27

"I have given them thy <u>Word</u>; and the world hath hated them, because they are not of the world, even as I am not of the world. I pray not that thou shouldest take them out of the world, but that thou shouldest keep them from the evil." - John 17:14-15

"Ye adulterers and adulteresses, know ye not that the friendship of the world is enmity with God? whosoever therefore will be a friend of the world is the enemy of God." - James 4:4

Worshiping

Who - Is – Show – Sing – Worship (Ph: War ship)

Why should we worship God? Is it because He needs for us to worship him? An emphatic no! In fact, it's us who needs to worship Him. We benefit enormously from worship. It brings us close to God, and equips us for spiritual battle. That is why worship sounds like war ship. The word worship comes from the Anglo-Saxon word worthship, meaning worthy. "Let them praise the name of the LORD: for his name alone is excellent; his glory *is* above the earth and heaven." (Psalm 148:13)

Real worship requires knowledge of the true God. When you know the creator God you know that God alone is worthy of worship. No created being should ever be exalted to receive worship. Worship is the way of acknowledging who He is in all of His glory and power. He is the all powerful, all knowing, all present, and eternal God. Worship is us giving back love straight from our hearts, for the love, grace and mercy that He regularly shows to us. God is not impressed with vain repetitions. Love is the heart of worship, and true worship is from the heart, soul, and spirit of the worshipper.

So, if worship is directed toward God, why is it us who are on the needing end of it, and not God? It's because God doesn't need anything. He created the universe and because of the three persons of the Godhead, He has love and fellowship! But we do need Him, and everything we do in worship benefits us. Through worship we get to know God better and learn to hear His voice. Through worship, we acknowledge the fact that we do need Him, and in return, He provides. Through worship, we show that we are obedient to Him, which allows us to be used by Him. Through worship, we are saying "You are our protector and defender, and our sword and our armor. You are like a great war ship that defends us from the enemy!" It also shows that we fear (fear, awe, respect) the Lord, and we know that He is sovereign and greater than any other force or power.

Therefore, when we sing, pray, study God's word, and fellowship with others, we are obediently <u>worshiping</u> God. Even recognizing the beauty of a sunset or colors and patterns in the sky and attributing its splendor to God is a form of worship.

"Thou, *even* thou, *art* LORD alone; thou hast made heaven, the heaven of heavens, with all their host, the earth, and all *things* that *are* therein, the seas, and all that *is* therein, and thou preservest them all; and the host of heaven worshippeth thee." – Neh. 9:6

"The LORD is my strength and my shield; my heart trusted in him, and I am helped: therefore my heart greatly rejoiceth; and with my song will I praise him." - Psalm 28:7

"God is a Spirit: and they that worship him must worship him in spirit and in truth." - John 4:24

X

There are no X words in Scripture in English therefore; there is no hologram message from any word that starts with this twenty-fourth letter of the English alphabet.

Y

Yeshua

Shu (Ph. - Shoe) - Yes
Hebrew:
יֵשׁוּעַ – Yeshua
שׁוּעַ – Shua – A desperate cry for help
שַׁי – Shai – A gift

Jesus is the English name for Joshua, which was the Greek name for <u>Yeshua</u>. <u>Yeshua</u> was the actual name that Christ would have been known as in the land of Israel. Today, this is the name that is used for Christ in Messianic Congregations, and by a very small number of other Christians. Messianic congregations primarily consist of Jewish members that are believers in the Messiah or <u>Yeshua</u>. There are more Jews coming to faith in <u>Yeshua</u> now than at any other time.

The Book of Ruth was written about 3,000 years ago during the reign of David. Ruth was a Moabitess woman. She was a Gentile that was rescued from childlessness and poverty by Boaz, the Jewish kinsman-redeemer. This book of the Bible is an exciting account of romantic love between a Jew and a Gentile. Ruth epitomizes godly womanhood, beauty, devotion, gratitude, and spiritual sensitivity. Ruth's commitment to Naomi, her poverty stricken mother-in-law, and Naomi's God was rewarded. Ruth was blessed by the love of a wealthy husband, the joy of motherhood, and became a member of the Messianic lineage.

Therefore, her redemption was not just physical, but also spiritual. Boaz was a type of <u>Yesuha</u>, the kinsman-redeemer that would arrive a thousand years later and redeem man from sin. Boaz had to take off his shoe and give it to make his redemption official. As Ruth was so profoundly needy when she was redeemed by Boaz, so are all sinners profoundly in need of the Redeemer. Seek truth and say yes to the Redeemer.

The Hebrew word for Salvation is Yeshuah ישועה This is Yeshua's (Jesus) name with an extra letter at the end (ה). So in the word Salvation, we not only have the name of Messiah, but also Lamb – שה (Seh) but also the word for Work (Spiritual work) –עשה (Aseh). From a Jewish perspective, this is defined as a Positive Command. Jesus came to show us how to do good works (his whole public ministry was filled with these works). Also, on the word Shua – שוע which is a desperate cry for help, the Modern Hebrew dictionary defines it also as "to cry out to, to implore; *to need desperately.*" We all have a desperate need for Jesus or Yeshua for salvation.

"Then went Boaz up to the gate, and sat him down there: and, behold, the kinsman of whom Boaz spake came by; unto whom he said, Ho, such a one! turn aside, sit down here. And he turned aside, and sat down. And he took ten men of the elders of the city, and said, Sit ye down here. And they sat down. And he said unto the kinsman, Naomi, that is come again out of the country of Moab, selleth a parcel of land, which *was* our brother Elimelech's: And I thought to advertise thee, saying, Buy *it* before the inhabitants, and before the elders of my people. If thou wilt redeem *it*, redeem *it*: but if thou wilt not redeem *it, then* tell me, that I may know: for *there is* none to redeem *it* beside thee; and I *am* after thee. And he said, I will redeem *it.* Then said Boaz, What day thou buyest the field of the hand of Naomi, thou must buy *it* also of Ruth the Moabitess, the wife of the dead, to raise up the name of the dead upon his inheritance. And the kinsman said, I cannot redeem *it* for myself, lest I mar mine own inheritance: redeem thou my right to thyself; for I cannot redeem *it.* Now this *was the manner* in former time in Israel concerning redeeming and concerning changing, for to confirm all things; a man plucked off his shoe, and gave *it* to his neighbour: and this *was* a testimony in Israel. Therefore the kinsman said unto Boaz, Buy *it* for thee. So he drew off his shoe. And Boaz said unto the elders, and *unto* all the people, Ye *are* witnesses this day, that I have bought all that *was* Elimelech's, and all that *was* Chilion's and Mahlon's, of the hand of Naomi. Moreover Ruth the Moabitess, the wife of Mahlon, have I purchased to be my wife, to raise up the name of the dead upon his inheritance, that the name of the dead be not cut off from among his brethren, and from the gate of his place: ye *are* witnesses this day. And all the people that *were* in the gate, and the elders, said, *We are* witnesses. The LORD make the woman that is come into thine house like Rachel and like Leah, which two did build the house of Israel: and do thou worthily in Ephratah, and be famous in Bethlehem: And let thy house be like the house of Pharez, whom Tamar bare unto Judah, of the seed which the LORD shall give thee of this young woman. So Boaz took Ruth, and she was his wife: and when he went in unto her, the LORD gave her conception, and she bare a son. And the women said unto Naomi, Blessed *be* the LORD, which hath not left thee this day without a kinsman, that his name may be famous in Israel. And he shall be unto thee a restorer of *thy* life, and a nourisher of thine old age: for thy daughter in law, which loveth thee, which is better to thee than seven sons, hath born him. And Naomi took the child, and laid it in her bosom, and became nurse unto it. And the women her neighbours gave it a name, saying, There is a son born to Naomi; and they called his name Obed: he *is* the father of Jesse, the father of David" - Ruth 4:1-17.

"For I know *that* my redeemer liveth, and *that* he shall stand at the latter *day* upon the earth:" - Job 19:25

"Thus saith the LORD, thy redeemer, and he that formed thee from the womb, I *am* the LORD that maketh all *things*; that stretcheth forth the heavens alone; that spreadeth abroad the earth by myself;" - Isaiah 44:24

"For thy Maker *is* thine husband; the LORD of hosts *is* his name; and thy Redeemer the Holy One of Israel; The God of the whole earth shall he be called." - Isaiah 54:5

"And when these things begin to come to pass, then look up, and lift up your heads; for your redemption draweth nigh." - Luke 21:28

Z

Zion

I (Ph. – Eye) – On

Because I care about the God of Abraham, Isaac, and Jacob, I keep a close watch and a close eye on <u>Zion</u>. Israel is the apple of God's eye, so He is keeping a close watch on Jerusalem, or <u>Zion</u> the Capital city. Israel is the only covenant nation on earth, and this small nation will receive divine protection when their existence is jeopardized by enemies. Israel was reestablished as a nation in 1948, and this event fulfilled a 2,500 year old prophecy to the letter.

<u>Zion</u> is an enigma because it has no river, no port, or no major industry, and yet it is highly valued by a majority of the worlds' population as represented by their religions. This ancient city has spiritual significance, first for the Jews, second for the Christians, and third for the Muslims. These three groups represent over three billion followers. It is a very important key to end time events, and is a truly important place. Even a casual observer of the news will recognize that the Middle East is prominent in reported activity.

Following the Battle of Armageddon that will occur near Jerusalem, Yeshua will be crowned King of Israel. His earthly throne will be a continuation of the Davidic monarchy, and Yeshua will rule the entire world from <u>Zion</u>.

There is ongoing spiritual warfare, and this will increase as the end approaches. Always above the physical battle that you can see, there is a spiritual battle that mortal eyes cannot see. As a student of eschatology, I am aware of the tremendous attacks that Israel will experience prior to the Messiah becoming King.

The land of <u>Zion</u> is part of an eternal inheritance of the Jewish people. I love America, but I am convinced that Israel is of far greater importance than the USA. Satan is God's enemy, and Israel and <u>Zion</u> is the prime target that he wants to conquer. Now is the time to join sides, and the right side will support <u>Zion</u>. "For <u>Zion</u>'s sake will I not hold my peace, and for Jerusalem's sake I will not rest." Isaiah 62:1

At this late hour, all believers should support the Holy Land with prayer, and financial support, especially to Messianic congregations. Just as Paul told the early churches to provide financially for the church at Jerusalem (<u>Zion</u>), we should do the same today. Churches and individual believers have a stake in this nation, and need to show God where you stand. Already the blessings that the world has received through God's chosen people is unequalled by any other nation or people in history. I am assured by Scripture that more great spiritual blessings are yet to come from <u>Zion</u>!

"Nevertheless David took the strong hold of <u>Zion</u>: the same *is* the city of David." - 2 Samuel 5:7

"Oh that the salvation of Israel *were come* out of <u>Zion</u>! when the LORD bringeth back the captivity of his people, Jacob shall rejoice, *and* Israel shall be glad." - Psalm 14:7

"Do good in thy good pleasure unto <u>Zion</u>: build thou the walls of Jerusalem." - Psalm 51:18

"Remember thy congregation, *which* thou hast purchased of old; the rod of thine inheritance, *which* thou hast redeemed; this mount <u>Zion</u>, wherein thou hast dwelt." - Psalm 74:2

"Behold, he that keepeth Israel shall neither slumber nor sleep." - Psalm 121:4

"For thus saith the LORD of hosts; After the glory hath he sent me unto the nations which spoiled you: for he that toucheth you toucheth the apple of his eye." - Zechariah 2:8

"And it shall come to pass, *that he that is* left in <u>Zion</u>, and *he that* remaineth in Jerusalem, shall be called holy, *even* every one that is written among the living in Jerusalem:" - Isaiah 4:3

"Thy watchmen shall lift up the voice; with the voice together shall they sing: for they shall see eye to eye, when the LORD shall bring again <u>Zion</u>." - Isaiah 52:8

SECTION THREE

Chapter One gives the author's personal testimony, experiences and God's twelve step plan with words that all start with "re."

Chapter Two discusses how the universe began and supports the Genesis creation world view by using the spiritual meaning of thirty-eight words.

Chapter Three provides a perspective on the importance of Israel from a Biblical point-of-view.

CHAPTER ONE

THE MIRACLE OF SPIRITUAL BIRTH . . .

The following is my personal testimony about the conversion experience that I had over twenty-five years ago. Neither you nor I are Christians because we were raised that way, because of belonging to a church, or because of having a high standard of morality. The only way to be a real Christian is to have had the supernatural experience of being spiritually born again. "Jesus answered and said unto him, Verily, verily, I say unto thee, Except a man be born again, he cannot see the kingdom of God." John 3:3

You are not a Christian because you think that this would provide a nice lifestyle. If the teachings of Jesus are not true, then Christians should be pitied above all people, because we would have used our life for a false cause. However, the Apostles and countless thousands of Christians from every corner of the planet have followed the faith, even to death when necessary.

Becoming a member of God's family is supernatural and similar to getting Gmail because God, the Holy Spirit, must draw you and give you the faith that is life saving. "For by grace are ye saved through faith; and that not of yourselves: *it is* the gift of God." Therefore, true spirituality is a profound and supernatural experience. Once you have true faith in God I am convinced that you will never lose it.

> "Nor height, nor depth, nor any other creature, shall
> be able to separate us from the love of God, which
> is in Christ Jesus our Lord." - Romans 8:39

The two thieves crucified on crosses along with Jesus reviled him. People revile God because the natural man is in rebellion against God. One of them, as the day progressed, went through a change, "And Jesus said unto him, Verily I say unto

246

thee, To day shalt thou be with me in paradise." (Luke 23:43) I believe this converted criminal and all believers will ultimately have twelve total experiences in the following order:

1. <u>rebellion</u> against God;
2. <u>recognized</u> God (including the Holiness of God);
3. <u>repented</u> (changed his mind) about God;
4. <u>responded</u> (called out to God - public proclamation of the change that had happened); was
5. <u>reconciled</u> to God (regenerated by God - new birth) and inherited the promises of God;
6. <u>rejoiced</u> in celebration of salvation from God (when I knew I was regenerated I rejoiced for several days); and then experienced the ongoing
7. <u>renewing</u> of his mind (Romans 12:2); God's children go through a
8. <u>refining</u>; and like Jesus those born again will have a
9. <u>resurrection</u>. Believers will receive a
10. <u>reward</u> that is based on works of eternal value, and Believers will
11. <u>return</u> to earth with the Lord where they will
12. <u>reign</u> with Him for a thousand years.

That made twelve words starting with "re" and twelve is the number for fullness of completion. I think this is God's twelve step plan of grace for mankind.

None of this was by works, but all by grace. I am currently experiencing numbers seven and eight (renewing/refining). I know all non-believers rebel against God. If they become believers they will also experience God taking them through this process of receiving eternal life, sanctification (refining) and living in paradise or heaven. God starts and finishes this work (process). Without the cross, there is no gospel message. Do you know where you are in this divine process of grace that brings salvation and eternal rewards? Once you truly believe, you may be disappointed by people, churches, and even yourself, but not by God. Through genuine faith, you believe in God with your head and more importantly with your heart. The heart represents the center and essence of your soul; of who you are. True Christians are convinced by supernatural faith, as well as empirical evidence and experience, that truth is found in the person of Jesus Christ, the only begotten Son of God the Father.

One day when I was a young boy around age eight, I was walking down the street within a few blocks of my home (in the 1940's kids had more freedom to play throughout their neighborhood and I had extensive freedom of this kind.) I saw an older man sitting on a front porch with a Bible in his lap and our eyes connected. I immediately had the thought that some day this book was going to be very important to me. It was impacting enough that I never forgot the experience. In reflection, I think that it might have been an angel because he seemed to know me. If it had been an angel, no one else would have even seen him. Did this possibly indicate that God knew I would be called to write a book about the Bible over fifty years later?

My parents required regular Sunday school and worship service attendance for me, but many times they did not attend themselves. I do not remember discussions about God from my parents or from any of my many relatives. I know I must have been taught to pray because there is a photo of me praying as a young boy. I do not remember hearing family accounts of answered prayer, etc. There was a Bible in the home, but I did not see it read. I had heard that I had a great grandmother that read the Bible daily. There was neither a library of Christian books nor any Christian radio. There was no evidence of a passion for God. I had a grandfather who started life in Ireland. He went to church every Sunday, but he did not talk to me about God. He took a food basket to someone needy every Sunday afternoon. He was a believer and helped many families. He has now been with the Lord for over fifty years and my father followed him at the age of eighty-six.

At age eleven I was baptized with my whole immediate

family. This was not believer's baptism because I was told we were getting baptized. That type of baptism just gets you wet. Later, the pastor of this church called me into his office and talked to me about going into the ministry. He said that when I spoke in front of the church that everyone in the church sat up and listened. He said they did not even do that for him. At that time I had not given a thought to ministry.

Around age twelve, while sitting in a Sunday school class, I wanted to know so badly if what they were telling me about Jesus was true. I felt like every cell in my body wanted to know if He was really God. I just was not able to know if it was true or not. I just could not take the teachers at their word and I was not able to believe.

When I was a junior in high school I was attending a Presbyterian church that was liberal. They had a youth group and I was given an assignment to present a lesson on the parable of the talents. The lesson was going over the allotted time and Sara Jane, who was a very popular girl in my high school said, "Don't stop."

There was a church leader there and because of the impact of this lesson I was added to the church Evangelistic Committee. I was amused because all of the other members were adults and had important positions in the church. I never attended a meeting or went on a visitation (Years later I did do church visitation). This liberal church did not draw me into believing because I felt that the teaching was not consistent and therefore not the truth.

At age twenty-one my immediate supervisor at work was a committed soul-winner. Later he became a pastor. He was the most convincing Christian I had ever met, and I was around him regularly. After months of his witnessing, I made a decision that I would become a Christian. I prayed the sinner's prayer. The problem with that was I had made the <u>response</u> where I needed the step of <u>recognition</u>. It was premature because I responded before I had truly recognized God.

I was a true Christian, I thought, and I did "Christian things." I did not drink alcohol, rejected sexual advances from young women, and read the Bible daily. I put up a good front, but in reality I had some confusion, doubts, and unhappiness. I prayed every night but was not aware of any prayers answered. I did not consciously experience God. Still, I had some influence on others because they saw something that they felt that they did not have. In reality, I did not have it either.

This brief period of my life as a practicing Christian became extremely difficult for me. I knew the Bible taught about Satan sifting a person and I felt like that had happened to me. I felt loneliness with an intensity that I had never known. I had tried Christianity, and it did not work for me. I had experienced more difficulty and unhappiness than I had ever known. Since I had not been a true believer I became secular and skeptical, not wanting anything to do with God, religion, and certainly not church. Therefore, if you are not truly born again I would not recommend calling yourself a Christian.

A very secular life was my condition for the next seventeen years, but I was experiencing a life that I really enjoyed. I was physically fit (could easily run 10 miles without stopping), I owned a successful insurance agency, which provided an excellent income with ease. I owned my home, had friends and a good social life, I dated attractive women, and I had a very promising career in politics. A Christian would say I was blessed.

I thought I had a great life, and I did except spiritually I was lost. That means that if I died in that condition I would go to the place that was prepared for Satan and his angels. That is eternal separation from God in the "lake of fire." But, if God was not relevant then who cares? I certainly did not. I was thirty-eight years old and I had a good hedonist lifestyle. I was good at reviling God, church and Christianity.

When we experience real recognizing of God we have a natural response through faith. Then, God in His way and in His time shows that we are indeed regenerated. For the man on the cross the process took hours, but he found out he was saved immediately after he called out to Jesus.

I have known some individuals that wake up lost and get through the salvation process or steps in one day. My personal experience and observation is that for many it takes longer than a day and trying to hasten the process can be detrimental to faith rather than beneficial. I think the get saved fast and selling of response is a possible problem of modern evangelism. I have heard a statistic that only 3% show evidence of a real conversion.

Jesus did not ask the thief to make a response. No one asked me either when I had my real conversion. It came naturally from following the process of the other steps. The pray and get saved or give your life message has been so prevalent I wonder how many others have made the same subtle premature substitution of response when they must first experience the real recognition of God.

Probably the best Biblical model showing how individuals respond is in Acts 17. The Apostle Paul preached at Mars Hill in Athens, Greece and there were three different responses. Some mocked; others were interested in hearing more later and some believed and "clave unto him." Those that believed were the ones saved in one day. Some of the others would eventually be saved as well. Paul was anointed to preach and there are ministers and evangelists still today that are anointed and empowered by the Holy Spirit to preach and offer salvation through the Lord Jesus.

The Bible uses the term self-will. Unfortunately, it is man's nature to want to be on the throne himself, and not answer to a higher authority. Now I know if he/she is born again it is the best life. A spiritual life is a better life than any secular life; even that of a popular celebrity, king, or billionaire. Actually, your eternal life inheritance begins here on earth after you have saving faith. You inherit an 'abundant life' that starts after salvation and I have now experienced that new life in countless ways.

I have an analytical mind, and I was contemplating the question: What is life? I realized that humans were more than a mass of trillions of cells. Human life was more than that. I remembered the Bible verse about, "What did it profit a man if he gained the whole world and lost his soul?" I had analytically determined that we must have a soul, and realized that I agreed with the Bible. I think that gave me pause, but it did not produce any action on my part.

Not too long after that I was in a *secular* book store with a close friend, and he started to say something about a rack of books. He caught himself and just dropped the subject. Had I known this book, *Late Great Planet Earth* by Hal Lindsey was a Christian book I would not have gone near it. But I did not know and I was curious about this paperback book, because for some reason my friend did not want to tell me something he knew about it. I went back by myself and bought a copy.

I started reading this book and I could not stop. This was a book about prophecy concerning the last days. I realized that if the Bible was able to accurately describe events hundreds or even thousands of years in advance, that I might have made a serious mistake about God. As stated in Scripture, "work out your own salvation with fear and trembling." (Philippians 2:12)

I immediately went to church on Sunday. I picked a nondenominational church with a reputation for being conservative and Bible believing. The attendance there was about 1,000 on Sunday mornings. I do not think I missed a Sunday for an entire year. The Sunday school class that I was in had a teacher that had been teaching for twenty-nine years. I only listened; I did not feel worthy or knowledgeable enough to contribute so I did not talk during the class lesson.

It was a fairly large class and there were some members of this class that held leadership positions in the church. A deacon member of this class stated that he thought I might be there just for political reasons. I knew my motive, so what he said did not bother me. There just might be a good lesson here for church leaders. Why did he not ask me why I was there? No one in this church ever asked me that question. I think every person that attends a church for the first time should be asked that question. Just shaking someone's hand is superficial and not real friendliness.

Right after I began attending the class, they started studying through the book of Revelation. After *Late Great Planet Earth* and the book of Revelation, I had gotten a baptism in prophecy and end time events. This gave me an interest in Eschatology, so I continued to study and follow material relating to the end times from then to the present. I am jumping ahead here, but in April 2001 I had an expectation. I verbalized to a Sunday school class, that in the near future something momentous might take place on earth. When I saw 9-11 unfold on television, I felt that this could have been the end time event I was expecting. 9-11 did not just affect America. The end time is all about the second coming of the Lord and Israel is a key to prophetic events. I like the way this was stated by Dr. David Reagan in *God's Plan For The Ages*. "Are you yawning or yearning for the Lords return?"

The "Day of the Lord" is fast approaching. This is a period of judgment on the whole earth. Lot was vexed in his soul daily prior to judgment coming upon Sodom and Gomorrah. Do events taking place locally and around the world today vex your soul? Are you able to be thankful that God has the power and the will to one day bring judgment and correct all the sin, injustice, corruption, and false religion on planet earth? Are you ready?

The pastor in this Bible church I attended used the KJV and was a tremendous expository preacher. The Scriptures were presented in a way that I felt clearly demonstrated that the Bible could only have come through God's inspiration. The truth and power of the Word astonished me and humbled me. I had no choice but to believe. Faith this time was easy for me because I realized that the Bible is the word of God (not as sure for some newer translations) and I believed it all. That has not changed in over twenty-five years. "Faith cometh by hearing, and hearing by the word of God." (Romans 10:17)

However, I did not have an understanding of the gospel, and I was confused about salvation. In the final days leading up to Christ's arrival in Jerusalem and His crucifixion, He gave His sternest of messages. One of these statements made me think that I was "not worthy of the Kingdom of God," and that I could not be saved. I certainly did not feel at all worthy or deserving of inheriting an eternal life in the presence of God.

I realized that "Who was I to question the God that was intelligent enough to design and create this universe?" I did not want to be condemned to Hell, but if God determined that was where I belonged I needed to accept it. God must know what He is doing and I needed to accept my destiny. I was motivated to pursue God and to learn all I could about God. I reasoned that since I would be separated from God after death, that this life was the only chance I was going to have to learn about Him. Heaven or hell did not matter. I just pursed God with passion and determination. I went to church because they knew a lot about God. Neither you nor anyone else will learn all he/she should learn about God without church.

In my earlier religious experience I was focused on me and only a little focused on God. This time it was very different because I was insignificant and irrelevant. I pursued God with determination. It was all about God, and by God's grace I rapidly gained biblical and spiritual knowledge. God had allowed me into the reality of truth and that experience is very special. Once you find truth you know that there is nothing else that satisfies the same way. So, I continued my quest to know about God, and little did I know that I was going to be able to know God - to really know God. That close relationship did not begin for me until a little over a year after I had returned to church. The Bible states, "But seek ye first the kingdom of God, and his righteousness; and all these things shall be added unto you." (Matthew 6:33)

God deals with us individually, so we all have testimonies that are unique. The experience is not exactly the same for everyone. I had learned a lot at this church, but I did not feel that I fit in well. I later found out that because they required a committee interview and approval for membership, that only about 400 of the thousand attending were actually members. They were serious committed Christians, but I think there was a need for members to fit their precise Christian view or mold.

When I left, I immediately changed to another church and unfortunately, it had very weak preaching. But I had some great experiences while there. Shortly after I left the first church, and through a connection from the first church, I was invited to join a home Bible study that was made up of doctors, lawyers, and their wives. This group had some seasoned Christians, and this was a real spiritual blessing for me. It was unusual that I would have this privilege, and it was the beginning of my starting to experience God on a personal basis. My spiritual confidence began to grow and I became more outspoken in Sunday school. I, in fact, was a believer and a child of God.

I had experienced God enough by this time that I felt my faith in God was very strong. It did not seem to me that others in this second church experienced faith in the same way that I now enjoyed. This church had a picnic that I attended and I decided that I wanted to do something during this picnic to demonstrate faith. I made it a prayer request. One event was an uncooked egg toss contest. I got a partner and went next to last. I asked where the mark was for the current longest toss. I had my partner start there and I kept telling him to go back farther. I had him continue backing up until his distance from me was several times the current record. It was a really long distance. Someone observed that is too far to throw the egg underhanded. I said, "You are right." I drew back and threw the egg over handed like a baseball, as high and far as I could. It went right to my partner's hands and he caught the egg without it breaking. People were astonished! A lawyer realized what he had seen, and he said that he had not really been a Christian. He made a profession of faith and told me he would never forget the experience. I do think it was miraculous.

After about six months I left this second church, because I just could not tolerate such a weak worship experience. I went to another church, but only stayed for a few months because I realized that I was in disagreement with too much of their doctrine (dogma). There were some people there that I did like very much and the young pastor became a friend while I was there. He regularly came by my office.

Earlier, I mentioned that I had encouragement in politics and had been referred to as 'a rising star.' I won the primary my first try, and barely lost in the general election to serve in the state legislature. I was invited to a 'political' party a few weeks after the election. I noticed that I was the only candidate there that had lost in the last election. The highest elected official to attend was the Chief Justice of the State Supreme Court. When he arrived, everyone stood, and when I left, he stood for me. These people knew protocol, and I saw how surprised they were to see this Chief Justice stand for a non-elected official.

I experienced profound accomplishments during my campaign for elected office. One person told me that political action committees did not know what to do with me because I was the only candidate that gave an intelligent answer to every question. I received many endorsements and gave some speeches that impressed veteran politicians. In looking back, I think that God may have allowed me this success to set up a test for me. God does not tempt us, but He will test us. I was certain that I would win if I ran for office again, but I chose God instead.

I saw politics as a great temptation for me. There is something about having power that is addictive. I experienced enough from winning the primary to know that this could really get in your blood. Politics could be both very rewarding and very consuming. For me, as a young believer in Jesus, I felt that I could not be in politics and grow spiritually. I decided that the real power was with God, and political power was only a sort of illusion. I chose to continue to pursue God rather than return to politics. I am very glad I made that choice. The right God is always the right choice.

I think that this may have been a crossroads decision for me - not affecting my salvation, but my future of having increasing power with God. The Bible says you cannot serve God and money, and I was not going to be able to serve God and politics. I do not mean to say that some individuals cannot serve both. I know they can if they are able to put God above their political career. Pontius Pilot failed. He tried hard, but finally gave into the pressure from the Jewish leaders and the crowd when his standing with Caesar was threatened.

King David demonstrated clearly that he put God above the throne of Israel; however his predecessor King Saul did not. How strong could America have become if all politicians would have put God first throughout their political life?   It seems that today politics is a lot less about serving, and a lot more about personal interests. Elected and appointed officials may not have considered God or do not believe, but this will happen anyway. One day they will stand before Almighty God, and they will be held accountable for every official action they have made.

The church that I chose next was a good fit for me for the next several years. It was a conservative, Bible believing (KJV only in the pulpit), preaching church that was growing on a regular basis. The pastor was an authority on spiritual gifts and he was intrigued by the gifts that he knew I had demonstrated. For those that do not know, every believer receives at least one spiritual gift at the time of their salvation. The gift(s) you receive are chosen by God for the benefit of the church. You do not lose them until death, because they are not needed on the other side. It is important to use your gift(s) for God's Kingdom, as long as you have that opportunity. I find gifts to be humbling because they increase your responsibility. Based on all we had been given, do we know how well our accomplishments please God?

I served this church and eventually held various leadership positions. I ushered, did some teaching, served on committees, chaired a committee, etc. The whole church knew that I had spiritual gifts. I could connect with God in a way that I could demonstrate to others. I found God to be very accessible, especially when the request was in line with His will and purposes. I had some profound experiences with God during this period and was able to understand exactly how God designed the New Testament church to function. It is a supernatural organization with Christ as the head.

I stated that in my religious experience years earlier, I was not aware of any answered prayer. I remember just one prayer that I believe God answered years later. God knows our hearts, and I did pray earnestly that I would not be a false teacher. I am a person that is persuasive, and I usually am able to convince others to my point of view. I remembered how people in the church would listen to me even when I was a young boy.

When I was in my early twenties, I knew that I lacked a lot of spiritual understanding and I did not want to mislead others. After becoming a believer, I received spiritual gifts equipping me with discernment, the ability to recognize sound doctrine. That is a prayer that would probably be good for many religious leaders to pray – especially legalists and liberals.

The legalists want to add one or more plusses to "grace through faith," and some want to add to the Ten Commandments. Many of these professing Christians are probably saved, but not representing the gospel accurately. I do not understand how anyone that has experienced grace would not understand it. On the other hand, I do not know how anyone that has not experienced grace could understand it. One point that I want to make for those with legalist tendencies is that liberty is not license. God is long suffering, gracious and loving, but there is accountability with the God that is a "consuming fire."

The liberals are upset by the fundamentals of the faith. They will accept about any belief position except conservative Christianity. Some do not even like the question, "do you know where you will go when you die? They do not respect the Bible as the authentic, inspired, sacred Word of God. Most would not take Genesis as historic and literal. Some are even very conservative in their lifestyle, but their theology is liberal. They do not seem to be able to recognize truth as truth. Some years ago, I was talking with a young Jewish lady who had attended a very liberal divinity school. I asked her why she went there. She said that she was looking for answers. I told her that she would not have found them there. She did not disagree.

One day during my time of membership at this church, I was sitting in the state cultural center building watching a free movie. About two-thirds of the way through the movie I had the feeling that I needed to get up and go home. This was not logical, and I was enjoying the movie. I walked outside and saw a mixed race gang of four young men severely beating a young white male that was slightly built. I started walking quickly right toward them. I just felt that God was going to let me win. I thought it might be with supernatural strength like Sampson. I was wrong about that, but right that God would allow me to prevail. God used a technique that He has recorded in the Bible. When they saw one person coming after them they immediately stopped, and then ran in four different directions. I wanted to go after at least one of them, but the victim was unconscious and bloody. I knew I needed to help him first.

Months later, a detective came to my office for insurance. I brought up this incident, and he explained that he had solved the crime. The detective said it was a totally unprovoked attack. He said that all four assailants had been convicted, and were now serving time in prison. He told me the victim had been beaten so badly that the next day he was still not coherent. I relay this account to share an example of a demonstration of faith. Faith is evidence of things unseen. I could not see God there, but felt that it was He that brought me out of that movie. If I had not been a Christian, I would not have been able to go toward this gang unarmed. If David had not been a believer with faith and a personal relationship with God, he would not have been able to challenge and defeat Goliath. I fell short of David's victory over Goliath because he ran and I only walked.

My last year at this church was disappointing because of some things I saw. Also, I strongly disagreed with the pastor every Sunday during the invitation saying, "Make a total commitment and be saved." The gospel is grace through faith, and not by works. I did not really understand, but I felt that God wanted me to sell my business and leave the state. That is what I did, and that is when I left this church that had been so meaningful to me for a long time. I can understand Abraham having to leave and go to a new country. It was not an easy experience, but it did not shake my faith.

I went to northern Georgia, and spent a few weeks (rent free) in a new vacation home that was owned by a married couple that had been insurance clients. I loved the area and visited several churches and had many spiritual discussions with those that I would meet. It was from this area that I later got the comment from one of those people I had met. A 70 year man that became a Christian, said, "Around here you are known as John the Baptist."

The next phase was confusing, because I just was not able to decide on a new location and begin to get established. It took three years for that to happen and many different experiences occurred during this time; including becoming a grandfather for the first time. I was a young grandfather, and looked even younger. At the hospital the staff would not believe that I was the grandfather, and not the father.

A few months after I started my transition to life in a new place I was driving through Nashville, Tennessee. It was evening and I saw that the next exit had a Hotel. After I exited the interstate I recognized the exit as belonging to the only family I knew in Nashville. I thought if I can find their house, I probably would get to visit and get a free room for the night. I did find their house and stay; but not before spending a little time looking and driving around the area where they lived. One street that I drove on while looking for them is where I ended up living about four years later. I met my future wife in a Cracker Barrel restaurant three years later, and she lived on that street. Was that God's way to show that he knew my future? I think that it was.

When I met my future wife she was not a Christian, and as she says she was a "happy heathen." I called her for a date about a week and a half after we met; she told her best friend that she knew something had to be wrong with me. And she said that she hoped it was not that I was religious. At dinner, I ordered a glass of wine and she thought this is a good sign. Later, I brought up the subject of God. She thought, "I knew it." I saw God building her faith, but did not want to say too much. After she became a believer, I saw her quickly begin to enjoy a close relationship with God. I knew that I had experienced this for years, but I marveled at her personal relationship with God. She became spiritually empowered and loved church, other believers and Bible studies.

I want to share an experience we had early in our relationship. We were visiting out of state at the home of friends that I had known for many years. The family matriarch, now a widow, told me after I became a Christian that she had prayed for me for years. During this visit there were some theology conversations because everyone there was a professing believer. This was Saturday, and that night when I prayed I asked God which church I should visit the next day, my old church or this old and dear friend's church. The next morning I overslept and it was too late to go to either church. During this period in my life, I was used to getting prayers answered, and I was disappointed that God had not answered this one. I actually silently fussed at God – "I wanted to go to church and You did not awaken me."

Later, my wife and I were having lunch at a restaurant in a small town, located between where the two churches are that I had prayed about. I saw an older retired pastor that had attended my former church. This was a man that I really liked and respected. I asked him for his opinion about us going to my old church for a visit. He did not recommend that I go back to the old church. He said it had really gone down after I left, but he highly recommended a new church in a rural area about ten miles from where we were having lunch. When he told me the pastor's name, I recognized it, and I knew he had been the pastor at the city church where my friend was a member for years. When I went back to the table, the acoustics, or something, had carried our conversation to our table, so my wife heard it all. She said we needed to go to that church.

We spent the afternoon visiting with my daughter and her husband. I was getting tired and was not dressed well for church, but agreed that God wanted us to go to the Church in the Valley. So, we drove there and arrived before the Sunday evening service started. I was surprised that the church was full for an evening service. It was an excellent sermon and a good one for my wife, because her church experience was one of works and not one of grace. Even so, I was disappointed because I was expecting something really special from God.

The pastor was at the back of the church and was greeting everyone as they left. I shook his hand and said that I knew a lady that was a member of his previous church. I told him who and he said, "No, she is a member here." I was just stunned because she had not said a word about this new church. Also, it was at least a 30 minute drive from her home and she did not drive. He saw I might not believe him so he told me her vacation schedule. My wife had a big laugh, "God played a joke on you and I got see it." God actually had answered my prayer. I did not realize how complicated the prayer was, because I did not know about the church change. I did learn a lesson. I do not think I have complained about an unanswered prayer since.

This pilgrim's spiritual journey has been a varied and interesting adventure. I have experienced the joy of everything from a mission trip to Brazil, to coaching church league basketball. I am very skilled at coaching at this level; which has gotten pretty competitive. I loved coaching young men along with teaching them about God. My wife and I have had countless personal experiences with God and answered prayers. We have learned to hear God and see God's providence at work many, many times.

Years ago, we realized that many professing Christians were not aware of these same kinds of experiences. There were times that if we tried to share an experience of this type we were looked at like we were aliens. We came to the conclusion that Christ had many disciples, but only a few inner circle disciples. "Many are called, but few are chosen." We decided that some of our experiences were for us only and that we should not share this information with others. This book has been an exception, because I think that the evidence presented in *Amazing God* for revelation and inspiration should be obvious. We have found that all churches are not equal in this regard. Some have more understanding about a personal relationship with God, and are more receptive regarding sharing experiencing God.

The powerful Hurricane Katrina was America's greatest natural disaster. Was this destructive force a random act of nature or was it a purposeful act of God? This is an account of my experience relating to this event. I have a strong interest in Israel because I have a strong interest in God. Israel is the only covenant nation on earth, and it is of primary importance in this final phase of history. Is there a connection between a hurricane in America and Israel?

The Bible has a strong warning against dividing the land that God gave the Jews for an inheritance. Many Evangelical and Messianic believers were very upset that plans called for the Gaza Strip to be turned over to the Palestinians. I was one of those that were very concerned, and I wrote a letter to Prime Minister, Ariel Sharon, making a case that this not be done. Days after I sent the letter, my wife got a Gmail on the Prime Minister's name; Sharon – share own. He was in fact going to give away land that Israel owned. I sent another letter nine months before Gaza was turned over by the Prime Minister to the Palestinians. In this letter, I indicated that I knew the Gaza giveaway would take place. It was not right, but it was going to occur. I advised a Messianic ministry in Israel to calm down about this because it would happen. The United States government "Road Map for Peace" put a lot of pressure on Israel to give up the Gaza Strip. (Gmail – Gaza - sounds like gauze that you put on a wound; strip – strip away).

A few days before Katrina, I told my wife that God was soon going to bring a judgment on America because of our role in the Gaza giveaway. I had been spiritually concerned and involved with this issue for a year. While Katrina was out in the ocean, but getting quite strong, I told my wife that this hurricane was the judgment event that I was expecting. The night before it hit land (Saturday or Sunday), I knew the situation was serious and I made an intercessory prayer. I agreed with God that this nation had gone against His warning about Israel and that we deserved to suffer judgment. I pleaded for mercy in the midst of His judgment. The night before the hurricane was to reach the coast, when I went to bed, the hurricane was a category five and heading straight toward New Orleans. I felt that God was going to do something special, but I did not know what it would be.

The next morning when I woke up, I turned on the television and the first thing I heard was, "the meteorologists are scratching their heads because a puff of warm air out of nowhere changed Hurricane Katrina from a category five to a category four and moved it below New Orleans." I believe I know the source of that warm air. I believe that prayer(s) brought mercy to New Orleans residents. I am glad that I was one of those that had prayed on their behalf.

As bad as it was, do you have any idea what the death and destruction would have been if New Orleans had gotten a direct hit category five? Destruction and death would have been total. I would say that God did show mercy in the midst of judgment. We knew that Rita; that came after Katrina, also involved judgment because the letters for Rita are in Katrina. The reports from Israel about the refugees from Gaza, and the news reports about the refugees from New Orleans had many remarkable similarities. God showed mercy, but still made a direct hit that was felt all over America. We all paid when we went to the gas pump, and many of us made financial contributions for relief. Also, it was costly for our government in both money and reputation.

I have heard the question, "Was New Orleans reputation for sin, for corruption, and for the scheduled gay parade responsible for this tremendous destruction?" I do not think that this was the cause, but probably was the reason that this area was targeted. The primary cause was ignoring God's word regarding dividing the land of Israel; that is a bad idea for any nation or any person. Actually, the progression of sexual immorality that started in the 1960's is just one evidence of judgment on America.

Several days before Prime Minister Sharon had the massive stroke; I had heard from God that he was finished politically. I did not know any details, and I do not know why God gave me that information. Yes, I do think the timing of his loss of power was the result of his Gaza decision. He was a great field general, and I admired and respected this man. The Gaza situation provides a good lesson for America, other nations, and other political leaders. That is why I included this account; and I do have a love for intercessory prayer. I highly recommend not dividing Israel, and also recommend earnestly making intercessory prayers for this covenant nation.

The question that you should consider is whether there is a connection between 9-11, Katrina, Rita, earthquakes (the tsunami that killed over 120,000 people), droughts, floods, destructive tornados, plagues, famine, the Iraq War, Iran developing nuclear weapon capability, importance of oil, economic uncertainty, increasing anti-Semitism, etc. I am persuaded by research from the Messianic Levite Michael Rood that probably the seventh millennium began in April 2001, and we are in the judgment period that is the "Day of the Lord." Regardless, time for serving the living God, Maker of Heaven and Earth, is running out. Today is the day and now is the time for salvation.

There have been numerous Bible prophecies fulfilled just since I was born. This is a time of many spiritual opportunities. It is a bad time to be secular, because the problems of this world will continue and increase until the return of the Lord. Evil will increase and spiritual blessings and power will increase. A biblical world view, based on knowing that God will prevail and be victorious, is an encouragement in difficult and challenging times.

Culture is learned and ethnicity is skin deep. In heaven there will be people from every color, language, and nation on earth. I pray that faith will increase and especially all those that read this book will be among those joyous millions in God's Kingdom. Amen.

Gmail using 38 words will be in this chapter: Adam, began, breath, character, creation, dimension, dominion, earth, elements, evolution, galaxy, genes, genesis, heart, history, image, individual, knowledge, life, live, moon, nature, origin, person, planet, philosophy, reality, rule, science, serpent, sound, species, stars, sun, time, universe, wisdom, and world.

When I was a young boy lying in bed at night, I sometimes would meditate on the question, "What would be here if what is here did not exist?" I just could not understand how I and everything else came into being. This question and one other, have held the fascination of philosophers, scientists and most of mankind for centuries. These two questions are: From where did everything originate? And what is the meaning of life?

This chapter presents direct evidence from the thirty-eight English words listed above to assist you in exploring answers to these two age old questions. This presentation should provide you with much to think about, and some interesting new insights into both theology and present day science.

Over twenty-five years ago, I realized that the written Bible was the inspired revelation from God for the benefit of man and the glory of God. A year later, I became fascinated in learning more about creation. I logically accepted Genesis as being accurate HISTORY (page 115). This first book in the Bible explained how the universe got here, the origin of all life on the earth, and man's fall by disobeying God.

I thought I would study creation, and learn a lot more about God's word over that summer. A few days after I decided to start my studying, I got a call from a dear Christian lady that taught a high school Sunday school class in a Lutheran Church. She asked me if I would be able to teach her class because she had temporary blindness. Their next lesson started with the study of the beginning of Genesis, which covered the account of creation. Her blindness continued for the four weeks that I taught the verses from the Sunday school lesson plan. After I had finished, her sight returned. Just as I believe that God called me to teach twenty-five years ago, I am convinced that God wants me to teach about creation again.

Origins present a particular difficulty of uncertainty because they were not observable. The scientific attempt to explain the universe and many life forms on earth, without direct evidence, seems to blur into philosophy and therefore, becomes a type of faith or belief that is based on a person's particular view of reality. Many start from the world view position that there is no God; therefore some other explanation must be sought. Science has the letters for the word seen, because if it is not seen it is not science. Let me repeat that, IF IT IS NOT SEEN IT IS NOT SCIENCE!

In *Scientific American*, in 1959, two-thirds of those scientists surveyed, said when asked the age of the universe, "Beginning? The universe is eternal." Now the Big Bang is accepted, and science believes the universe had a beginning. The Bible stated that the universe had a beginning. It is profound to me just how much science is getting right when compared to Biblical statements. Science and the Bible go hand in hand, and do not contradict each other, as many people have been misled into believing.

For many years, scientists have used this Big Bang theory to try to prove that the universe was created by an explosion of matter from a single point. It states that there was nothing in the beginning. It goes further to say that a process known as Vacuum Fluctuation created a dime-sized singularity, or a dense mass of matter, which exploded to form the ever-expanding universe we see today. An expanding universe gets into complex and interesting physics. Does space and time dilate with expansion? Oh the mysteries and complexities of creation.

Was the universe formed from a big bang? On the surface, the Big Bang theory as stated by scientists looks like an absolute mockery of God's divine blueprint of the universe. And that generally is their whole aim: To try to remove God from His creation. However, they may be closer to the scriptural truth of creation than they realize! Again, in accepting the Big Bang theory, these scientists also accept the event of a beginning, but they do not acknowledge God as the creator. We know that in the beginning there was "nothing," as the scientists say. That compressed mass of matter that exploded had to come from somewhere! Matter is not eternal and it did have a beginning. God, not matter, is eternal. God is not matter. God is a spirit.

> "God is a spirit: and they that worship him must worship *him* in spirit and in truth." - John 4:24

> "For the invisible things of him from the creation of the world are clearly seen, being understood by the things that are made, *even* his eternal power and Godhead; so that they are without excuse." - Romans 1:20

Now, if matter had a beginning where did it come from? Genesis, the first book in the Bible, was inspired by God, and written by Moses about 1,400 BC. The "beginning" Moses described was an absolute beginning before anything existed: except God and eternity, because God states that he is eternal. "The eternal God is thy refuge…" - Deuteronomy 33:27

The thing that confounded me for years was my understanding that God brought the creation into existence ex nilo, out of nothing. My analytical brain could not understand that, because, how do you get something out of nothing? This issue also confounds science and philosophers because they do not have an answer. God did not use his essence to make the matter or material of Creation. I prayed for years for God to reveal to me how he brought something out of nothing.

There was a bumper sticker that said, "I Believe in the Big Bang Theory: God said "Bang" and there it was!"

> "By the Word of the Lord were the heavens made;
> and all the host of them by the breath of His mouth.

He gathereth the waters of the sea together as an heap: He layeth up the depth in storehouses. Let all the earth fear the Lord: let all the inhabitants of the world stand in awe of Him. For He spake, and it was done; He commanded, and it stood fast." - Psalm 33:6-9

Finally, I got an answer I liked, and I think that the bumper sticker was right. I heard a preacher on Christian radio; I did not catch his name, but he was explaining that God made the Creation out of sound. The Bible record does state that God spoke it into existence. The more he talked, the better I liked the explanation. Could God speak everything into existence? That night when I prayed, I asked God to show me what the building block of matter looked like. I instantly saw a vision of a perfect circle with uniform waves going all the way around the circle. The circle with the perfect symmetrical waves was connected, just like a ring that symbolizes eternity because it has no beginning or end.

Astronomers in the 1970's theorized that the universe was thick and gassy just after the Big Bang and that the heavens rang with sound, like cosmic bells. Dr. Daniel Eisenstein has continued studying this theory, part of the Sloan Digital Sky Survey and he has concluded that the distance of the many galaxies today, and the pattern of the sound waves of the early universe, match up precisely and the early cosmic sounds were like pebbles being thrown into a pond. Again, a scientist may have inadvertently found the result of God's speaking the universe into existence.

There is your "Big Bang." I believe that this sound from God might have extended for a trillion times a trillion miles. That would have made a really loud bang. Just in case you are still wondering – BEGAN has the letters for *bang*. One more little bit of evidence is the word SOUND. It contains *son* and *sun*. Therefore, this author's position is yes, there WAS a really big bang. Halleluiah, praise God!

"In the beginning was the Word, and the Word was with God, and the Word was God. The same was in the beginning with God. All things were made by Him; and without Him was not any thing made that was made." – John 1:1

A recent poll showed that in the United States only twelve percent of the population does not believe that life came from God. Recently, I read about a DNA study by researchers from the Broad Institute of MIT and Harvard. The study hypothesized that an ancestral ape species split into two isolated populations about ten million years ago, then got back together after a few thousand millennia. One thousand millennia would be a million years. They suggest that the human-chimp split was no earlier that 6.3 million years ago, and more likely in the neighborhood of 5.4 million. They also say that their data suggests this human-chimp split probably took millions of years to occur.

I have an idea for these researchers. Since they think that the species split and re-united once, shouldn't it be about time for them to do this again. Yes, it is about time for these ancient relatives to re-unite a second time. These guys should just either move in with the chimps or have the chimps move in with them. If given a few million millennia they just might be able to produce another new species for their family tree.

The previous paragraph was, of course, satire because the author of this book thinks that evolution research is a questionable use of valuable resources, and in fact I have a few questions for the researchers. First, where did the apes come from? How many splits did it take to get the apes and monkeys? How many thousands of millions of years did that take? What millennia did man get the gene for language? When did we get our gene for abstract thought? How many splits did it take to get the 5,000 species of birds on planet Earth, with a range in weight from a couple of ounces to 300 pounds? Sorry, this author prefers the inspired Bible, a divine designed language, the enormous variety of complex life, and the astonishing human DNA code to your suggested conclusions.

How can evolution scientists explain C14; which has a radioactive life of a million years? It is found in virtually all forms of carbon. This alone would limit the earth to a million years or less. That is significantly lower than the billions of years that are proclaimed by supporters of evolution. There are multiple other scientific proofs that support a young earth.

The research conclusions on evolution frankly sound just plain impossible, and therefore ridiculous. It would be like throwing pieces of a watch into a field and waiting for them to evolve into a watch, instead of trusting in the careful hand of a watchmaker to craft the intricate masterpiece. How ridiculous a thought! And how impossible! We know that a watch would never just come from a pile of watch parts, unless crafted by the watchmaker. Even if we waited billions of years, like the evolutionists say. So, why would anyone think the complexity of life would happen that way?

If you want to believe in phenomenal species complexity, improvement, and advancement that occurred over thousands of millions of years; and that you are related to apes and chimps, you are free to do just that. But those of you doing evolution research are the blind leading the blind. Jesus healed a blind man and he said, when questioned by the Pharisees, *"One thing I know, I was blind and now I see."* Everyone that is born again, born spiritually, is able to make that statement. You are justified, not by works, but by faith. Faith is not blind. You must hear from God to have faith. The real blind are those without faith and therefore without hope. I would not trade real faith for tons of gold.

The word veil is in evolution and it does cover the truth for many. Evolution is called a theory, but it lacks the observed phenomena to justify that scientific designation. It does not even have the foundation for a hypothesis. It is actually just a <u>notion</u>; which is a vague thought. I have one word for those that promote EVOLUTION, which is an *evil* <u>*notion*</u>, and those words are in evolution (use letter twice). The UNIVERSE exists because of <u>one</u> <u>*verse*</u> and it is the first verse in the Bible.

271

"In the beginning God (Elohim) created the heaven and the earth." - Genesis 1:1

This verse answers one of the first two questions, "From where did everything originate?" by plainly stating that matter did have a beginning. Evolution is not only false, but it is evil. Those that promote this flawed feeble theory would be better served to seek eternal life.

Fortunately, there have been evolution scientists that did see the light, and have become strong defenders of the Genesis creation account. One such well known scientist that supported Genesis was the published author Dr. Henry Morris (10/6/1918-2/25/2006). His doctorate in paleontology provided an academic evolution background. He became a creation apologetics (defender) author. If you do not believe this author please read a book or two written by Dr. Henry M. Morris. Currently, his son Dr. John Morris is President of the Institute for Creation Research in Dallas, Texas. The web site is www.icr.org. Recently, a DVD with Ben Stein was released titled *EXPELLED*. This quality DVD provides an in depth look at the subjects of creation, intelligent design and evolution.

There was a CREATION because of the Creator, the eternal God. This word was used because the creation demonstrates <u>art</u>. Mankind was created to be creative. Also, CREATION includes the word <u>eat</u> in the middle of the word. "And he said, Who told thee that thou wast naked? Hast thou eaten of the tree, whereof I commanded thee that thou shouldest not <u>eat</u>?" (Genesis 3:11) Because of that sin of disobedience to God the whole creation is under a curse.

"For we know that the whole creation groaneth and travaileth in pain together until now." - Romans 8:22

There is a theory called "theistic evolution" which states that evolution and the Bible can both be believed at the same time without contradicting each other. About twenty years ago, I was riding in Virginia with a Navy Seal and he asked me this question, "John, can you believe in evolution and be a Christian?" My answer was simply, "Yes." He drove a little further and asked, "Would you be on the first team?" I said, "No." He drove a little further and said, "I have always been a first team guy." I said, "Good." Evolution and the Bible are really not compatible.

> "And God called the light Day, and the darkness he called Night. And the evening and the morning were the first day." - Genesis 1:5

In the Genesis account of creation, numerals are used for each day. This means that it is a literal twenty-four hour day and the entire creation, including man, was completed in six literal days. I believe that the Bible supports a young earth of thousands of years and not an earth of billions of years. I do not believe that real science has any way of contradicting that position. I like real science, but I do not like the philosophy of applied materialism represented through the theory of evolution, as being science.

I am convinced that the millions or billions of years "scientific theories" hold require circular reasoning, conjecture and/or false assumptions. Circular reasoning goes something like this: The fossil is ten million years old. How do you know? The rock where it was found was ten million years old. How do you know the age of the rock? The fossil found there is ten million years old. Okay!!

I would like to offer a little Gmail insight into Charles Darwin's book, *"Origin of the Species."* ORIGIN has *groin* because that is the area of the body where reproduction is initiated. SPECIES rearranged gives you *pieces,* because there is no "missing link." And there is not any chain, or any transitional species. If they had existed, thousands should have been found by now through archeology.

"And God said, Let the earth bring forth the living creature after his kind, cattle, and creeping thing, and beast of the earth after his kind: and it was so."
- Genesis 1:24

That is what man and animals do. They always reproduce their own kind from a genetics pool that provides for variety. That is what has always been observed, and that is also what the fossil record shows. Macro evolution, simple changing into complex, is not science. And if you like evolution I am so sorry, because you have accepted a lie and have fallen into darkness. There are no less than **seven** disciplines of science that disprove evolution.

"And the light shineth in darkness and the darkness comprehended it not." - John 1:5

I am not being judgmental because I also needed to be convinced of sin and saved by God's marvelous grace. I just hope and pray that those of you, who have not before, will see the light of truth and believe before it is too late. Faith is not blind as some suppose. You receive faith by hearing from God. I do not know of anything that is clearer than real Biblical faith.

"So then faith *cometh* by hearing and hearing by the word of God." - Romans 10:17

We got our *genes* on the sixth day of GENESIS. The genetic information coded in human DNA is so extensive, that in a microscopic cell it is a gigabyte of data. The human body contains billions of miles of DNA. That is a message and anytime there is a message there is a messenger. The information is more complex than a Saturn rocket. That is compelling proof for design. I submit to you that in this case the messenger is none other than the eternal God. Wisdom (page 247) is intelligence that is different from knowledge.

"The fear of Lord is the beginning of wisdom." - Proverbs 9:10

What is more important to you, the world or your soul? You are not just a big pile of arranged molecules that developed by accident. You have purpose and value. HEART has the letters for the word _rate_ for both physical and spiritual reasons. You need a heart beat (rate) to be physically alive, and you need the right heart rate or rating by God to be spiritually alive. God said let us make man in our image, after our likeness.

". . So God created man in his _own_ image." - Genesis 1:27

IMAGE contains _I Am_ and _me_. The image of you and me is in the likeness of I Am. God has revealed to man that He is one Godhead but with three distinct and equal persons – Father, Son, and Holy Spirit. So, if we are in his likeness, does man exhibit anything similar to this? We have a soul, a body and a spirit, or three in one. The Father represents the soul, Jesus, the body, and the Holy Spirit, the spirit. To quote Ravi Jacharias, "Our mind is to our souls, as our brain is to our body." The brain controls and directs the body, and our minds direct our hearts and souls. Has your mind directed you to Christ? If not, what is hindering you?

We also received BREATH, and from these letters you can spell _heart_.

> "And the Lord God formed man _of_ the dust of the ground, and breathed into his nostrils the breath of life; and man became a living soul." Genesis 2:7

> "Jesus said unto him, THOU SHALT LOVE THE LORD THY GOD WITH ALL THY HEART, AND WITH ALL THY SOUL, AND WITH ALL THY MIND." - Matthew 22:37

I was a non-believer (not a Christian), but I still knew, as most people will also acknowledge, that there was too much complexity of design for random events to have been responsible for creation. I realized that a God, or some power and intelligence much greater than man existed. God makes no attempt to prove His reality rather He says it this way,

"The fool has said in his heart *there* is no God." - Psalm 14.1

The Bible states that man does not fail to recognize God in nature because of reason or intellect, but because of his heart. The word CHARACTER contains *heart chart*. God knows you better than you know yourself, and has a chart of everyone's heart. Do you have a heart for the creator God? I was once this way: I did not know God and was not interested in God, because I enjoyed a hedonistic secular life.

"And this is the condemnation, that light is come into the world, and men loved darkness rather than light, because their deeds were evil." - John 3:19

By the way, for all the nature worshippers, it is called NATURE because it provides a glimpse into the *nature* of an all powerful and sovereign God. Be careful what you worship.

There is something about truth with which nothing else compares. Once you really experience truth, you would never want to live again without it. Jesus said,

"I am the way, the truth, and the life: no man cometh unto the Father, but by me." - John 14:6

What a profound statement. My prayer is that if you do not have truth now that the Spirit of God will draw you. I hope that you will find truth as I was blessed to do many years ago.

"For the wages of sin is death; but the gift of God is
eternal life through Jesus Christ our Lord." -
Romans 6:23

It is okay to be in the WORLD because it contains *Word*
and *Lord*. EARTH rearranged spells *heart* because this is where
God's heart is focused. It is a PLANET because it was from a *plan*.
You were also planned and designed unique from anyone else that
has or ever will live.

Moses had his first encounter with God on Mt. Sinai, "And
Moses said unto God, Behold when I come unto the children of
Israel and shall say unto them, The God of your fathers, the God of
Abraham, the God of Isaac, and the God of Jacob, hath sent me
unto you; and they shall say unto me, What is his name? What
shall I say unto them?" (Exodus 3:13)

"And God said unto Moses, I AM THAT I AM: and
he said, Thus shalt thou say unto the children of
Israel, I AM hath sent me unto you. "- Exodus 3:14

These words express absolute and eternal being. About
1,400 years later you find that Jesus or Yeshua, his actual Hebrew
name, arrives on the scene and is the I am. Jesus said, I am the
bread of life, I am the good shepherd, I am the way, etc. Is it a
coincidence that the name of the first human, ADAM contained
am? I do not think that it was a coincidence, because God breathed
life into Adam that made him a living soul. God <u>added</u> AM when
he created man.

Why do we have a LIFE? Because when you rearrange the
letters you get *file*. Before you are saved or born again you are an
enemy of God, but after spiritual birth you immediately receive
eternal life. God has a file on every person that ever lived. The
files of those that are saved have no sins recorded, but what is
recorded is for the purpose of rewards. Every single thing that you
have done that has any purpose for God's Kingdom will be in your
file. Scripture states,

"For where your treasure is, there will your heart be also." - Luke 12:34

If you are a believer you should be about building treasure in heaven. One of the standards for that is what you have done to help others.

"He that believeth on the Son hath everlasting life: and he that believeth not on the Son shall not see life; but hath the wrath of God abideth on him." - John 3:36

You are who you are as a person *per* the *son*! You will either have an eternity with God; or an eternity of separation, loss or despair solely based on your standing with God per his only begotten Son. You LIVE because the letters rearranged spell *evil*.

"Behold, I was shapen in iniquity; and in sin did my mother conceive me. Psalm 51:5

"For all have sinned, and come short of the glory of God." - Romans 3:23

We are not born good and then corrupted by parents or the environment. We are not capable of righteousness within ourselves, and that is why we need to have righteousness imputed to us through faith in the Savior.

"For I am not ashamed of the gospel of Christ: for it is the power of God unto salvation to everyone that believeth; to the Jew first and also to the Greek (gentile)." - Romans 1:16

I would like to get back to the question of what, if anything would be here if the universe was not. I do have an answer to offer.

God has revealed that He is omnipresent. God is everywhere at the same time, and God was here before time, space, and the universe. God is in eternity and is not limited by time, space, past or future. TIME is a _mite_ to God. I find it interesting that time provides a type of space. We are in time and space with a spirit, a soul and a body. Time is present with matter, and eternity is not just lots and lots of time. The spirit of God, the Holy Spirit, is like an invisible sea that extends throughout this entire expanse of universe. God is omnipresent. We _see_ because of that _sea_ of the Spirit of the Holy eternal God.

Adam, the first man, was given DOMINIOM over the animal kingdom, but one of those animals, a serpent, was used by Satan to cause a _domino_ effect of sin in man. SERPENT has _step_, _repent_, _tree_ and _see_. Since the serpent did this, God cursed him, saying he would crawl on his belly and,

> "And I will put enmity between thee and the woman, and between thy seed and her seed; it shall bruise thy head and thou shall bruise his heel. – Genesis 3:15

Satan used the serpent to trick Eve into eating the fruit of the _Tree_ of Knowledge of Good and Evil, telling her:

> "your eyes (see) shall be opened, and ye shall be as gods, knowing good and evil." - Genesis 3:5

Man's fall came through Adam because he was not deceived, but rather made a willful decision. Adam and Eve ate the fruit and then, "they knew that they were naked."(Genesis 3:7) Nakedness is now a problem (sin), because sin is passed through the genitals by reproduction.

This Tree of Knowledge is a big deal to God. Why might God have forbidden something that does not appear that serious? The letters in the word rule spell lure. The only RULE God gave was used by Satan to lure Eve to first eat the fruit that was forbidden. Besides a test, being the only sin Adam could have committed, that he and mankind failed because Adam represented the human race. Why would a Tree of Knowledge be so bad? I think that the tree represents a false and perilous pursuit. It is human nature to be curious and to seek knowledge. The Bible even encourages man to search out the hidden. But this tree apparently represents seeking knowledge apart from God. Is it any surprise that countless millions of people still seek their understanding by this method and apart from God? Science (means knowledge) so this tree could be called the "tree of science." Unfortunately, this seems to be the Tree of Knowledge that so many think will advance man; and make humans the measure of all things instead of God, the Creator of this universe, and the Sovereign Supreme eternal being.

Knowledge, apart from humility through a relationship with God, can puff you up and make you prideful. Some theologians consider pride to be one of the worse sins. Many pursue knowledge and neglect God. Are you a doctor, lawyer, professor, scientist, jet pilot, CEO, etc. that has knowledge which gives you advantages? Your knowledge may have made you a multi-millionaire or even built a $25 billion foundation, but I would not trade places with you if you do not know God. And I promise God is really worth knowing!

> "For what is a man profited, if he shall gain the
> whole world, and lose his own soul? Or what shall a
> man give in exchange for his soul?" – Matt. 16:26

Man's wisdom is foolishness to God, so WISDOM apart from God is _we is dumb_. The Bible warns against vain philosophies. PHILOSOPHY, separate from God, is _full of loss_. Science has the letters for seen, because if it is not seen it is not science. Science that is not seen is really philosophy. "Faith is the evidence of things not seen." Faith does not need to actually see, but science must see. Therefore, science is good, but faith is best.

Wake up; wake up America and the rest of the world! Millions upon millions have continued to eat the forbidden fruit, and it is the same dead end now as it was for Adam. If you are one that has neglected God and followed only knowledge and philosophies of man, you need to repent (change your mind). You are not prepared to meet God. You should fall on your face and apologize to the One that designed you and gave you life.

KNOWLEDGE is for _now_ and has a _ledge_ because it only goes so far. Wisdom helps you understand the proper application and limited aspects of knowledge. Textbooks constantly need updating and technology is still exploding. Intel had stated that each year ninety percent of sales at the end of the year are for products that did not exist at the beginning of that year. Today, much of current technology and products produced fast become obsolete. It is so pronounced that the effect is that time and space are being compressed.

How many stars do you think are in the heavens? Until Galileo invented the telescope the number of observable stars was about 1,000 to 1,500. This seemed to contradict the Bible that stated that the stars were as the sand of the sea. Abraham received a word from the Lord in a vision.

> "And he brought him forth abroad, and said, Look
> now toward heaven, and tell the number of stars, if
> thou be able to number them: and he said unto him,
> So shall thy seed be." - Genesis 15:5

Scientists now know that GALAXIES (_axis_ –yes, galaxies must have an axis or it would not be in the word) contain millions or billions of stars, and with powerful modern telescopes they look out across many trillions of miles of space. They have determined that there are innumerable galaxies estimated at about a trillion. The Milky Way galaxy has approximately 200 billion stars. It is considered to have more than the average number in all the galaxies. However, the galaxy 3C 236 is two hundred times the size of the Milky Way. Therefore, not only could Abraham not count the stars, but they still cannot be counted with modern super computers. God not only knows the number, but: "He telleth the number of the stars; he calleth them all by their names.– Ps. 147:4

That is an omnipotent and powerful God. Man is not able to count the stars, but God knows them by name. Our greater light source is called *sun* because of the *Son*. Both the sun and the Son are the light of the world.

Well this writer decided that since man could not count the stars that I would, in faith, just ask God in prayer for the answer. I instantly had a vision of 10^{10}. I thought that this might just be the format of the answer rather that the correct answer for this question. This number is only ten billion, so it is not the number of stars. About three months later on May 1, 2006, I believe that God revealed to me the answer. It is 10^{24}. That number represents a septillion. Starting at a million, then billion, then trillion, etc. to a septillion is a thousand times each and there are seven. Seven is an extremely significant number appearing numerous times in Scripture. Seven represents covenant completeness. The four for the world (four limbs, four chamber heart, four seasons, etc.) plus the three for the trinity gives a total of seven.

> "And round about the throne were four and twenty seats: and upon the seats I saw four and twenty elders sitting, clothed in white raiment; and they had on their heads crowns of gold." - Revelation 4:4

In May 2008 I learned that scientists had now counted 70 sextillion stars throughout the universe. I was surprised that they are now that close to the correct answer of a septillion, being only 930 sextillion short.

Could it be that each elder (Revelation 4:4) has the responsibility and privilege for oversight of 1/24 of the universe? Twelve is the number for fullness of completion, so then possibly twenty-four is the number for the complete universe.

STAR has the letters for the word *art*. The stars in the heavens have been an inspiration for poets and artists for thousands of years. About a 1,000 to 1,500 stars are visible to the naked eye on a very dark night. Are these stars randomly scattered in the sky as you would expect from an uncontrolled explosion, or might there be some order of design? Also, earth has the word art as well. Would you agree that all human art and all colors come from the observance of nature?

> "The heavens declare the glory of God; and the firmament sheweth his handywork." - Psalm 19:1

Recently, physicists have theorized there are actually 10 dimensions. The foundation for this is the mathematics of geometry. The word *dime* means a tenth, and that is why a dime is ten cents. Therefore, I conclude, based on the word DIMENSION that the physicists are correct; and that there are ten dimensions. Heaven may provide the complete experience of all ten dimensions.

If our very existence is by chance, then what real purpose, hope, or future could anyone have? Life would have no meaning. The agnostics and atheists can just eat, drink, and be merry, for after death there will be nothing. I have some news for them that may come as a surprise. Even though they do not realize it, they have an appointment scheduled with God. The worst possible event will be these words heard spoken by the King of Heaven.

> "And then will I profess unto them, I never knew you: depart from me ye that work iniquity. - Matthew 7:23 "And these shall go away into everlasting punishment: but the righteous into life eternal." - Matthew 25:46

The following words (4) will be used in this chapter: Israel, Gentile, Liberal and Revelations.

The Bible states that God made a covenant with Abraham.

"Now the Lord had said unto Abram, Get thee out of thy country, and from thy kindred, and from thy father's house, unto a land that I will shew thee: And I will make of thee a great nation, and I will bless thee, and make thy name great; and thou shalt be a blessing; And I will bless them that bless thee, and curse him that curseth thee; and in thee shall all families of the earth be blessed: - Genesis 12:1-3

Abraham was visited by God about 4,000 years ago, probably in an area near the Persian Gulf. The questions are, "Did God keep this covenant?" "Did a nation come from Abraham?" "Have all the families of the earth been spiritually blessed by Abraham's seed?"

Yes, many nations came from Abraham; but the great nation from God's perspective is Israel. This little nation was predestined by Almighty God to bring divine blessing to the entire world. ISRAEL was named this because God _is_ _real_. The true God is the God of Abraham, Isaac, and Jacob. The nation of Israel was to be a blessing to both Jew and Gentile. This means Jews and the inhabitants of all other nations of this world. What did God give to the entire world from this little nation?

The contributions have turned out to be by far the most important in human history. They are as follows: Prophets (spoke divine revelation), Old and New Testaments (inspired word of God), Yeshua (actual Hebrew name) or Jesus (God's son that was fully man and fully God), Apostles, and the Church (the body of

Christ which is the true believers). God's plan for divine spiritual blessing to the entire human race was brought forth through this covenant with Abraham. This people group fulfilled this promise to Abraham through a crucified (sacrificial Lamb of God) and resurrected Messiah. Direct words of the Messiah:

"Ye worship ye know not what: we know what we worship: for salvation is of the Jews." John 4:22

To qualify, your lineage would have to go back to one of the original 70 descendents of Abraham that entered into Egypt. I am thankful for Israel and to God, for His wisdom in providing a way through this nation, ISRAEL, to reconcile people from all nations to Himself.

"After this I beheld, and, lo, a great multitude, which no man could number, of all nations, and kindreds, and people, and tongues, stood before the throne, and before the Lamb, clothed with white robes, and palms in their hands; And cried with a loud voice, saying, Salvation to our God which sitteth upon the throne, and unto the Lamb." Revelation 7:9, 10

I pray that you will be at this tremendous event from your nation, and that you will take part with this great multitude that have been so blessed through the covenant made many centuries ago with Abraham. You might be surprised to know that the letters for the word *Israel* is contained in the word REVELATIONS. That should be a clue that Israel is definitely important; especially as the end approaches. Thank God for Israel!

Yeshua said, "Think not that I come to destroy, the law, or the prophets: I am not come to destroy, but to fulfill." (Matthew 5:17) The current rabbinic system is at its heart in rebellion against Yeshua, the Messiah and second person of the Godhead. Though the Rabbi's have many areas of wisdom and truth they miss the heart of God's revelation and His only way of salvation. I am doubtful that even the pious ultra orthodox Rabbi's have a relationship with God. They are the blind leading the blind.

Israel is the "apple of God's eye," so I need to be respectful and very careful how I give them a poke in the eye. After that bad news I have some good news (Gospel = good news). The Apostle Paul who is almost certainly the greatest Christian that ever lived was Rabbi Saul before he believed in the Messiah and became a completed Jew. Yeshua is the completion of the law, and He is able to save you, but the law is not. Rabbi's still make tremendous completed Jews when they recognize their Messiah. I believe that this is a transition period and more and more Jewish spiritual leaders will seek truth and find Yeshua. The Messiah is the consolation of Israel, so Israel please turn to Yeshua when things look bleak and you desperately need consolation.

Christianity is completed Judaism and that is why God has used the Christians to take the Torah and complete Jewish Bible all over the world. Again, He has proved His word that there would be a "times of the Gentiles." Christianity did lose something from institutional church anti-Semitism from the second to the seventh century. Church separation from Jewish festivals and rejecting Messianic Jewish communities was wrong. It was not following Biblical teaching. In Christ, Jews and Gentiles are equal. In Christ they become the "one new man."

The world needs for the nation of Israel to have their spiritual blindness removed. This should be a prayer from Christians worldwide. The broad church community should align themselves with and support the Messianic Jewish community. These Jewish believers are crucial to Israel's restoration to faith.

God has provided so much evidence supporting Jesus to be the true Messiah that it astonishes me that it is still less than one percent of Jews that recognize their Messiah. Even the instructions to Moses for the tabernacle with the Levites on the north, south, east and west and the specific location for each of the twelve tribes in four camps forming a perfect cross at Sinai. The tribes were in four camps and the four standards (flags) they used represented the four gospels of the New Testament (Lion, Ox, Man, Eagle).

God did say that a remnant would believe and thank God for every one of them. This remnant is very special to God, and I do believe their sacrifice is preparing the way for faith to greatly increase among the Jewish people. Again, all believers and churches should support Messianic Congregations in Israel and America because they are a high priority of importance to God.

Israel has many enemies just as Bible prophecy stated they would. Their primary enemy seems to be nations that are Islamic. I must admit I only know a little about Islam. There are Christian scholars and authors that do know a lot about this religion; especially those statements in the Qur'an about Christianity. My main resource about Islam is a publication by Mark Water titled *Understanding Islam and Christianity*. Apparently, the form of Christianity and the teaching about Jesus and the trinity that made it to the Middle East at the time of Mohammad had been rejected by mainstream church leaders. Most Christians in other parts of the world would have called this teaching heresy and/or apostasy. Based on this bad information it is understandable that Mohammed would reject what he was told about Judaism and Christianity. Even today not all of Christianity is true, but Christ is truth.

Today, about a billion people follow a misleading religion that is ambiguous and with known errors in what Christianity actually believes. Fortunately, the gospel is reaching lost people in every culture, even in the Islamic world. However, no cultures are as restrictive on religious freedom as Islamic cultures. Leaving Islam is even punishable by death. The word culture has cult in it. Does hatred, violence, oppression of females, radical jihad, and the subjugation or killing of non-Muslims sound reasonable or more like a cult. Islam has the words "I slam", and that is what they did on September 11, 2001 when two hijacked commercial jet aircraft "slammed" into the World Trade Center buildings. Planes were also slammed into the Pentagon and a field in Pennsylvania. Also, Islamic leaders verbally slam the West and Israel.

Islam is a horrendous force against religious freedom. Islam denies the incarnation of God in Yeshua; therefore it is the spirit of Antichrist. My understanding is that Islam teaches that it was Ishmael (Islam is in Ishmael) and not Isaac that Abraham was going to sacrifice. My question is if this sacrifice was not a type for the sacrifice that God was going to make through His own Son what was the point or purpose? The sacrifice type makes sense through the line of Isaac, but how would it make sense through the line of Ishmael because he was not in the Messianic lineage?

Islam teaches that a man may have four wives. This was not the model for marriage that God established in the Garden of Eden for mankind. Monogamy is probably one of the primary reasons that Western civilization had success that far surpassed other cultures. Have Islamic cultures made any significant contributions to advance mankind, like arts, technology or science, in the last one thousand years?

Islam rejects original sin, and believes that children are born with an innate disposition toward virtue. Psychology also teaches that man is basically good. This position contradicts the writing of Moses and other prophets in the sacred scripture. Christianity teaches that man sins because he is a sinner, and not the other way around. All of mankind has a sin nature and that is why this world is full of evil deeds that include murder, lying, greed, wars, corruption, etc. Mohammad exercised revenge and had people murdered – ten in Mecca.

Islam teaches that Jesus was not crucified on the Roman cross in Jerusalem. The problem here is that this event is recorded in history by more documentation than anything else from that period. It is simply a denial of history and of prophetic scripture (one hundred fifty prophecies of the first coming of the Messiah and Jesus fulfilled them all). Satan is very subtle at deception (Gmail – deception = deep pit), so he does not completely deny Jesus. He just changes him from the Son of God to a prophet that is not divine. Jesus claimed to be equal with God. "He that has seen me has seen the Father." "Before Abraham was I am." (John8:58)

My understanding is that Islam is a religion that promotes a combination of good works and faith for salvation. The theological term for salvation by works is called "Legalism." One problem with this is that it puts God in debt, and the other problem is works have never saved anyone. The Islamic view of heaven has lustful pleasures, including sexual relations with virgins, and exotic food and drink. This seems to be an earthly view of paradise extended to heaven. Muslims want to show up in the presence of a Holy God bringing along with them a suitcase of corruption. A Holy God is unable to be in the presence of that which is not holy.

I look forward to heaven with a resurrected incorruptible and glorified body. Also, I know there will be many other profound rewards and experiences that God has for His children. The Christian understanding of heaven is very different from the view offered by Islam.

There are apparent differences between Christian prayer and Islamic prayer. The Muslim religion instructs the adherents to have prayer five times a day. Concerning prayer Jesus warned against vain repetitions and public show. Jesus did an enormous amount of praying in quiet private places. The Bible states that it is good to pray night and day without ceasing. This represents an attitude of prayer that is habitual. Christians have direct access to the throne of God through prayer and are instructed to come there boldly. I have had countless prayers answered, and some of those answers have been astonishing. The common position is that practicing Christians, Jews, and Muslins all support time in prayer.

God sacrificed His Son for all people groups and the peoples of all nations. Now, the God of Abraham seems to have everything set in place for a great clash and challenge involving the restored nation of Israel, a growing Islamic population, and a West that has been slipping from a Christian world view to relativistic view with increasing decadence and materialism.

Some Muslim nations have a lot of oil (wealth), and some of their governments are Islamic Kingdoms. These tend to have less tolerance for non-Muslims, and some want to defeat Israel and overthrow Christianity. This mission will not succeed. Israel is the only covenant nation on earth, and God said His church would prevail against the gates of hell. Jesus said "love your enemies" and Islam says to kill your enemies. Which is the highest standard?

If you are opposing Israel and Christianity, your fight is with God. I know how this turns out – I have read the Bible and God wins.

Muslim numbers are growing and currently represent over 21% of the world's population. Currently, America has a Muslim population of five million and growing. Muslims know that God can save them, but they do not know about the assurance of salvation now. Muslims know that God should be given first priority, and religion in the Islamic language means "the way." Maybe these two things will help them to search with an open mind. If they would just compare the Jesus in the Qur'an with Mohammed they would be amazed by the supremacy of Jesus. Followers of Jesus want Jews, Muslims and all people groups to experience the love of God, the abundant life and a sure salvation.

Jewish accomplishments are not in proportion to their demographic numbers. No other people group comes close to their enormous accomplishments compared to their numbers. This is because the true God is the difference. They are receiving blessings, even in their unbelief; which is temporary because God has stated that their blindness (unbelief) will end. "The gifts and calling of God (to Israel) are without repentance." (Romans 11:29)

America has also made many discoveries to advance civilization. This nation had received the blessing like Judah in their Golden Age under the reign of King Solomon. American political leaders say they support Israel, but they give twice as much aid to the enemies of Israel. Is that really supporting Israel? The American government support for Israel is inconsistent and ambiguous. Dividing the land of Israel carries a very strong Biblical warning. Liberals are in a culture war with conservatives and they support many issues like legal abortion that lead to the Spirit of God departing. The pornography industry is basically unregulated and I do not think there is any sin tax. The Bible states that in the end times there will be people committing unnatural affection and others taking pleasure in the activity. It states, "they which commit such things are worthy of death." Romans 1:31-32

Unfortunately, many of these "freedoms" are actually bondage to sin and will hasten God's judgment. When God leaves the glory departs at the same time, but the people do not realize this change has occurred. They do not immediately know that the glory has departed. Sadly, the USA has followed Judah in making mistakes and in displeasing God, so God's judgment will intersect America's folly. Are you prepared for God's judgment? I see evidences that America must repent or perish. That needs to start with the people of God.

Israel had a leader who was simultaneously both Judge and High Priest named Eli. The letters for Eli are in Israel, Gentile and liberal. I do not think that is an accident or coincidence. This leader was representative of the entire nation of Israel because his unfaithfulness to God brought severe judgment on the whole nation of Israel. 1st Samuel 4 His two sons were priests, but they did not know the Lord. This man's unfaithfulness caused the Spirit of God to depart from Israel. It also brought judgment (death) on himself, his sons, and a curse on his descendants. He and his sons (priests) put their greed above God and the people they had a responsibility to serve.

Israel no longer walks with God, and I am not able to name one nation that is walking with God at this time in history. America is now facing an unprecedented economic crisis. A majority of the American people have lost confidence in the political and corporate leaders. Also, some religious leaders today may be like Eli and put personal gain above true service. Do you think that many elected officials, CEO's and other leaders are putting their careers and lifestyle above true service? Greed was the major cause of the Great Depression and history seems to be repeating itself. All leaders, Jewish and Gentile, should pay attention to the account of Eli and make very sure that they are not making his same mistakes because they are not getting away with anything. There is still accountability with God, and one day they will all stand before Him and answer for their leadership behavior. America remains a nation with many churches and a lot of Christian faith. God is more concerned with the spiritual side of a nation than with the secular. The spiritual is far more important than the secular, because it produces fruit that has eternal consequences. The world's image of America, I believe, is more influenced by the secular side of America. They see our movies (including pornography), music, military actions, and materialism.

This is a very prophetic rich period of time and a perilous period of time. Many prophecies have been fulfilled since I was born. True spirituality is always a major advantage, but I think more so for this end time period. The spiritual opportunities for Jews and non-Jews are enormous. Remaining secular is like being an Ostrich with your head in the sand. Just because you chose to ignore the situation of judgment and peril it's not going away. If God did not focus on the spiritual side of America this nation might have already suffered a final judgment. The Christian believers in the USA are probably the only thing that is delaying the full justice and wrath of God. God judges nations and you will find an important prophecy about America in Jeremiah 30:11.

Many more Americans and people from all nations need to wake up and turn to God before it is too late. Many of those that already know God should consider being more engaged. There are huge battles being fought in the spiritual realm and individuals and nations are involved in that war. There is no neutrality in this war because you are on one side or the other. Christians do not want to call down fire from heaven on anyone. That is not how spiritual warfare should be fought. Souls being saved from a common enemy (Satan) is the goal of Christians and the purpose of the "Great Commission." "Go ye therefore, and teach all nations, baptizing them in the name of the Father, and of the Son, and of the Holy Ghost." (Matthew 28:19) All nations need teaching about God and His Christ, but sometimes there is strong resistance, persecution, and even the killing of the messengers.

There is a lot of talk of peace, but Yeshua (Jesus) said that there would be war until He returned and destroyed the weapons of war and established His Kingdom. I recently read a statistic from the World Jewish Congress Foundation stating that twenty years of conflict in the whole of the Middle East has caused the region to lose a staggering $12 trillion. The countries and people of this region are paying a steep price for conflict and instability.

Jesus gave the disciples instruction in prayer and one of the things He included was to "deliver us from evil." I pray that Almighty God will deliver us from evil: evil government rulers; evil business leaders; evil false religious leaders/teachers; evil moviemakers, actors and other celebrities; evil doctors; evil lawyers; evil authors; evil professors and other teachers; evil journalists; the evil practice of slavery; evil judges; evil law enforcement officers; evil nations and all of the evil worldwide Satanic systems.

I have the assurance from the word of God that one day this entire prayer will be answered. Jesus will be on the Throne of David, and He will rule the world from Jerusalem for one thousand years with a rod of iron. During this period there will be individual sin, but no organized system of evil nor any corrupt nation. There will not be any false organized systems of religion. There will not be an abortion industry or pornography industry. There will not be any atomic bombs or any other weapons of war. This planet will experience a lot of evil and a lot of war before this thousand year reign by the King of Kings begins. His reign is the new world order that I want, and I do expect to be included.

I consider this to be a most important time to genuinely seek truth, do your own searching and make sure you are on the side of the true God. Hopefully, the illumination in this book will be helpful for many of you. I look forward to seeing you on the other side in eternity with that incorruptible glorified body.

Jesus has been more studied, written about, and had songs sung about than anyone else that has ever lived. The Bible, a 100% Jewish book, has for centuries outsold all other literature. You might say that you do not believe or trust the Bible. What is that based upon? There are millions and millions of people that would disagree with you. The Bible is a book (66 books) containing hundreds of miracles called prophecy. This is because it is God's book, his only book on planet earth.

Amazing God has made the effort to demonstrate through many words that even language verifies the powerful God of the Bible and His unique Son. I pray that this information presenting words from the letters in words has been a blessing to you. And believers worldwide please pray for the peace of Jerusalem (Shaalu Shalom Yerushalim). Amen.

Photo by J. S. Governor

After your body is in the grave do you know where you will be?

A Tribute to the Memory and Mission of

✞ <u>Chris Samuel Nedumkandathil, Evangelist</u> ✞

Chris, a man age twenty-five taught a Vacation Bible School class in Kerala, India the day he died.

This remarkable young man made an impact for Jesus in Kerala, and everywhere he traveled in India and in America. Many people have been inspired to get involved in ministry because of Chris. Tina, his younger sister stated, "All of this is **amazing** to me, and provides a source of joy."

Yes, Tina God definitely is **amazing**.

I quote from his journal, "If you can preach or teach you are needed. If you can distribute clothes you are needed. If you can give proper medical care you are needed, there are millions in India and around the world in dire need of some spiritual food, the Bread of Life and the Living Water. How long will we ignore them? How long will we continue to worry only about ourselves? Brothers and sisters let us awaken from our stupor and emerge in the world following the footsteps of our Master and walking the paths of our forefathers. The time is now, the opportunities are endless, and the responsibility is ours."

His message and mission needs to continue throughout this nation and other nations around the world. Chris's mission was to assist the needy and increase the Kingdom of God. Will you help?

Chris Samuel Ministries - 723 Beacon Cove - Lawrenceville. Georgia 30045

http://www.chrissamuel.com

The author is not affiliated with this ministry organization.

Order Form

Email orders: amazingministry@bellsouth.net

Website: **www.leewordcodes.com**

Postal orders: Amazing Ministry
John A. Lee
P. O. Box 3211
Brentwood, TN 37211

Book Price is discounted from retail and the Prices subject to change at anytime.

Amazing Book $17 ☐   CD Lexicon $5 ☐
(4 or more $4 each)
Amazing T-shirt $22 ☐   Book & CD $21 ☐
Amazing Annual Membership (newsletter and access to lexicon updates) $20 ☐

Shipping by USPS or UPS ground. Add $4.00 for first product and $2.00 for each additional product up to ten. No additional shipping charge above ten products.

Add 8.75% sales tax for shipments to Tennessee addresses.

Please send more FREE information on: Bible Prophecy Conference ☐

Speaking/Seminar ☐   Premium (volume) discount ☐   Interview ☐

Send Gmail submissions to email address. If new and added to the website lexicon you will be identified by up to three initials and your state. Example: HDW-VA

Name ____

Address _______________________________________

City___________________________State________Zip__________

Telephone_________________________Email:_______________

CHURCH INFORMATION

Church name: ____________________________________

Address   City   State   Zip

Comments: ____

____

____

Printed in the United States
153913LV00001B/2/P